Margaret Cook holds a PhD in history from The University of Queensland. She is a member of the Professional Historians Association, has a significant body of work in environmental and social history and heritage conservation, and has worked in cultural tourism and the museum sector. Margaret is a Research Fellow at the Australian Rivers Institute, Griffith University, and an Honorary Research Fellow at La Trobe University. Margaret lives in Ipswich with her husband and two sons.

A River with a City Problem was shortlisted for the Scholarly Non-Fiction Book of the Year in the Educational Publishing Awards, and for *The Courier-Mail*'s People's Choice Queensland Book of the Year Award in the Queensland Literary Awards.

www.margaretcookhistorian.com.au

A RIVER WITH A CITY PROBLEM

A HISTORY OF BRISBANE FLOODS

MARGARET COOK

First published 2019 by University of Queensland Press
PO Box 6042, St Lucia, Queensland 4067 Australia
Reprinted 2020, 2022 (three times)
This edition published 2023

University of Queensland Press (UQP) acknowledges the Traditional Owners and
their custodianship of the lands on which UQP operates. We pay our respects to their
Ancestors and their descendants, who continue cultural and spiritual connections to
Country. We recognise their valuable contributions to Australian and global society.

uqp.com.au
reception@uqp.com.au

Cover design by Christabella Designs
Author photograph by Nick Cook
Typeset in 12/16pt Adobe Garamond Pro by Post Pre-press Group, Brisbane
Printed in Australia by McPherson's Printing Group

University of Queensland Press is assisted
by the Australian Government through
the Australia Council, its arts funding
and advisory body.

ISBN 978 0 7022 6606 5 (pbk)
ISBN 978 0 7022 6699 7 (pdf)
ISBN 978 0 7022 6705 5 (epub)

A catalogue record for this book is available from the National Library of Australia.

University of Queensland Press uses papers that are natural, renewable and recyclable
products made from wood grown in well-managed forests and other controlled sources.
The logging and manufacturing processes conform to the environmental regulations of
the country of origin.

Contents

Introduction: A Meandering River

IT IS THE smell of the mud that I remember. I was five when the 1974 floods devastated Brisbane, but my home was on a ridge, safe from the floodwaters. My father skipped work and doorknocked in Graceville to volunteer his labour. For several days he scraped, swept and hosed mud out of family homes. My mother collected washing and returned it clean, along with home-cooked food. My task was to hose linen hanging on our backyard Hills Hoist and remove the worst of the stinking mud before it saw our washing machine. I also recall taking in homeless fieldmice and sheltering them in a shoebox; there are few opportunities to help in a disaster when you are a child. Our relatives in Yeronga and Jindalee, along with thousands of others across Ipswich and Brisbane, were rescued and spent largely sleepless nights in community halls, their homes and possessions threatened by floodwaters.

Almost 40 years later, while I was holidaying in Western Australia in 2011, I sat glued to the television, watching in horror as floodwaters again raced towards Brisbane, having already devastated Toowoomba and towns in the Lockyer Valley, including Murphys Creek, Withcott, Helidon and Grantham. The Bremer River rose, inundating streets and houses in the city of Ipswich. I felt more useless than in 1974, unable to assist and a long way from home and family, some of whom were evacuated or isolated.

Following the 2011 floods, many Brisbane residents expressed incredulity that their city could experience such extreme flooding, despite the wide, muddy river that their suburbs and properties overlook. As lives were lost and possessions destroyed, people looked for someone to blame. Many had pinned their hopes on Somerset and Wivenhoe dams to prevent such a tragedy, and when the dams seemingly failed to do so, allegations of mismanagement quickly circulated and both the dam operations manual and flood engineers faced scrutiny. This response was not born from an ignorance of climate or riverine history but instead reflected Queensland's long-standing cultural and political values in relation to the environment. Human action created the disaster – the hazard in part due to settling on a floodplain – yet this systemic problem was largely overlooked in the Queensland Floods Commission of Inquiry in 2011 and 2012. This prompted my research, and the title of this book; *A River with a City Problem* acknowledges that the river came first, long before humans occupied its banks.

As the 2011 floods receded into memory, South East Queensland was again inundated in February 2022. Extreme rainfall, in excess of 1,000 millimetres in some Brisbane suburbs, fell over three days, pouring into the river and creek systems and causing extreme overland flows. This time I was at home in Ipswich, watching in horror as the rain started running down my brick chimney, creating an unexpected and unwanted water feature in my living room. The rain seemed incessant, and I constantly checked my mobile phone for weather reports, dam levels, friends' texts, and social media updates about rising waters and swelling creeks. The week following 26 February was a blur of pumping stormwater and cleaning floodwaters and flood-damaged property at my home and at friends' places nearby. While the floods followed some familiar patterns to those of the past, houses and suburbs flooded this time that did not flood in 2011, proving the adage that 'no two floods are the same'. The unpredictable weather caught everyone, even the weather monitors, by surprise, as the city's creeks inundated homes.

Brisbane residents were left wondering why this flood was different, and why it occurred so soon after the last one, and these questions have led to this updated edition.

Riverine territory includes both the riverbed and the banks, and the floodplains created by sand, silt and mud deposited during floods. More than a boundary between land and water, a floodplain is an 'ecosystem in its own right, dependent on water level fluctuations', and is an area that changes with the seasons.[1] Flood is a 'highly anthropocentric term'.[2] Many rivers naturally overflow their banks, but it's only when settlements are inundated that this overflow is labelled a flood.

The Brisbane River is characterised by its meander. In his description of Brisbane in *A First Place*, poet and novelist David Malouf explains how the river winds across the city, creating 'pockets' and 'elbows' and cutting in and out of 'every suburb'. From every vantage point the river is 'inescapable'.[3] While the river does not weave through 'every suburb', a quarter of suburbs within the Brisbane City Council area can claim riverside land. The river's serpentine nature has greatly extended river frontage. The outward bends have created knots or nodes surrounding pockets for suburban development, even the central business district is wrapped by a river bend. But Brisbane's terrain often obscures the river from view. It is visible from the hills, but on the lower ground the river can disappear, only to reappear in an unexpected and disorienting way. This topography makes it difficult to understand which areas are susceptible to flooding. Similarly, in Ipswich, the Bremer River bisects the city and meanders through the suburbs. Low-lying areas some distance from the river are less evident as belonging to the floodplain. For most observers it requires a flood to delineate the floodplain. In the words of Indigenous artist Tex Sculthorpe, 'the water shows us the country'.[4]

The Brisbane River system is approximately 40 million years old, and its present course was established in the late Miocene era, about

10 million years ago. Water cut gorges through the hard Devonian and Jurassic rocks and formed sinuous patterns characteristic of slow-flowing rivers. The Brisbane River catchment, the land that contributes run-off to the river, is 13,560 square kilometres, bounded on the west and south by the Great Dividing Range, on the north by the Cooyar, Jimna and Conondale ranges, and on the east by the D'Aguilar and Teviot ranges. Much of the catchment is rural, used as grazing, cropping and forestry land. Within the catchment are the towns of Kilcoy, Fernvale and Lowood, the urban centre of Ipswich on the Bremer River, and Brisbane, Queensland's capital city, which is bisected by the Brisbane River.

For millennia the Brisbane River system followed its own hydrological rhythms with floods replenishing the estuarine environment and regenerating the floodplains. For 60,000 years the Turrbal and Jagera people had a spiritual connection with the country, respecting and accommodating the river's life cycles. British colonisation in 1824 brought a problem for the river: settlement of a city on the floodplain by a society imbued with notions of human superiority over nature, a mindset that viewed nature as bounty for progress. To the colonists, riverine floods brought a moment of 'disorder' as the river left its 'proper place with catastrophic results'[5], shattering the ideal of the linear path of progress.

The British settlers perceived flooding as a problem of water control. As they had done for centuries throughout Europe, hydraulic engineers were employed in Australia to 'control', 'tame' and 'harness' rivers to mitigate floods. Australia became another 'hydraulic society', a society that is reliant on technology to manage water.[6] Technocratic strategies were called on to regulate the flow of the Brisbane River system, provide potable water and prevent floods. As British colonial engineers began dredging, straightening and truncating the Brisbane River, its transformation into an 'envirotechnical landscape', a blend of ecological and technological systems, a fusion of culture and nature, began.[7] Dams, the ultimate solution, became the largest and most visible manifestation of progress and human power over nature. With the construction of Somerset Dam, and later Wivenhoe Dam, the river's flow regime was controlled by mechanical gates, turning the Brisbane River into an 'organic machine', a phrase coined by historian Richard White to describe rivers modified to a hybrid state between nature and technology.[8] Yet, despite human intervention, hydrological rhythms have persisted and are demonstrated most forcefully in times of flood.

In histories of South East Queensland, the Brisbane River system has been largely overlooked and generally relegated to a passive role in the background of the central story of human action.[9] This book places the river centre stage as I draw on the key floods of 1893, 1974, 2011 and 2022 to explore the relationship between the river and its human floodplain dwellers. Other floods have occurred, most notably the larger flood of 1841, but the scarcity of records allows me to do little more than acknowledge their occurrence. Although individual floods are relatively short-term catastrophic events, they expose the evolution of the hazard created by humans over a longer term. Historian Stephen Pyne suggests that a bushfire offers a lens for historical understanding, as it creates a time of crisis that reveals an interplay between humans and the environment that 'illuminates the character of each'.[10] Floods evoke similar responses and reflect deep-seated and entangled 'technological, cultural, economic and political factors'.[11] It is the contested space of the floodplain where the competing interests of the river and humans are most exposed.

This book focuses on the history of riverine flooding in the Brisbane River catchment and outlines alterations to the river system implemented by engineers, and demanded by politicians and the community, between 1893 and 2022. As such it does not take account of Aboriginal people's ongoing relationship with the river. It is also not an ecological biography of the river system that charts water quality and estuarine habitats, nor does it discuss the more frequent creek flooding that has limited impact beyond the affected catchment. Instead it is an account of the unique behaviour of specific floods and their impact on an ever-expanding human environment, and the attempts by successive governments to control the river, rather than control development on the floodplain.

The history of floods in the Brisbane River catchment is more than another global example of riverine flood control due to the unique combination of climate, geography and hydrology in South East Queensland. Brisbane's subtropical climate is characterised by summer rain and comparatively dry winters. Within Australia, the driest vegetated continent on Earth, Brisbane is the third wettest capital city after Darwin and Sydney. Its average annual rainfall is 1,149 millimetres, with extremes of both drought and flood. The Brisbane River catchment is generally regarded as dry, with a low average rainfall/run-off ratio but, like many Australian streams, it has a highly variable streamflow. Even by Australian standards, variations in the Brisbane River's flow regime are extreme. Before the river was regulated with the completion of Somerset Dam in 1959, 8 per cent of records showed a flow rate of zero, but the flood of February 1893 recorded a peak discharge of 13,700 cubic metres per second.[12]

The greatest cause of climate variation in Australia is the El Niño–Southern Oscillation, which brings extreme weather. The name El Niño, Spanish for 'little boy' or 'Christ child', reflects its time of arrival around December when there is unusually warm water in the eastern Pacific Ocean. The El Niño phase can bring cyclones, intense rain, storms and floods in South America, while in eastern Australia it is associated with droughts, bringing periods up to a decade long of dry weather. Its counterpart, La Niña ('little girl'), brings below-average sea temperatures in the eastern Pacific, and above-average ocean temperatures in eastern Australia, resulting in extremes of wet weather. South East Queensland is further affected by the Madden–Julian Oscillation, a global weather pattern that influences tropical rainfall and brings a higher probability of rain on a weekly to monthly cycle.

Cyclones are often linked with floods in Queensland. Although the official cyclone season is November to April, they most commonly cross the coast in January and February. The warm air around a low-pressure system can bring intense rainfalls, characteristic of subtropical climates. In January 1974, decaying tropical Cyclone Wanda forced a monsoonal trough towards Brisbane, dumping 872 millimetres of rain in 26 days, the city's wettest January ever recorded. A cyclone in February 1893 produced Brisbane's wettest month on record as the city received 1,026 millimetres in 25 days. To provide perspective, Brisbane's mean January rainfall is 159.6 millimetres and 158.3 millimetres for February.

Along with great variability, South East Queensland's rainfall is remarkable in its intensity, which is the factor most likely to cause floods as it produces the greatest rainfall/run-off ratio. The town of Crohamhurst on the Stanley River still holds the Australian record for the highest daily rainfall, receiving 907 millimetres in 24 hours in 1893. Ipswich rainfall reached an estimated 341 millimetres in 24 hours in 1974, the city's highest ever recorded daily total, although the Amberley gauge received a record 345 millimetres in 24 hours in 2022. Also in 1974, New Beith, on Oxley Creek, received 250 millimetres in six hours. In 2022, Brisbane set a new rainfall record with three consecutive days of over 200 millimetres.

Individual floods are unique, reflecting the quantity and intensity and distribution of rainfall, as well as changes in the river and floodplain (both natural and human). Although floodwaters may follow familiar paths, floods are not predictable in their timing, location or outcomes. State agencies have created models in an attempt to codify and regulate flood behaviour, but nature does not follow rules. Each flood behaves differently, its overall impact determined by both weather and the ever-changing human activities on the floodplain.

A recognition of the entangled relationship between humans and nature was largely missing from the 2011 flood debate, with much of the rhetoric repeated in 2022. A reliance on technocratic solutions to control floods endures in South East Queensland, which has led to the misguided belief that floods will not happen again. Vested interests of property owners, land developers and governments has promulgated a myth that Somerset and Wivenhoe dams can prevent floods so that development on the floodplain can continue. This history of flooding in the Brisbane River catchment offers a timely intervention in our understanding of the environment, especially because the current trend of climate change increases the likelihood of floods becoming more frequent and severe in the future. It is imperative that we understand the dynamics between nature and humans on the floodplain, and that this understanding informs future flood debates and policies.

Despite being major disasters, the 1893, 1974 and 2011 floods are often overlooked in accounts of South East Queensland's history. They, along with the 2022 floods, should not be forgotten. We owe it to those who lost lives, property and treasured possessions in past floods to acknowledge their suffering and record these events. The Turrbal and Jagera people lived in harmony with the river for centuries, but permanent settlement on the floodplain created a hazard. Perhaps with greater understanding of rivers, we will learn to adapt, and to manage human behaviour rather than attempt to control the river. At the very least, we must understand that future floods are inevitable and we would be wise to get out of their way. Nature will prevail.

Glossary

AEP   Annual Exceedance Probability

AHD   Australian Height Datum

AMTD   Adopted Middle Thread Distance

ARI   Average Recurrence Interval

BoM   Bureau of Meteorology, a Commonwealth Government agency

Cumec   Cubic metre per second, stated as m^3/s

DFE   Defined Flood Event

DFL   Defined Flood Level

EL   Elevation (in metres) above the Australian Height Datum

FSL   Full Supply Level – maximum normal water supply storage level of a reservoir behind a dam

ML   Megalitre (ML): 1,000,000 litres or 1,000 m^3

Q100   This term is used interchangeably with a 100 year ARI flood, 1% AEP or 1 in 100 year flood

QFCI   Queensland Floods Commission of Inquiry

QRA   Queensland Reconstruction Authority

The Brisbane River Catchment:
Map and Facts

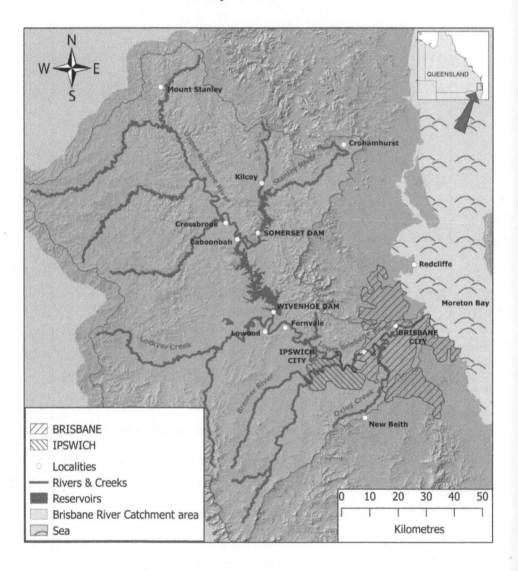

Brisbane River catchment contains the sub-catchments of the Stanley, Brisbane and Bremer rivers and 22 creeks, the largest of which is Lockyer Creek.

Stanley River (112 kilometres long; catchment area of 1,330 square kilometres) has 18 tributaries and is a significant contributor to Brisbane River floods.

Lockyer Creek (113 kilometres long; large flat catchment fed by areas of heavy rainfall) is hydrologically complex.

Bremer River (100 kilometres long; catchment area of 634 square kilometres) is not dammed and rises rapidly within hours of heavy rainfall.

Brisbane River (309 kilometres long) includes Moggill and Breakfast creeks (left bank), and Oxley, Norman and Bulimba creeks (right bank).

River heights are measured by stream gauges at fixed points. Since the 1840s, flood heights in Brisbane City have been recorded at the Port Office Gauge (Station no. 540684) on the right bank diagonally downstream of the Port Office and since the 1970s at the City Gauge (Station no. 540198) in Edward Street. A flood height of 3.5 metres at either gauge is considered a major flood.

Since 1971, flood heights in the lower reaches of the Brisbane River downstream of Mt Crosby, and the Bremer River downstream of Berrys Lagoon, have been recorded in Australian Height Datum (AHD). Dam levels are also recorded in AHD. At most other gauges flood heights are recorded as local gauge height. Metres AHD are used throughout this book unless otherwise noted. Flood or water release volumes are given in megalitres (1,000,000 litres or 1,000 cubic metres) and flow rates are measured in cubic metres per second. This book uses the measurements quoted in primary sources, except where metric units are required for clarity or comparison.

1

Encountering the Floodplain

BRISBANE IS TURRBAL country, with land stretching from the mouth of the river to Moggill, north to North Pine and south to Logan. The language group in Ipswich and the Lockyer and Fassifern valleys is Jagera or Yuggera. The Turrbal and Jagera people have a symbiotic relationship with rivers and land; for them, the river is the giver of life and needs care in return. Different Dreamtime stories tell how the Brisbane River was created. One tells how Moodagurra, the rainbow serpent, became stuck as she made her way up a dry creek. Moodagurra called on Yara (the rain) and Ngalan (the cloud) to help. As the storm thundered and rain flowed into the creek, the water seeped under Moodagurra's belly, allowing her to wriggle from side to side. This movement formed the sinuous river called Maiwar. Now Moodagurra decides when the big rains come and brings the floods, and Maiwar provides sustenance and recreational activities.[1] In Turrbal and Jagera culture, floods are appreciated as an essential part of the river's life cycle that shape the country, create floodplains and sustain all life in the river's catchment.

The Turrbal and Jagera people are fishing people. For over 60,000 years, the rivers and streams provided them with a bountiful source of water and food – mullet, flounder, crabs, shellfish, turtles, eels and water birds among the seasonal foods on offer. Attuned to the environment, the Turrbal and Jagera people moved with the seasons, relocating before exhausting food sources. As Jagera man

Neville Bonner explained in 1995, 'We rotated around allowing nature to provide and crops to rejuvenate.'[2]

Aboriginal camps were located near water crossings, including present-day Enoggera, Breakfast Creek, Kurilpa Point (South Brisbane), West End, Toowong, Oxley Creek, and upstream near Ipswich at Colleges Crossing and Kholo Flats. Prior to colonial dredging, the river depth varied greatly, offering both deep waterholes for fishing and swimming, and shallow crossing points. A large waterhole near the present-day City Botanic Gardens was used for swimming, fishing and catching dugong, while Hamilton's large sand islands and low water offered a favoured crossing point. At low tide the river at Kurilpa Point was waist deep. The Turrbal and Jagera people used the river as a transportation route, traversing it in rafts and canoes, or swimming using logs for flotation when fatigued. Reminiscing in 1909 about South Brisbane in the 1840s, settler William Clark recalled Turrbal people crossing the river on rafts, or up to 60 people swimming across at a time, holding spears above their heads and rotating them in a motion like sculling a boat.[3]

The Turrbal and Jagera people were well aware of floods. They built camps near water under trees to provide shade, but they built these camps 14 metres above watercourses to prevent flood damage.[4] As early as 1842, Aborigines warned the McConnel family, new settlers in the Brisbane River valley, that an inundation had occurred the previous year.[5] After a flood in 1890, the Cooyar people of the upper Brisbane River told journalist Archibald Meston of a large flood on Magenjie, 'Big Flowing Water' or 'Big River', an alternative name for the Brisbane River.[6] Meteorologist Inigo Jones wrote in 1929 that Aboriginal oral tradition described how Brisbane floods could originate in the Stanley River, a fact validated by his own hydrological analysis.[7] The Turrbal people also recalled a flood that broke the river's banks at North Quay, flowing through the present-day Brisbane City Hall site (Adelaide Street) and into Creek Street, an old river tributary.[8]

The recollections of Thomas Petrie, who from 1837 grew up among Aboriginal children and learned their language and customs, provide a rare insight into Indigenous culture in the early years of the colony. Petrie reveals the climatic adaptations and agricultural practices of Aboriginal people in the area as they responded to the changing environment. In drought, Aboriginal people dug wells in swampy areas for water and constructed weirs across the river or tributaries to regulate the water flow. Aboriginal men would build dams of stone or brush and make traps to block streams to catch eels or fish. They piled wood on the water's edge to rot and attract cobra or kambi (*Nausitora queenslandica*), a long white worm, for harvesting.[9] The Turrbal and Jagera people had learned to live with the river, using it for food and transportation, but also allowing it to replenish the lands through flooding. They tried to warn the colonists of the changing nature of the land alongside the river, but these warnings went unheeded.

A 'Magnificent River'

The first British record of floods in the Brisbane River area is from botanist Joseph Banks on board the *Endeavour* in May 1770. Travelling as part of Lieutenant James Cook's expedition, he observed a 'dirty clay colour' in Moreton Bay waters, suggesting a flood from a large river.[10] However, the river remained hidden to the British until explorer John Oxley was charged with finding a site for a new penal colony for the New South Wales (NSW) Government in 1823. He encountered escaped convicts John Finnegan, Thomas Pamphlet and Richard Parsons at Bribie Island who alerted him to the existence of a river.

Despite fighting exhaustion from the environmental challenges of a 'vertical sun', mosquitoes and sandflies, Oxley's expedition located the river. His crew shared his enthusiasm for this 'magnificent river'. Expedition member John Uniacke noted the banks of 'rich black loam' forming 'rich flat country, clothed with large timber', which he expected would prove 'a valuable acquisition to the colony'. The expedition, Uniacke pronounced, was 'successful beyond our expectations'. Oxley's field notes on 3 December 1823 record that he had found an eligible place for settlement, served admirably by a navigable river. He said that the river 'promises to be of the utmost importance to the colony from the very fertile country it passes through, affording the means of water communication with the sea to a vast extent of country, the greater portion of which is capable of producing the richest productions of the tropics'.[11] Reflecting the priorities and worldview of the British Empire, Oxley recognised the river's maritime potential and the economic value of its contiguous fertile land. Colonisation soon followed – a transformative event in the relationship between the river and its human neighbours.

Oxley charted the river's course upstream to present-day Goodna, assigning British names to pockets of land and topographical features, and honouring the NSW Governor, Sir Thomas Brisbane, by bestowing his name on the river. Historian Peter Read describes how explorers and cartographers inscribed maps 'as if the rivers flowed waiting for a European to name them'.[12] By charting the river and its surrounding landscape, Oxley supplanted Aboriginal history. Cultural anthropologist Veronica Strang notes the symbolic importance of naming places as it 'humanises the landscape' and imbeds the identity of the new settlers on the land, 'bringing it into their perceived sphere of control'.[13] With its naming, the Brisbane River became part of the British Colonial Empire.

Initially, Oxley misunderstood what he saw. He erroneously believed the Brisbane River to be the largest river in New South Wales, its source the 'Interior Waters' (the much-desired inland sea that many imagined lay at the heart of the continent).[14] Regardless of this error, Oxley had fulfilled his brief, finding a river necessary for settlement and a potentially economically advantageous outpost. Ignoring the conspicuous presence of Aboriginal people and the assistance they provided to explorers, the British regarded the country as terra nullius, empty and ripe for the taking. Oxley's glowing accounts prompted Governor Brisbane to establish a penal settlement at Redcliffe, on the shores of Moreton Bay, in 1824.

Oxley's second voyage in 1824 charted more colonial land and rivers upstream with the assistance of Allan Cunningham, the King's Botanist. Cunningham, who was more attuned to the environment, saw beyond the area's economic advantages. His journal records species of flora and fauna, geology and navigational obstacles, providing an early account of the river prior to settler alterations. He also dispelled the myth of an inland water source, suggesting the nearby ranges as the river's origin.[15] Oxley and Cunningham described the riverbed as mostly sand and shingle. At the bar of the river the depth was 1.5 metres at low water, with a tidal rise of 2 metres. Upstream between the bars at Luggage Point and the rocks at Lytton the river reached a desirable depth for navigation. After the flats at Eagle Farm and the Pinkenba-Colmslie area the river remained clear and deep to Seventeen Mile Rocks, 27 kilometres from the mouth. Shoals were recorded upstream as far as the confluence of the Brisbane and Bremer rivers, beyond which the shallow Brisbane River was unnavigable. The Bremer River, with its snags and rocks, provided a shallow channel only as far as the future site of Ipswich.

While the Turrbal and Jagera people had respected and worked with the rhythms of floods and drought, the British colonists, with their notions of human superiority over nature, regarded the environment as existing for the British Empire to exploit by creating agrarian and urban settlements. The settlers, with little understanding of subtropical floods, ignored both Indigenous and their own fledgling knowledge of floods in South East Queensland and built to the water's edge, sowing the seeds for future flood hazard. Floods were ignored by colonial administrators who were preoccupied with establishing a colony, navigational improvements and providing potable water in a drought-prone settlement.

Newspaper and explorer accounts promoting the new colony fixated on the beauty and economic potential of the rivers and their banks, viewing the world 'through the fiscal lens of revenue needs'.[16]

Accompanying Governor Brisbane on a visit to Moreton Bay in 1824, a journalist marvelled at the 'truly picturesque' scenery, with one bank 'high open forest land', the opposite 'comparatively low country covered with close vegetation'. The banks abounded with 'promising' pines, some '8 to 10 feet in circumference' (2.5 to 3 metres) and '90 to 100 feet' (27 to 30 metres) in height.[17] As well as noting the vegetation for potential timber trade, in 1828 Colonial Botanist Charles Fraser recorded the elevated and rocky riverbanks in Brisbane – the distinctive ignimbrite cliffs at Kangaroo Point, and the limestone and abundant coal seams near Ipswich – as bounty for the Imperial treasury. While enthusing about the magnificence of the vegetation, the product of a fertile floodplain, how aware were these explorers of evidence of flood?

Although in 1823 Oxley found 'no appearance of the River being even occasionally flooded', on his second voyage he noted that the bank near Kholo Creek had been 'at some period washed by an inundation: a flood would be too weak an expression to use for a collection of water rising to the height (full 50 feet), which the appearance of the shore here renders probable'.[18] This flood height may well have exceeded his previous experience, causing him to declare the term 'flood' an inadequate description. Cunningham also observed evidence of past flooding, meticulously recording evidence of 'water-borne debris well above the banks'. The noted sand and gravel banks 'over which the River in great floods impetuously sweeps, its marks on the Outer Bar furnishing us with the proofs of its being at those periods 500 yards wide' offered evidence of large floods. Later, when exploring the river in flood in September 1825, Major Edmund Lockyer noted upstream from Fernvale near Lockyer Creek discoloured water rising 'a foot in less than an hour'. He recorded earlier floodmarks 'upwards of one hundred feet', further commenting that 'tremendous floods' had at times occurred in the Brisbane River.[19]

Explorers also recorded evidence of the region's susceptibility to drought. Dry weather in the nine months between Oxley's expeditions had reduced Brisbane River heights and increased the salinity further upstream. Pondweeds covered the surface.[20] Rocks and sandbars, exposed in low water, impeded navigation. Although the cycle of floods and drought had been duly noted by Oxley, Cunningham and Lockyer, and could have raised concerns for future settlement, this did not dim the dominant narrative. Diaries and official reports of explorers and penal colony administrators expose a colonial preoccupation with the navigational potential of the river and its banks' economic value as a source of free timber and fertile, alluvial farmland. The riverbanks presented an untapped potential for settlement. With their Eurocentric understanding of the environment and their utilitarian mindset, the British colonised the floodplains of the Brisbane River.

Creating a Colony

The penal colony first settled at Redcliffe in 1824 until problems of poor water, mosquitoes and an unsuitable port forced its abandonment the following year. Commandant Henry Miller chose the new site of Brisbane, 27 kilometres up river, ignoring John Oxley and the Governor's endorsement of Breakfast Creek. Reasons for this choice are unclear, but perhaps the elevated ridge above the river, waterholes on the north bank, fertile land on the south and building stone in the nearby riverside cliffs offered incentives. The original overseers of Brisbane Town exploited the topography and chose a site surrounded on three sides by the Brisbane River and bounded to the north by a ridge (now Wickham Terrace). Its self-contained character made an ideal prison. Buildings were constructed on the high ground along the ridge of William and George streets and on the spur (now Queen Street). The Brisbane River provided the ingress and egress to the town, primarily via the wharf behind the Commissariat Store in William Street, and settlement was restricted to the north side of the river. In a rare newspaper insight into the flood hazard created by settling on a floodplain, *The Brisbane Courier* remarked in 1893 that the convict settlement had been located with 'sublime disregard of fluvial footprints'.[21] By leaving little open space for floodwaters, town planners created a permanent environmental risk.

Despite the potential for flooding, riverside land helped address the pressing need for food, prompting dramatic changes to the landscape. Settlers cleared the lush vegetation the explorers had enthused about. Land in South Brisbane opposite the main settlement, described in 1930 by a former convict as a 'tangled mass of trees, vines, flowering creepers, staghorns, elkhorns, towering scrub palms, giant ferns, beautiful and rare orchids and the wild passion flower', was cleared for agriculture.[22] In 1828, the Government Gardens (now the City Botanic Gardens) were laid out beside the river and planted with vegetables and arrowroot. Captain Bishop, Commandant of Moreton Bay, reported in 1826 that 34.5 hectares of arable land had been cleared for tobacco, sugar cane and maize. The development of 404 hectares at Eagle Farm made further incursions into both riverside and Turrbal and Jagera lands. Redbank Plains, 53 kilometres upstream from Brisbane, provided grazing land for cattle after 1832. Farther upstream, lime was mined at Limestone (renamed Ipswich in 1843) for building construction.

The penal settlement closed in 1839. In preparation for free settlement, Andrew Petrie, Superintendent of Public Works, and military engineer Major George Barney made the first attempt to regulate land development, surveying Brisbane in 1838 to accommodate the existing riverside settlement. Surveyor Robert Dixon's town survey, completed by March 1840, created a grid pattern of square blocks with 66 foot (20 metre) wide streets. He imposed the accepted rectilinear street pattern already used in America and other Australian cities, a system that offered a 'cheap and rapid' method of surveying a town, and provided homogeneity, administrative order and control. The standard plan's application afforded the landscape minimal attention, as it was merely rotated to cater for a meander in the river with streets terminating at its edge.[23] Early plans for a wide riverside esplanade were abandoned, removing an opportunity to create a small flood buffer between river and settlement. Sir George Gipps, appointed Governor of New South Wales (including Moreton Bay) in 1837, dismissed the idea. Grandiose boulevards were not required in a town that he believed had little future beyond 'an ordinary provincial settlement' or 'a paltry village'.[24] With the town already restricted in size to half a square mile by the Spring Hill scarp and the river, authorities did not intend to constrict development any further. Little effort was made to preserve the river frontages for public use or keep structures off the floodplain. Writing with hindsight in 1866, Andrew Petrie expressed his regret at Brisbane's poor planning:

> [A]ny citizen who is interested in the progress of the City must feel touched with regret to see that every bit of river frontage is, as likely to be, locked up in private hands. Were Brisbane, as it ought to have been, planned after the model of the best seaport towns at home, the whole of the river front would have been reserved as public property, with sufficient breadth of ground, for wharves, sheds, and streets.[25]

A riverside esplanade or public reserve would have reduced the flood hazard. Instead, in 1844 surveyor Henry Wade subdivided the land to the edge of the river, allowing maximum development in the floodplain.

Upstream, Ipswich was developed at the farthest point a large vessel could reach before the river became too shallow and rocky. To the Governor, building a township at what he described as the 'head of navigation' made perfect sense. He dispatched Henry Wade to survey the town in 1842. Wade did not share the Governor's enthusiasm for the location and expressed concern that known floods at the chosen site had reached a little over 16.8 metres and the brackish water would threaten future water supply.[26] Although correct, both concerns were disregarded by authorities. The navigational appeal of the Bremer River and the fertile land along its banks outweighed all.

When Moreton Bay opened for free settlement in 1842, the Sydney press advertised riverside land with its rich alluvial, undulating banks, extensive timber supplies and coal for sale.[27] But in 1841, before Brisbane's first land sales had been held, the settlement flooded. Although records are scarce, the flood height has been calculated at 8.43 metres, the first major flood since British colonisation and the largest in Brisbane since records have been kept. Perhaps such an enormous inundation should have prompted a pause to consider the implications of subdividing land on the floodplain. Did the government feel no moral imperative to reconsider these actions and move the settlement to higher ground? Governor Lachlan Macquarie had already warned early settlers of the perils of settling on flood-prone land after he witnessed floods on the Nepean and Hawkesbury rivers in New South Wales. Not mincing words, Macquarie declared in his General Orders of March 1817 that:

fatal Experience of Years has shown the Sufferers the inevitable Consequences of their wilful and wayward habit of placing their Residences and Stock-Yards within the Reach of the Floods (as if putting at Defiance that impetuous Element which is not for Man to contend with); and whilst it must be still had in Remembrance, that many of the deplorable Losses which have been sustained within the last few Years at least, might have been in great Measure averted had the Settlers paid due Consideration to their own Interests, and to the frequent Admonitions they had received, be removing their Residences from within the Flood Marks to the Townships assigned for them on the high lands.[28]

Settlers, Macquarie argued, should not try to defy nature. Yet floods and the principle of placing structures beyond their reach appear to be have been far from mind when land at Moreton Bay was declared open for sale. Environmental ignorance offers one explanation of why floods may have been overlooked and raises questions of settler understandings of a climate vastly different from Britain's.

Settlement in an Unfamiliar Environment

New settlers to Australia brought British climatic knowledge as cultural baggage, against which they measured and analysed their new environment. To their eyes Australia seemed strange, with foreign Indigenous people, flora, fauna and soils, and a subtropical climate with temperature and rainfall vastly different from Britain. As NSW astronomer Henry Chamberlain Russell noted in 1896, these settlers had left a country where drought was defined as a period of days or weeks without rain. In Australia, drought could be measured in years.[29] United Kingdom (UK) rainfall records from Oxford between 1770 (the year Cook explored Australia) and 1903 indicate only three months when rainfall exceeded 200 millimetres. Brisbane's current mean January rainfall of 159.6 millimetres and 158.3 millimetres for February are close to the United Kingdom's record-breaking rainfalls. This rainfall mean is made more remarkable by some very dry months; for example, in February 1874 Brisbane received only 64 millimetres. Extreme monthly rainfalls most likely exceeded settlers' comprehension. A Brisbane River catchment that received 1,148.8 millimetres annually seemed unrealistic when compared with the Thames River catchment's average of 706 millimetres.

A new climate must be learned through 'time, through averages and extremes' and cannot, as historian Tim Sherratt argues, 'be mapped and comprehended like a new continent'.[30] Colonial experience of India's tropical climate and Sydney and Melbourne's temperate climates may not have prepared settlers for South East Queensland's extremely variable climate and rainfall. In the absence of written records and lived experience, and with Aboriginal knowledge unheeded, initial ignorance and misunderstandings were inevitable. Settlers may have regarded the floods in 1841, 1843 and 1844 as aberrations, rather than as a climatic characteristic.

The 1841 flood (8.43 metres) went largely unreported in both the Sydney and Moreton Bay press. Rivers offered the promised land of untapped economic potential; accounts of floods did not sit comfortably with the prevailing narrative of prosperity and progress.

Settlement: The Utilitarian Dream

As British settlers colonised Australia, they imported ideals of 'improving' the land, exploiting the environment in the utilitarian pursuit of progress, as they had done throughout their empire. The language of progress offered exaggerated promises of prosperity assured by the gifts of nature. Humans and nature were deemed separate, the former imbued with a sense of superiority, the latter the provider of essential resources. Floodplains devoid of farms, houses or industry were considered wasteful. Land had to be organised and improved through productive use, with empty land perceived as the antithesis of progress. In Australia, 'improvement' was a culturally laden term, whereby altering the land to 'look like the old country', settling it with 'an idealised yeomanry of self-sufficient family freeholders', was regarded as 'the true measure of progress'.[31] Settlement and cultivation, colonists believed, improved nature.

These values were unambiguously expressed by a self-described 'traveller' in *The Moreton Bay Courier* in 1859, who bemoaned the 'wasted' rich scrubland along the river, a potential 'poor man's purchase'. With Queensland now separated from New South Wales, but still a British colony, the traveller hoped the new government would change land regulations so that 'sale of these waste lands will be both rapid and profitable to the colony and the purchaser'. Warming to his theme, the writer continued, 'millions of acres of productive land is unsurveyed and unsold, affording ample space for the industrial exertions of thousands of our fellow creatures'. He added that along the river 'immense tracts of maiden soil lie upon their margins only waiting for the occupation and labors of man to convert them into productive wealth'.[32] In the traveller's opinion, the value of riverside land was economic, the key to progress. In

1860, the passage of the *Occupation of Unoccupied Crown Lands in the Unsettled Districts* that dealt with 'waste lands' made this link between land and economic progress clear at a legislative level.[33] Unoccupied, non-productive land failed to extract a desirable annual licence fee for the impoverished Colonial Government.

Imperial Britain favoured closer settlement, a policy designed to subdivide large land holdings into smaller agricultural farms, as Queensland's yeoman farmers would produce food and raw material for industrial Britain. Reverend John Dunmore Lang, a Presbyterian minister and advocate of British immigration to Australia, championed closer settlement. He viewed Queensland as a vast colonisation scheme whereby British immigrants would buy and convert unused land to cotton-fields for England. His 1861 promotional book on Queensland, subtitled 'a highly eligible field for emigration, and the future cotton-field of Great Britain', employed much of the rhetoric used by the land promoters or boosters in America, New Zealand and other parts of Australia. Commenting on the navigational potential of the river, described by Lang as 'glassy water, exhibiting all the romantic beauty of a Highland or Swiss Lake', he noted that 24 kilometres from the river mouth cottages had already been built on riverside land 'appropriated by colonists of taste and enterprise'. The lush vegetation on the riverbank provided proof of 'spots of extraordinary fertility where the hand of man is perhaps erecting his future dwelling and transforming the wilderness into smiling farms and fruitful fields'. He had seen no other Australian city, apart from Sydney, with a 'greater number of interesting and beautiful sites' along its river.

Lang acknowledged the 'considerable' flood-prone rich alluvial land along the flats on both sides of the main river and tributaries but promoted it as easy to clear and cultivate. This land would 'prove admirable localities for the settlement of small farms to raise productions suited to the district'. Encouraging British migration to Brisbane, Lang declared it a 'pity' that 'such a region should be lying comparatively waste and unoccupied, when there are so many thousands of our fellow-countrymen struggling with poverty and privations at home!' Lang had a dream. He could not 'conceive anything either in natural or in moral scenery more interesting and beautiful than this noble river would unquestionably be, if its banks were thus lined with the neat cottages and well-cultivated farms of a happy peasantry'.[34] Lang's view of the floodplains as an untapped resource, awaiting the 'hand of man' for improvement, was shared by many settlers and immigrants who were keen to capitalise on the floodplain's bounty.

'Improving' the Land and River Through Settlement

Early Brisbane land sales were concentrated in the inner-city areas as riverfront land sold in 1843 at Kangaroo Point and New Farm, then in South Brisbane and Breakfast Creek in 1844. The 1840s floods did not diminish the acquisitive appetite for floodplain real estate. By March 1846 there were 614 people residing in North Brisbane and 346 in South Brisbane. *The Moreton Bay Courier* declared in July 1846 that the district 'which so very recently echoed only to the foot-fall of the wandering savage, now exhibits all the signs of civilisation', the towns indicating 'future prosperity and progress', thus fulfilling the settler utopian dream.[35] *The Moreton Bay Courier* ignored the hydrological reality of floods and in 1849 advertised riverside land overlooking the 'calm and placid waters of the River Brisbane'.[36] Floods were not to interfere with development. As trees were felled and dwellings constructed, the settlers, who had purchased land more cheaply than in Sydney or Melbourne, looked on with pride at the culmination of progress.

In the colonial settler mentality, as the river provided a regular route for local and inter-colonial transportation and trade, it, like the land, had to be productive. By 1866 the Brisbane and Bremer rivers were important highways with 18 steamers, 18 sailing vessels, 23 barges and 70 market boats plying their trade between Brisbane and Ipswich.[37] Settlers were soon aware of river obstacles including shallow bars, rocks and bends, all restrictions to navigational efficiency as they impeded larger ships. The creation of the Queensland Pilot Board and Steam Navigation Board to control customs and shipping as early as 1853 reflected the importance of maritime trade to the local economy. The appointment in 1862 of a Marine Board and the first Colonial Portmaster (Lieutenant George Heath) not long after the formation of Queensland illustrated the importance for the colony to manage the river. So did the elevation of the Marine Board to the Department of Harbors and Rivers in 1865 (renamed the Department of Harbours and Rivers in 1877), led by Joseph Brady, an Irish engineer with experience in Victoria.

Engineers were called on, as they had been throughout the western world, to 'improve' the river, a term meaning navigational improvement, rather than ecological. The phrases 'improving the river', 'taming' and 'training' became the frequently cited euphemisms for dredging, deepening, cutting and straightening. In 1862, dredging at the river mouth created a deeper shipping channel, enabling ships to berth at Lytton. The resultant Francis Channel, named after the dredging superintendent Thomas Francis, became the first engineered alteration to the Brisbane River. Modifications to the Bremer River included removing obstructions, deepening the channel and wharfage area, and constructing a 76 metre-long retaining wall to train the river's flow. Seventeen Mile Rocks presented the greatest transportation obstacle for Ipswich as the rocks created two channels. Their removal took many attempts, first in 1863 and again in 1865–66, and not finally achieved until 1965.

Dredging upstream became a priority for the Department of Harbors and Rivers with a concerted program commencing in 1874. Between June 1878 and March 1886, the *Groper* removed over 2 million cubic metres of sand and gravel from the Brisbane River. Over four years (1882–1886) the *Octopus* extracted a staggering nearly 3 million cubic metres.[38] By straightening Francis Channel and cutting Hamilton Reach and Pinkenba Flats, vessels drawing 6.4 metres could berth at the Brisbane wharves after 1886, which made the river more productive.

These engineering alterations changed the river's flow regime in small floods and formed the initial steps towards a hybrid river – a mix of nature and human intervention. But the river refused to be tamed. Floods in 1863 deposited up to 1 metre of silt in the newly dredged channel at the river mouth bar. The floods of February 1887 and 1890 deposited silt and snags and created shoals, undoing much of the dredging and reshaping of the riverine environment. Engineers redredged and by the end of 1892 the river channel had been deepened to 4.5 metres, a desirable draught for shipping.[39] With dredging the river could fulfil its promised navigational potential. Attention then turned to another utilitarian use of the river – a source of urban water.

The Want of 'a Constant and Dependable Supply'

Since 1846, residents had complained about the fetid, 'nauseous' and unreliable water supplied by a rudimentary system of dams and wells in the settlement.[40] With the creation of the Municipality of Brisbane in 1858, citizens called on council to provide 'a constant and dependable supply' for a growing settlement in a region with uncertain seasons.[41] Council's Water Supply Committee was instructed to report on the 'most efficient and economical plan' for supplying 'pure' water. Council commissioned Thomas Oldham, a British civil hydraulic engineer who had recently arrived in Brisbane after gaining experience in Victoria, to investigate supplying Brisbane with water from a permanent source. Oldham looked to the river for traditional nineteenth-century solutions for water supply: dams and pumping to reservoirs. He believed a dam across the river above Brisbane, accompanied with locks and waterwheels, 'would convert what is now a river of brackish water into a pure fresh stream, navigable for some 40 miles' (64 kilometres).[42] Such a scheme had been adopted on the Thames River in London, and considered on the Yarra River in Melbourne before construction of the Yan Yean scheme. Council rejected Oldham's river dam in favour of a dam on Enoggera Creek, which would feed into town reservoirs. From the limited rainfall data available, Oldham calculated this system would supply a frugal 20 gallons (roughly 90 litres) per person per day to 150,000 people for one year.

Disputes soon erupted over the yield estimates and the expected cost, culminating in the creation of the Brisbane Board of Water Works under the *Brisbane Water Works Act 1863*. The board functioned as an ad hoc government authority until the Metropolitan Water Supply and Sewerage Board was established in 1909. This administrative arrangement revealed the complex relationship and ongoing tension between council and state in managing water resources. The board replaced Oldham with Joseph Brady from the Department of Harbours and Rivers, who finalised the design and supervised construction of Enoggera Dam, completed in 1866. Relations between council and state were further strained in 1890 when the Colonial Government commissioned hydraulic engineer John Baillie Henderson to head a Water Supply Department to advise local authorities.

Ipswich shared this tension, with the first municipal council (declared in 1860) considering schemes for both the Brisbane and Bremer rivers before abandoning the latter as the river, 'subject to huge changes in level and water quality', would provide a dirty and less reliable supply. Aborigines considered Bremer River water 'bad', the 'wrong colour' and a poor supplier of food.[43] Since settlement, there had been complaints about the Bremer's poor water, reported in 1847 as 'too brackish even for culinary purposes'. Finally, a scheme designed by engineer William Highfield for a pumping station at Kholo on the upper Brisbane River was constructed in 1878 at the Colonial Government's expense. Council was unhappily left with the management and debt.[44]

Floods and drought disrupted technological advancements in water supply. The 1867 flood forced the abandonment of plans to supply South Brisbane, and drought suspended reticulation extensions in 1886. In December 1885, during Australia-wide drought years (1880–1887), the Brisbane River ceased to flow.

Concerns about supplying the growing population, combined with a commensurate increase in water usage, prompted the construction of Gold Creek Dam (1882–1886) and Mount Crosby Pumping Station (1890–1893). With the river flowing again, Mount Crosby Pumping Station extracted over 27,000 litres each day, further intervening in the river's hydrology.[45] Heavy rain brought problems of silt and debris, and drought strained pumps and produced insufficient supply. Despite the setbacks, these engineered solutions offered some environmental security, allowing development on the floodplain to continue.

'The March of Progress'

In the 1840s, settlement was concentrated on the north side of Brisbane with a scattering of dwellings in the nearby areas of Spring Hill, Fortitude Valley, Petrie Terrace, South Brisbane and Woolloongabba, and a few beyond. Expansion slowed until 1854 when dense foliage was cleared, and booming land sales saw settlement spread farther to Yeronga, Bulimba, Moggill, Indooroopilly, Enoggera, Milton and Toowong. In 1856, the Ballarat *Star* reported that in Brisbane 'rapidly did the tide of immigration roll onward, and into these fertile lands'. With 'the march of progress', according to the *Star*, 'the country was thus becoming the abode of civilisation'.[46] The links with wasteland and productivity, settlement and civilisation had remained strong. Brisbane's 1861 population of 6,051 people reached 18,455 in 1871, but the central concentration had continued, only extending into Kangaroo Point. Between 1876 and 1881 Brisbane's population grew by 70 per cent, with 31,522 residents spreading to adjoining suburbs.

Most settlers lived within walking distance of work, with ferries providing limited public transport. The river offered the most economical means of transporting goods between Brisbane and Ipswich until the opening of a railway line between Ipswich and Oxley in 1875. Construction of the Indooroopilly Bridge enabled the railway extension to Roma Street in 1876. Settlement followed the railway and, after 1882, the tramlines. The urban sprawl began in earnest as the subdivision of large estates further encouraged gravitation to the suburbs. This growth extended in three directions from Brisbane's city centre to the north-east, south-east and the west, following previously established trends. Outer areas beyond transport terminals were sparsely settled and mostly used for farmland.

The 1880s brought a building boom and widespread land speculation to Brisbane, as they did in many Australian cities. Land sales brought the state taxation reward and a larger rate base for councils. Concerns about floods seemed foolish when an economic bonanza awaited. The auction houses promoted undeveloped riverbanks as an untapped resource, waiting to be realised by astute investors. At the February 1885 auction for Orleigh Estate in West End, the auctioneer promoted 240 'magnificent building sites', 66 of which had 'large river frontages'. Billed in the auction advertisement as aimed at 'capitalists, speculators, trustees' and 'others', this land was declared 'the cream of South Brisbane'. The effusive language continued with government auctioneers Arthur Martin & Co. promising a 'charming and enviable position', with 'grand and picturesque views, having such a noble river frontage'. The auctioneers assured the potential buyer that with the completion of the tramline, it was 'no stretch of the imagination, or in any way an extravagant assertion, to state that no matter what prices these lots realise at present, they will at least be worth double the same amount within the next twelve months'.[47] The advertising promoting these riverside sites with the promise of a doubled investment return had changed little from John Dunmore Lang's 1861 sales pitch. Many perceived land ownership as guaranteed economic success, a measure of human progress. More than 600 people attended the auction with nine river frontages (deemed the most desirable), realising the highest prices of the 71 allotments sold.

Newspapers encouraged floodplain land sales, with *The Telegraph* in 1884 promoting the sale of Bulimba Estate, its

29 riverside lots 'well known to be the pick of the Bulimba suburb'. Encouraging swift purchase, the paper noted a 'very great' rush to obtain riverside land with 'every available spot along the banks of our river being taken up at once when placed on the market'.[48] Proximity to the river, and nomenclature on the estate maps such as River Estate, or River, Creek and Wharf streets, were not regarded as a warning of possible flood but as a promise of cooling breezes and valuable, aesthetically pleasing real estate.

By 1891 Brisbane boasted a population of 101,554 inhabitants and was Australia's fourth largest city. Most people lived within 16 kilometres of the city centre with 92.2 per cent living within 8 kilometres. North Brisbane and South Brisbane were rival settlements, both attracting industry and commerce, but the north side provided the government hub. Elevation segregated the classes, with the heights overlooking the river occupied by the elite, the middle classes on the slopes, and the lower classes in the valleys and flats. The less attractive flats, susceptible to flooding, offered cheaper land for industry and industrial-class housing.[49] Ipswich followed a similar pattern, with much of its population of 7,625 people living within an 8 kilometre radius of the post office. Workers' homes were concentrated in low-lying land around industry: coal mines, wool mills and the railway workshops. The middle and upper classes occupied the higher ground.

Throughout early settlement, floods continued in the area, most notably the 1887 flood (3.78 metres and the highest since 1870) and a flood in 1890, which peaked at 5.33 metres. In Brisbane, the 1890 flood claimed at least four lives, left thousands homeless and inflicted over £700,000 damage to buildings.[50] After this flood, journalist Archibald Meston expressed no sympathy, but rather criticised human behaviour. Writing in *The Queenslander* on 29 March 1890 he declared:

> all over this colony are townships created by 'vested interests',
> unscrupulous speculators, or criminal foolishness, laid out in the

bottom of valleys, the flats of rivers, and low-lying plains, within short distances of magnificent situations free from the remotest danger of floods. All this is storing up trouble gainst the day of wrath, for assuredly Nature's laws know no mercy.

Meston forewarned that nature would 'inflict penalties that will be paid in bitter sorrow and tears of blood'.[51] He acknowledged that the defiance of nature and poor planning had created a conflict on the floodplain, one humans would not win. His view remained in the minority as settlers encroached farther onto the river's floodplain, ignoring Aboriginal and recent British experience.

These late-nineteenth-century floods did not temper growth; Brisbane's expansion was only halted by an economic depression that culminated in 1893 with bank crashes and registered unemployment peaking at 5,743 people. Land and rent values dropped to their lowest point, the problem exacerbated in Brisbane as the 1880s speculators had created a building oversupply. But by then the two urban settlements of Brisbane and Ipswich were firmly established on the floodplain, surrounded by private agricultural holdings. Transport systems, governments and speculators had encouraged the spread of settlement to the perceived picturesque and profitable riverside land. The goal remained progress, with the community giving little thought to the river's natural propensity, and need, to flood. The river, 'improved' by dredging and the removal of impediments, offered better navigation. River and stream waters could be stored in Enoggera and Gold Creek dams to provide potable water and offer some protection against the vagaries of drought. Dredging, training and cutting would alleviate minor flooding, but the public soon demanded an engineering solution to prevent major floods. South East Queensland's reliance on technocratic flood solutions had begun.

2

Mighty Outbreak of Nature's Forces: The 1893 Floods

ON BOARD THE steamer *Buninyong* near Mackay on 31 January 1893, Clement Wragge, Government Meteorologist for Queensland, experienced winds of 160 kilometres per hour as a cyclone developed. Wragge, who might today be described as a storm chaser, expressed the thrill of being in the eye of the cyclone, after years of 'longing' to do so, declaring it a personal 'red letter day'.[1] He telegraphed Brisbane on 2 February, reporting: 'passed though centre of terrible hurricane when off Northumberland group of islands; barometer at sea level and corrected about 28.60 inches. Providential escape, due to most skillful navigation; never seen such awful weather before.'[2] The cyclone crossed the coast, forming a rain depression that dumped record rains over the entire Brisbane River catchment. It deposited 1,026 millimetres of rain at the Brisbane Regional Office in February, Brisbane's highest ever recorded monthly total.

As the rain depression tracked south, it hovered above Crohamhurst, a settlement 87 kilometres north-west of Brisbane near the head of the Stanley River. Perhaps fortuitously for the historical record, Crohamhurst was home to meteorologist Inigo Jones, a protégé of Wragge. Jones recorded 35.714 inches (907 millimetres) of rain on 3 February. Wragge informed the scientific journal *Nature* that this extraordinary rainfall had 'beaten the world's record'.[3] While not an international record, it remains Australia's highest rainfall recording in 24 hours.

The rain flowed into the headwaters of the Stanley and upper Brisbane rivers, flooding the Brisbane River. The lower reaches of the Bremer River also flooded, the water outflow trapped by backwaters from the Brisbane River. Later estimates by the Bureau of Industry in 1933 concluded that '201,000 million cubic feet' (5.6 million megalitres) fell across the Brisbane River catchment in the first week of February 1893.[4] Extreme rainfall fell in the upper eastern catchment (Stanley River) with relatively low rainfall downstream around Fernvale, Ipswich and Brisbane. This meant Lockyer Creek and the Bremer and Brisbane rivers did not substantially add to the combined Stanley and upper Brisbane river floodwaters, otherwise flooding in the capital would have been much worse.

Grazier Henry Plantagenet Somerset watched the events unfold from his home, Caboonbah, on a cliffside 2,000 hectare holding roughly 4.8 kilometres below the junction of the Stanley and upper Brisbane rivers. He had previously experienced floods in 1890 when water submerged his house to shingle height. As the 1893 water levels rose, Somerset realised severe floods were imminent, recalling, '[I] heard a tremendous roar like a train coming out of a tunnel [...] I looked up the river and saw a wall of water coming down 50 feet high, it struck the cliff and shook the house [...] fully 300 yards back from the cliff.'[5] The tale may have become overdramatised in 40 years of telling, but Somerset knew the extreme localised heavy rainfall he saw in the Stanley River catchment had already produced a 'flood of unprecedented height in a remarkably short space of time'.[6] Somerset's wife, Katherine McConnel, a descendent of the same McConnels who had been warned by Aborigines of flooding at Cressbrook Station, lay in her bed awaiting the birth of their daughter, Doris. She was well aware of the danger as she watched the waters rise.

Somerset telegraphed John McDonnell, the Under Secretary for the Post Office in Esk, at 4.50 pm on 2 February: 'Prepare at once for flood. River here within 10 feet of 1890 flood, and rising fast;

still raining.' At 8.10 pm the McConnels of Cressbrook similarly telegraphed Brisbane: 'River within 1 ft of highest flood mark known, and still rising. It has been raining heavily since 6 pm. If the same rain has been falling at the head of the Stanley, look out.'[7] The intense localised rain caused the Brisbane River at Kholo to rise 3 metres in three hours before 9 am on 3 February. The river continued to rise rapidly at 600 millimetres per hour and peaked at 26.4 metres at Lowood, 32 metres at Mount Crosby, 22.8 metres at Goodna and 17.9 metres at Jindalee. Backwater from the Brisbane River also caused the Bremer River to flood to 24.5 metres. It took 36 hours for the flood in the headwaters to reach the inner city and, on 5 February, the Brisbane Port Office recorded a peak flood height of 8.35 metres.

The floodwater surged onto the floodplains, destroying settlements in its path. As water rushed downstream it swept through Cressbrook House, carrying bullocks and debris to Lowood. In Lowood, 20 houses were washed away, with a further 32 destroyed within a few kilometres of Fernvale. George Taylor from nearby Bellevue described his homestead as a 'complete wreck', the average inundation 0.6 metres to 1.5 metres above all buildings. The adobe (clay brick) walls of Taylor's home were washed away, with hundreds of cattle and horses killed. At Hay's Scrub, a nearby property, the flood left a 'mass of dead cattle, horses, pigs, fowls and sheep', with 35 cattle and 12 horses left in a heap 'as if they had been stacked'.[8] George Harris, a resident at Kholo since 1855, recalled that farmers living along the river 'not only lost their homesteads, but most of their stock as well'. He considered it remarkable that there had not been a greater loss of life given 'the deluge of water that rushed down the river and its tributaries'.[9]

Ipswich 'refugees' sought shelter on high ground at both grammar schools, the courthouse, the school of arts, churches and other public places on hills above the city. Sympathetic residents accommodated the 'less fortunate' in their homes.[10] Locals took extraordinary measures to prepare for the flood, including moving the Goodna Primitive Methodist Church building to higher ground, a futile act as it still flooded. By 4 February floodwaters inundated Ipswich. The Bremer Bridge (connecting north and south Ipswich) was rendered unusable, the train lines lay underwater and the telegraph line was cut. Ipswich was isolated (Figure 2.1). With the gasworks and the Mount Crosby Pumping Station submerged, Ipswich had no gas and the water supplies of both Brisbane and Ipswich were threatened.

Figure 2.1: Ipswich under water, Denmark Hill, 1893. (Picture Ipswich 8824)

Industries that provided employment in the predominantly working-class city of Ipswich were devastated. Floodwaters submerged the railway workshops and destroyed Hancocks' sawmills. The wool mills, left half-submerged, suffered £4,000 damage and the Ipswich Cotton Company lost £700 with work suspended through lack of water supply.[11] All coal mines, except Swanbank Colliery, suffered considerable damage, the worst at John Wright's Eclipse Mine at Tivoli where seven men were drowned and entombed, including John Wright's own adult sons, Tom and George. The local *Queensland Times* described the colliery disaster as 'one of the most lamentable occurrences' of the flood.[12]

The main thoroughfare in Ipswich, Brisbane Street, lay 4.5 metres under water and up to 9 metres in lower areas, crippling local commerce (Figure 2.2). The floods created a 'deplorable' situation in the suburbs where houses had been 'twisted into every imaginable position', with many homes swept away and piled on top of others.[13] In Basin Pocket, one of the worst affected areas, all but five houses were inundated, their residents saving nothing but the clothes they were wearing. Nearly all of Brassall and Woodend were submerged, and in Bundanba (now Bundamba) people walked around aimlessly, homeless and destitute.

Figure 2.2: Ipswich City in 1893 floods. (Picture Ipswich 9245)

Locals rushed to send telegraph warnings to the capital. Newspapers alerted Brisbane readers that 'a few hours will bring these waters past our doors', with floods 'imminent as soon as the waters from the Upper Brisbane and Stanley can get down'.[14] After 3 February no more warnings were possible as the telegraph lines at Goodna were submerged, cutting all communication with Queensland's southern and western districts and other colonies.

Citizens rallied with the warnings. As Brisbane's low-lying suburbs began flooding, 'great activity prevailed at the wharves', as consignees and agents worked day and night to lift their goods above the estimated flood line.[15] The colonial secretary organised crews for rescue boats and the defence, marine and police forces worked with volunteers to relocate people and possessions. The gunboats HMQS *Gayundah* and HMQS *Paluma* were moored alongside the Botanic Gardens to be 'clear of strong current and debris which is likely to swoop round Gardens Point'.[16]

However, the power and velocity of the floodwaters prevailed over human endeavours as the river accumulated debris and washed agriculture and homes downstream. Despite having piles deep in the riverbed, bridges were major casualties. A loaded train driven onto the Indooroopilly Railway Bridge to add weight offered no match for the water's force. The bridge succumbed to the river on 5 February with a 'great crash and a roar like thunder', as 'one of the 80 foot spans of the bridge canted over downstream, and then disappeared under the seething flood. The sound was heard distinctly nearly a mile from the site of the bridge.'[17] Brisbane was left without a cross-river railway bridge, its major freight route, for more than two years until Albert Bridge replaced the destroyed structure. Unstoppable, the floodwaters raced downstream, their passage graphically described by *The Brisbane Courier*:

> The produce of many a hard-working farmer went hurrying down the turbid waters. Hundreds of wooden houses, once the happy homes of owner or occupier, careered upon the flood, often remaining whole till they struck Victoria Bridge, when they crashed like matchboxes, and broke away into shapeless masses of wood and iron. Many of these houses contained furniture; and there is an awesome rumour that in some cases they carried the human inmates to hopeless death.[18]

Witnesses recounted hearing debris crashing against the pylons of Victoria Bridge 'above the roar of the water'. *The Brisbane Courier* reported that the bridge 'held on valiantly' until 6 February when the 'northern end yielded to the immense pressure of the water'. The account continued, 'there was one loud crash, which shook the very earth, and made the surrounding buildings shake in their foundations; one convulsive heave, and the wrecked portion went down the river' (Figure 2.3).[19] With the bridge completely destroyed, South Brisbane was isolated from the northern side of the city until the opening of a new bridge in 1897.

Figure 2.3: Crowds gather to see the destroyed Victoria Bridge, Brisbane City.
(State Library of Queensland 142118)

Railway station buildings were washed away, and boats were rowed along the submerged railway lines, now forming canals (Figure 2.4). Wharves were destroyed and the efforts to move the HMQS *Paluma*, hulk *Mary Evans* and steamer SS *Elamang* proved futile as they were washed aground, stranded on the banks of the Botanic Gardens. Low-lying portions of the city disappeared under water and boats traversed the main streets in South Brisbane. Floodwaters reduced South Brisbane's main thoroughfare, Stanley Street, to 'one long stretch of ruin and desolation', with an 'enormous' loss of property.[20] *The Brisbane Courier* reported on 6 February that only 'the top of a building here and there in South Brisbane could be seen from the Wickham Terrace observatory'. With perhaps unintended insight, the journalist continued that it 'might easily have been supposed that the waters were only occupying their natural bed'. Water submerged almost two-thirds of the business district, up to 4.8 metres deep in places, lapping verandah tops. Edward Street lay 'wholly under water' with 'no break' in the floodwaters 'from half way between Elizabeth Street and Queen Street to the Botanic Gardens' (Figure 2.5). In this principal shopping district, the floods left behind 'chaos, mire, and stench' and losses of between £1,000 and £10,000 for each warehouse.[21]

Figure 2.4: Low-lying railway cutting reduced to a canal at Toowong.
(*The Telegraph, Souvenir of Floods*, 1893)

Figure 2.5: Queen Street, Brisbane, February 1893.
(State Library of Queensland 64847)

Suburbs too fared badly. Across two South Brisbane wards, 198 buildings were destroyed (Figure 2.6), and a further 67 damaged, at an estimated cost of £48,985. In the western suburbs, only trees indicated where eight houses had once stood in Fig Tree Pocket. In North Brisbane, Breakfast Creek Hotel sat 2 metres under water and only the tips of the girder plates could be seen on Breakfast Creek Bridge. In Orleigh and Hill End estates in West End, 30 grand houses (approximately two-thirds of the houses in the estates) disappeared. The dreams of those who had purchased the 'large river frontages' from Orleigh Estate in 1885 with the promise of doubling their investment were shattered. Witnesses watched their homes 'move from their piles and go down the river', leaving the owners with nothing.[22] The family of 15-year-old Alexander Freese paid the ultimate price. His father, labourer John Freese, watched helplessly as Alexander drowned in the Orleigh Estate floodwaters while trying to prove how far he could swim.

Figure 2.6: Houses destroyed in Montague Road, South Brisbane, 1893.
(State Library of Queensland 6260)

The floodwaters subsided by 8 February, but South East Queensland had little reprieve. On 9 February a correspondent at Engelsburg (now Kalbar) reported, 'there is every appearance of more rain'.[23] Heavy rains were again falling by 11 February and caused a comparatively small second flood the following day. Low-lying parts of Brisbane were again inundated, and the railway line at Fairfield and Goodna was cut once more. The Brisbane River rose higher than the 1887 flood to 2.4 metres on 12 February.

As the flood passed and citizens breathed a sigh of relief, meteorologist Clement Wragge issued a special forecast on 16 February 1893 that a third 'tropical disturbance of considerable energy' (a cyclone) had developed north-east of Bustard Head, roughly 500 kilometres north of Brisbane.[24] Newspapers reported, 'abnormal rains are again falling in the south-east portions of the colony'. Witnesses at the head of the Brisbane River reported, 'another immense body of water is coming down. The river at Brisbane continues to rise slowly. It has been raining in Brisbane heavily all day with no signs of abatement up to tonight.'[25]

Henry Somerset again tried to warn Brisbane but with lines washed away, telegraphs from Esk were no longer possible. It has become a legend of the 1893 flood that Somerset sent William 'Billy' Mateer to North Pine (Petrie) to warn Brisbane of the third flood. The story says that Mateer, a 'good, game stockman' from Dalgangal Station, was staying at Somerset's property, Caboonbah Station. Somerset rowed Mateer with his horses Oracle and Lunatic in tow across the flooded Brisbane River. Oracle broke loose and swam back, but Mateer continued over the rugged D'Aguilar Range astride Lunatic until the horse became bogged near Petrie. Mateer arrived at Petrie on foot, sending his warning telegraph as the flood hit Brisbane. The outcome varies in different tales. Some claim the warning came too late. Others believe that the recipients discounted a flood warning from Petrie as a Petrie flood would have no effect in Brisbane. Thirty years later, Somerset remained bitter that his efforts were wasted. He received some recompense when the telegraph line was rebuilt after the flood and Caboonbah became the first official telegraph flood warning station until it was superseded by the telephone 12 years later.[26]

In this third flood, the heavy rainfall in the Brisbane River below the Stanley junction added significantly to the flood volume. On 17 February Fernvale received 13 inches (330 millimetres) of rain in 15 hours. Had more rain fallen in the headwaters, the flood would have been higher. Although the estimated rainfall of 3,960 million cubic metres was lower than in the first flood, the impact was much greater because the saturated land and swollen creeks and rivers could absorb little water, making the run-off ratio high.[27] The third flood, to quote *The Brisbane Courier*, 'did not quite reach its level of a fortnight previously, but it practically covered the same ground'.[28] The water came within 26 millimetres of the first flood at the Port Office, reaching 8.09 metres (Table 2.1). The river had reclaimed its floodplain.

Rainfall Event Date	Lowood	Mount Crosby	Ipswich (Bremer River)	Moggill	Goodna	Centenary Bridge	Port Office Gauge
29 January 1893	26.39	32	24.5	24.5	22.77	17.9	8.35
15 February 1893	na	31.28	23.6	23.6	21.88	16.6	8.09

Table 2.1: Rainfall events and flood peak heights (metres) on the Brisbane River in 1893 (except as noted in Ipswich).

The Disastrous Effects of the Flood

The effects of the third flood were devastating, not least because it followed the previous floods in quick succession and left little time for recovery. 'Disaster' was the word used most frequently by journalists to convey the damage. Theophilus Pugh noted the impacts were 'very similar' to the first 'calamity, only there were no bridges to carry away, and few houses, those within reach of flood influences having already succumbed'.[29] A Townsville newspaper offered hollow comfort: 'it is not likely that the flood will do serious damage, for there is scarcely any left for it to do'.[30] Recent flood experience had encouraged people to take precautions. Many had not returned to their homes or businesses, thereby minimising loss of life and possessions. But some weakened buildings succumbed to the third inundation and the sodden land and roads were more prone to landslides and collapse, so the damage was more visible.

The 'invaded' streets of Ipswich were left covered in debris, decomposing animals and mud, deeper and 'more obnoxious' than the last deposits and all emitting an 'abominable' stench. Houses had been twisted and 'strewn about in all directions', their verandahs removed as if by 'mechanical means' and the chimneys collapsed. Buildings that had collided in the floodwaters now 'huddled together as mere confused groups of timber'.[31] At Goodna, a suburb 'lamentably wrecked', 87 families (450 people) were left homeless with 'scarcely a single house having escaped the floodwaters'.[32] People living along the railway line were without food, including 25 railway men at Wolston and six or seven families at both Wolston and Darra.

Figure 2.7: HMQS *Paluma* stranded in the Botanic Gardens in 1893, before floating away in the third flood. (State Library of Queensland 43964)

Downstream, South Brisbane was the most affected, with unbroken stretches of water for kilometres. In Milton and Toowong, the 'actual course of the river could not be distinguished, save for the greater velocity of the current there'.[33] The gasometer in South Brisbane was overturned and coal supplies ran out, leaving Brisbane in total darkness for two nights. Food supplies diminished, and broken water pipes threatened potable water. Brisbane 'presented a wretchedly dismal appearance', covered in a thick layer of stinking mud, the much-prized alluvial soil the settlers had sought.[34] It was not all bad news, however, as the floodwaters helped to refloat the HMQS *Paluma* and SS *Elamang* from the Botanic Gardens (Figure 2.7).

The floodwaters ignored class distinctions, with newspapers reporting that 'cottage, bungalow, and mansion' vanished equally under the floodwaters.[35] The topography of the city meant houses were flooded some distance from the river itself, leaving both grand homes and workers' dwellings inundated. In Kangaroo Point, 'comfortable villas and cottages and the large foundries had been abandoned to the tender mercies of the flood water', and landmark elite houses and farms in Long Pocket were obliterated.[36] At the 'fashionable suburb' of Toowong, beautiful villas were destroyed. Water rose high in Sidney House, the residence of wealthy merchant Thomas Finney, and reached the upper floor of architect Richard Gailey's house. Eleanor Bourne, an affluent settler holidaying at Redcliffe at the time, was alerted to the extent of flood damage when she and her family were startled to find the front gate from their West End home, 'The Oaks', washed up on the beach.[37] The low-lying working-class suburb of Rocklea appeared to be a 'vast lake, hardly any home being visible above the water'.[38] Only 'one or two' cottage chimney pots 'peeped above the water' in the poor suburbs of Swan Hill and O'Conneltown (now parts of Windsor) on Brisbane's north side.[39]

Previous land clearances to provide sought-after property had made the land more vulnerable. Eighteen metres of the Domain at the Botanic Gardens slipped into the river and part of River Road (now Coronation Drive) collapsed in a landslide. Floodwaters and landslides deposited considerable sand, causing the Bremer and Brisbane rivers to silt up, with the river depth reduced by 2.74 metres at Hamilton. *The Telegraph* considered the reduced river depth 'one of the most serious results' of the floods.[40] Debris and sediment deposited throughout the river system stopped ferries and ships, a problem compounded by the loss of rail and road. Rubbish and other 'turbulent contents' in the floodwaters disgorged into Moreton Bay.[41]

After already experiencing economic depression, Queensland was left financially crippled by the 1893 floods. In his report on the devastating events, John Baillie Henderson, the Queensland Government Hydraulic Engineer, found the floods 'were severely felt along the whole course of the Brisbane and Stanley Rivers' and the Brisbane River's tributaries in the low-lying areas of Fernvale, Laidley, Ipswich, Goodna, and North and South Brisbane. In short, all the developed areas along the floodplain were affected. He estimated that 421 hectares in Ipswich, 348 hectares in South Brisbane and 128 hectares in North Brisbane were submerged. Agricultural areas fared worse, with an estimated 51,402 hectares inundated by floodwaters. Henderson calculated a damage bill between £1 and £2 million.[42]

The greatest toll was the loss of 35 lives. Some drowned trying to flee floodwaters as in the case of the family of Ipswich railway engine driver Peter Jackson whose boat capsized while they were escaping their flooded home on the Brisbane River, drowning four occupants. The only survivors were Peter's daughter Mary and labourer John Rowe, who sheltered on a house roof until it floated away and crashed into a tree. They tied themselves to the tree, clinging on overnight until rescued. Constable James Sangster drowned trying to rescue them when the tree he clung to uprooted and washed downstream. Others like John Jardine, a tinsmith at the Ipswich Railway Workshops, drowned rescuing property from houses in North Ipswich, his body washed up near the Bremer River Bridge. Others took foolish risks. Bricklayer James Florence, last seen on 4 February walking in water up to his armpits, was found by his son floating in 2-metre floodwaters near his home in Fortitude Valley.[43] *The Town and Country Journal* reported that 22-year-old John Power drowned in deep water while trying to rescue fowls, after having saved his father from the river. His inquest report makes much less heroic reading as Power disappeared into floodwaters after his father witnessed him 'skylarking in the water' catching chickens.[44] The sons of William Robertson, Secretary to the Civil Service Board, Launcelot (aged five) and Selby (aged two), were buried alive in a landslide at Indooroopilly where they were playing. Omnibus driver George Keogh, aged 23, last seen with three others in a boat until it capsized, was presumed dead as his body could not be found.[45] Other bodies were found floating in Moreton Bay, their identities unknown.

The psychological toll was considerable. Hinting at the extent of despair in the community, Margaret Crowley, a 40-year-old woman known to have had a 'melancholy disposition', suicided in March. The floods seem to have been the catalyst as they were for farmer Luke Fischer from Lockyer Creek, who suicided in March after losing all his crops the previous month.[46] Many people endured the heartache of losing all their possessions and faced the challenge of making their homes habitable. Community endurance and patience had been tested by the three floods and incessant rain. Over 21 days Ipswich received 738 millimetres, and 1,423 millimetres fell over Gold Creek Reservoir in Brisbane in 26 days. Newspapers reflected the mood as it degenerated: 'Brisbane has been afflicted with nearly seventeen days of rain this month and people are about beginning to despair of it ever becoming fine again.' A 'piercingly cold' gale increased the 'general wretchedness', especially for the homeless seeking makeshift shelter.[47] Many sought 'refuge in drink', with a correspondent in *The Worker* remarking that the level of intoxication had risen considerably in Brisbane as people grew increasingly desperate.[48] Casks of beer floating in the floodwaters must have increased that temptation.

From Incredulity to Blame

The 1893 floods fundamentally changed the human and riverine relationship. The river could no longer be regarded as a benign economic resource. It had a menacing side, one that threatened the prosperity it was meant to provide. The human response evolved from incredulity to practicality, then a sense of betrayal and conflict. These floods were unprecedented since free settlement began in 1842. The 1841 floods appear to have been forgotten with the 1894 *Pugh's Almanac and Queensland Directory* describing the 1893 floods as 'destructive and calamitous' and a 'pluvial visitation of extent never before experienced by white residents'. The 1890 floods had become the yardstick against which floods were measured, and, for some, knowledge of the 1890 height proved a liability. Imagining floods could go no higher, in 1893 some residents made 'no effort to move their goods or furniture' until too late. Others moved to the level of the 1890 flood and were forced to move repeatedly as the water continued to rise.[49]

Captain Robert Vernor, a British army officer with experience in the Crimea and India who lived with his family at Wivenhoe Pocket, about 30 kilometres from Ipswich, was one such person who found his 1890 flood experience a handicap. Vernor recalled, 'having weathered the flood of 1890 without much inconvenience, we felt no anxiety, and when we saw our danger it was too late, as we were then surrounded by a roaring torrent on all sides'. Eight people from his homestead were forced to flee in a rowboat on 4 February. When it overturned, the occupants clung to trees for 24 hours until they were rescued, tied on by strips torn from their clothing (Figure 2.8).[50] This belief that the last flood will never be surpassed was, and still is, shared by many, and, although scientifically illogical, it offers a sense of comfort to those living on the floodplain.

As South East Queensland slowly rebuilt after the 1893 floods, the opportunity arose for an examination of the floods and their causes. Floodplain occupants could no longer ignore the flood risk, nor the implications of building beside flood-prone rivers.

Newspaper accounts reflect the emotional and physical responses to the floods, but also highlight a major shift in attitude towards the river. The river had exposed its capacity to flood and destroy the manifestations of human progress. No longer perceived as an aesthetic fiscal resource or transport corridor, the river was instead regarded as a threat to civilisation that had to be controlled.

Figure 2.8: The Vernor family tied to a tree during the 1893 floods.
(State Library of Queensland 121166)

While amazement, shock and surprise had ranked high as initial flood responses, after the first flood in 1893 attitudes changed.

Newspapers reported on voyeuristic tourism with journalists describing the 'lively excitement' of railway passengers posted at 'every window [...] eager to catch a first glimpse' of the disaster.[51] Accounts marvelled at the spectacle of nature's performance, declaring the flood 'something to look on with admiration and wonder, as a sample of the wonderful forces of nature'.[52] Witnesses flocked to high vantage points 'gazing at the greatest spectacle of their lives'.[53] The flood 'fascinated and inspired the onlooker as do all the mighty outbreaks of nature's forces. But when the receding waters lay bare the ruin which their former majesty hid from view, wonder and awe are succeeded by horror and disgust.'[54]

In lieu of visual imagery to portray the disaster, journalists drew on poetic prose to capture the mood and drama of the moment. Newspaper descriptions reflect a sensory overload. Noise was noted – the roar of the floodwaters, the crash of debris and heart-rending screams – as a sharp contrast to the normally silent river, but smell dominated settler recollections. *The Brisbane Courier* reported on the 'nauseous filth' left behind, the streets 'coated with thick, slimy, stinking mud', and 'stench' and 'foul-smelling' were frequently repeated descriptions.[55] The smell of floodwaters and mud, full of dead animals, debris and raw sewage, in Queensland's subtropical February heat would no doubt have been memorable.

As the shock subsided, practical action came to the fore. The floods created enormous social problems, with homelessness, destitution, hunger and unemployment immediately apparent. The Brisbane Hospital dealt with 53 flood-related admissions with typhoid sufferers predominant, while drunkenness and looting presented a challenge for the police. Large recovery operations, including a 100-man gang in South Brisbane, were soon mobilised for the massive clean-up required. Aid was organised through the Central Flood Relief Fund of Queensland, a fund supported by community donations and administered by local government and churches, which was formed on 6 February. Funds poured into the Colonial Treasury from all over Australia and Britain. New Zealand

and neighbouring colonies donated large quantities of produce, as well as blankets and clothing, a ladies committee distributed clothing and seeds to replant 6,070 hectares, and the government provided free telegrams and railway transport. The relief work reached a 'magnitude that no person had anticipated', such was the total of donations. Yet applications for relief outstripped supply and stretched the Central Flood Relief Fund. By 18 August 1893, 10,945 families state-wide received at least some financial assistance, but with the funds exhausted many missed out.[56]

Despite the number of people affected and the economic impact, the floods did not attract political attention in the lead-up to the colonial election in April 1893. With election debate focused on the economy, imported labour and railways, reconstruction of Victoria Bridge provided a rare flood-related topic but was dismissed beyond the metropolis as fiscally irresponsible and too centred on Brisbane. Maryborough, Gympie, Bundaberg and Ipswich had all suffered flooding and Brisbane's floods were a local, not colony-wide, concern. Governments who had sold the flooded land were unlikely to encourage political attention on the subject. Rather than focus on the human actions that caused the hazard, some saw God as the culprit.

Many viewed the floods as an act of God, a response common to natural disasters. Robert Stewart of Toowong unequivocally connected the floods and God, informing *Brisbane Courier* readers, 'as a people, we have forgotten God' and asking, 'is it any wonder that calamity overtakes us? May we not expect even worse than the flood unless we repent?'[57] *The Week* received 'several letters from highly respected citizens' who shared Stewart's view that 'the absence of religious instruction in our State schools has led to the flood' and called for a 'Day of Humiliation' for society to repent and appease God. Several prayer gatherings were held on 14 June 1893 to pray 'in connection with the 'troublous times at present visiting the colony', with up to 300 people attending one meeting alone.[58]

However, not all were convinced that the floods were God-sent to punish sins. *The Telegraph* dismissed the need for a day of humiliation, arguing it wrong to blame Providence as 'natural causes have their natural consequences'.[59] Many happily attributed culpability to the uncontrolled and fearsome forces of nature that created natural disasters and destroyed human civilisation. *The Brisbane Courier* made light of the floods as 'freaks of the weather God' or the actions of 'Dame Nature'.[60] The labels 'act of God' and 'natural disasters' were used by those in power to clear themselves of responsibility. With divine intervention and accidents of nature beyond their control, political and administrative decision-makers could not be held accountable and could maintain social and economic control.[61] Admitting human error had the undesired potential to discourage development and prosperity and force social change. By framing the flood as a natural or God-ordained disaster, the event could be dismissed as an aberration or rare calamity. Instead of creating an environmental awareness that these floods were a climatic characteristic that would be repeated, the community clung to the hope that these floods were atypical. Growth and economic progress on the floodplain could continue, without adjustment to human behaviour.

'Bright Prospects so Cruelly Blasted'

Rather than accept responsibility, the government called on the people to rise to the challenge and recover from this adversity. *The Brisbane Courier* rallied Queenslanders: 'We have been taught distasteful lessons, but our resources have not been destroyed, nor our industrial energies weakened [...] We shall unquestionably benefit socially, morally, and politically by the adversity which we have lately encountered.' Settlers were inculcated with the notion that nature would not subdue human endeavour or the prosperity of settlement: the 'growth of Brisbane will not have been sensibly checked'.[62] The newspaper called on its readers to 'rise above' the disaster, 'develop our resources' and 'rejuvenate the colony'.[63] This narrative ran in tandem, and maybe in response, to newspaper correspondents who implied a sense of betrayal that nature had not made good on its bounty. A correspondent to *The Queenslander* reported that 'upwards of twenty years' of 'careful toil and industry' had delivered the promised productive farmland at Fig Tree Pocket, 'but, alas! the late floods have left them nought but grief and pain for promised joy'.[64] They had forgotten the cause of the fertile floodplain – the nutrient-laden, flood-derived sediments.

Writing to *The Worker* on 11 February, 'E. B.' vented his frustration: 'this is what we have been toiling and pinching and fighting and scheming for – these heaps of ruin and this absolute stagnation of trade'. The same day *The Darling Downs Gazette* declared, 'homes, secured after years of toil, gone in one night', and *The Australian Star* informed readers that in Orleigh Estate the river had carried away a 'vast amount of the wealth of Queensland – wrecked homes, furniture, cattle, produce' – the very things that humans expected nature to provide. If nature proved not to be a helper, a provider of wealth, it was only a small step for it to be declared an obstacle, the enemy of progress.

In the eyes of the colonial settlers floods made Brisbane a victim and the river an adversary, the enemy that had to be tamed. With this relational shift came the use of military metaphors in media reports. Historian Tom Griffiths says that 'in the face of an awesome natural force', militaristic language offers comfort, creating a belief that somehow these events can be controlled.[65] Newspaper articles from 1893 were littered with warlike phrases. Houses were 'invaded', factories took precautions to 'battle with the invasion', the 'dreaded invader would be seeking fresh conquests', property was 'destroyed' and businesses 'fell victims to the surging waters'.[66] Humans became 'fallen victims to the ravages of the unruly waters', with survivors like the Vernors, Mary Jackson and John Rowe celebrated and their rescuers awarded bravery medals as in wartime.[67] Queen Victoria conveyed her 'regret at the heavy loss inflicted on Queensland', a message not unlike post-battle commiserations.[68] A poem in

The Queensland Times eulogised Constable Sangster after he drowned in an attempted rescue, with language reminiscent of a soldier's tribute, professing his glorious courage, chivalry and daring 'deeds of glory' displayed in the 'field of battle'.[69]

The battle lines were drawn. The 1893 floods had brought death and devastation to much of South East Queensland and its citizens demanded the Colonial Government prevent a repeat of this perceived 'evil', 'calamitous' 'catastrophe'.[70] Brisbane residents regarded floods as an impediment to the progress of civilisation that must be removed. Land and business owners had no desire to move from the floodplain and the citizenry wanted the government to control floods. As settlers looked to science and technology to control the environment and tame the river, discussion turned to the most effective means by which to do so.

3

Taming the River

WITHIN DAYS OF the first flood, on 14 February 1893, a letter in *The Telegraph* declared if 'left to nature' the Brisbane River would 'continue to be a cause of periodical calamities'.[1] For many, leaving the river to the vagaries of nature was unacceptable, but not all were wedded to hydraulic solutions. Some dissenting voices suggested floodplain management to mitigate damage, yet these minority views were subsumed by the predominant desire to tame the river. Flooding was perceived as a problem of water control to be solved by engineering works, which reflected the late-nineteenth-century view that science and engineering could control nature and ensure human progress. South East Queensland looked to Britain, India and America to help implement technocratic flood solutions, including dredging and the construction of training walls, levee banks, canals and dams. Brisbane was an 'hydraulic society' in the making, a culture dependent on large-scale government waterworks.[2]

Although South East Queensland's faith in science and engineering reflected international trends, there were significant regional differences. Cycles of drought and floods delayed decisions over flood mitigation as tensions arose between the dual needs to provide potable water and control floods. As the memory of floods receded, and drought became the public's preoccupation, the administrative importance of flood protection diminished. The biggest delays, however, were cost and failure to agree on the most effective engineering structures, as locals and experts debated flood mitigation for over 40 years. While some settlers acknowledged the human-created flood hazard, the majority were focused on finding not *if* a technocratic solution should be implemented but *which* structural solution was the most appropriate path towards flood prevention.

Questioning Floodplain Development

The floods of 1893 offered an opportunity to re-evaluate settlement on the floodplain, which some did. Amid the language of exploiting and dominating the river, an alternative narrative appeared, revealing some settlers' understanding of the human-created hazard of building on the floodplain. As a *Telegraph* journalist reflected:

> these flood waters have come just where former flood waters have come. In the dim past flood waters found only gum trees on the ground and kangaroos as its inhabitants. Now we have built over acres and acres of this sort of ground, and we must not hastily conclude, having done so, that Providence takes the favourable opportunity so presented to punish us for our moral misdeeds by sweeping away our houses, our furniture, and gardens.[3]

The Week also exonerated God and the river, declaring human action accountable and cautioning:

> be careful how we blame Providence for permitting water to run again in old riverbeds and over areas of land actually formed by previous floods [...] If a man builds his house in the deserted bed of a river, can he complain should the water come again that way some day?[4]

Floods may be natural, but the hazard was anthropogenic.

Some also identified that the 'progress of settlement' with its land clearing and building construction had increased the height, velocity and damage caused by floods; land clearance and soil hardened by livestock had exacerbated floods, as the ground and vegetation could no longer absorb the water.[5] In 1898, the Brisbane Chamber of Commerce discussed the 'scientific fact' that the 'progress of settlement increases the frequency and severity of floods' by removing natural obstructions to the outflow of the floodwater, and providing new channels in drains and roads.[6] The Royal Society of Queensland added weight to this debate with a paper in March 1898 observing that in 'the early days of Brisbane, and before man's interference, Nature was naturally guarded by vegetation so that in times of long or heavy rains the lower reaches of the river's low-lying lands were saved from sudden overwhelming flood'. The paper argued that this changed with settlement:

> civilised man came: Governments without knowledge or experience sold the scrub land and the river bank reaches. The spirit of speculation in boom mirage set in, and the buyers or speculators chopped down and burned off or allowed the flood to wash away the timber, until the character of the country completely changed. Proportionately as this unwise work went forward, Nature's provisions for holding back the drainage waters were broken away, hence the waters unchecked had to come down in a rush in torrents.[7]

The boosters had ignored nature's own safety valves against flooding – trees and floodplains – instead clearing land, compacting the soil with cloven animal feet and building impermeable surfaces.

Others considered the lack of building regulations as the root cause of the devastation. A *Brisbane Courier* editorial in February 1893 declared, 'much of the misery lately endured in Brisbane has been the result of building beneath the known flood level of 1890'.[8] The newspaper called for legislative change to prohibit further building on the floodplain, suggesting flood-prone land be designated as parks and paddocks and provide breathing spaces for the city. A letter in

The Brisbane Courier, written under the pen-name 'Exchange no Robbery', advocated vacating the 'very considerable slice of the bed of the Brisbane River' sold by the government as town allotments and eligible building sites in South Brisbane. Removing settlement, the writer argued, would allow the river channel to 'devote' itself to the 'purpose for which nature, and not man, has designed it'.[9] Prominent citizen and merchant Nehemiah Bartley alerted *The Telegraph* readers to the fallacy of remaining on the floodplain, writing Brisbane's 'busy little human hive, all settled upon the treacherous "waste" ground where the river once flowed, and where it intends, periodically, to flow again' remained vulnerable to future flooding.[10] J. Kay expressed a similar opinion in *The Brisbane Courier*, saying 'nature has reiterated her warning to us wither to get out of her way or give her some other channel in which her exuberance may pass off without any one being hurt'.[11] However, at a political level the idea of vacating the floodplain fell on deaf ears, as no policy or regulatory changes were made.

Floods drew the attention of the Queensland Branch of the Royal Geographical Society of Australasia with society member James Park Thomson corresponding with John Wesley Powell, the Director-General of the United States Geological Survey. Years of experience had taught Powell to respect the importance of preserving a floodplain. He warned Thomson:

> There is one prominent fact which must not be over-looked – namely, that rivers of the character of the Brisbane must be allowed to retain a large territory in their own possession over or through which to discharge the waters of unusual floods. If man encroaches on these domains, he must take the consequences, from which no ordinary exertions can save him. In other words, the river must be allowed a fair amount of space of its own choosing. When by a large flood this space has been fairly well defined the borders may be thereafter protected, but encroachments beyond this must in the long run prove futile.[12]

While these opinions were made public in newspapers and journals, they remained a minority voice. Although some acknowledged the need to respect the floodplain, most settlers had their attention firmly fixed on preventing floods, not floodplain development.

The Faith in Engineering

The 1893 floodwaters had barely subsided when residents demanded flood prevention. Newspapers published the opinions of both amateurs and experts on the most effective engineering solutions to control the river and prevent floods. Gilbert Fowler White, regarded as the founder of floodplain management, noted in 1942 the 'common' trend in 'scientific and popular literature' to consider floods 'great natural adversaries which man seeks to persistently [...] over-power'.[13] Scientist Mark Everard describes how, as humans spread onto floodplains, floods were perceived as 'dark forces seeking to swamp, quite literally, a technocratic model of progress'.[14] It was a 'bitter battle', with the 'price of victory' being engineering works designed to control the floodwater and continuing flood disasters the 'price of defeat'.[15] Hydraulic engineers offered solutions to control the river and ensure environmental security. Historians Mark Cioc and David Blackbourn show how the language of control – tame, train, abate, ameliorate, straighten, regulate and improve – dominated nineteenth- and early-twentieth-century European engineering texts. Both argue the language implies warfare and nature's enemy status while also revealing a belief that free-flowing rivers were 'imperfect or defective' and therefore 'in need of improvement'.[16] A canal represented the ideal river – a single, straight channel, controllable and not flood-prone. Engineering would 'improve' the river, just as boosters believed settlement improved the land.

In 1879, Queensland employed its first hydraulic engineer, John Baillie Henderson. Known as J. B. Henderson or 'Hydraulic Henderson', he brought his vast hydrological knowledge, obtained through informal study and practical work as an engineer in Victoria since 1862. Initially contracted as a consultant to investigate

Brisbane's water supply, from 1883 to 1914 Henderson served as the Queensland Government Hydraulic Engineer in charge of the new Water Supply Department. His role included Superintending Engineer for the Brisbane Board of Water Works as well as a daunting work schedule managing stock routes, artesian water, and agricultural and urban water supply. These tasks reflected the imperatives of supplying water to assist agricultural and metropolitan development. In 1893, Henderson was commissioned to investigate the causes and extent of the floods, and recommend measures 'that might be taken for controlling floods or for mitigating their serious effects'.[17] Henderson understood the link between development and hydrology. In 1910, he declared, 'It is impossible to over-estimate the great value of this work and what a sound knowledge of the seasons means in connection with the prosperity of this State.'[18] As Henderson produced maps, hydrological graphs and tables, he codified weather and hydrology, thereby reducing complex natural systems to simple schematic representations.

Henderson faced an enormous task with limited resources as the 1890–1893 depression had forced staff retrenchments. Flood investigations increased an already overcrowded job list, a task made harder as the floods submerged his office by 3.4 metres, destroying records and maps.[19] Henderson also had little data to draw on for analysis. In 1880, Queensland had only 422 registered rainfall stations, most concentrated in the south-east corner. By comparison Victoria, a much smaller state, had over 450 stations and 15 years of data. River gauging (the recording of stream flow) was even more neglected. Victoria had gauged its streams since 1865 and New South Wales had done the same since 1890. Despite Henderson's repeated requests, the Queensland Government did not employ a stream gauger until 1909, and then only to inform water allocations for irrigation, rather than gather environmental knowledge. Between 1910 and 1919, gauge numbers increased from 14 to 50, greatly adding to available data.[20] The resultant data are still used in flood modelling and flow rate calculations for the Brisbane River.

While the water department collected data slowly, weather bureau meteorologists were hard at work. By 1893 Clement Wragge had established 97 meteorological and 398 rain stations in Queensland.[21] A quarrel with Premier Sir Robert Philp forced Wragge's resignation and the closure of the bureau in June 1903. The Water Supply Department absorbed the weather bureau, with the intent of collecting rainfall records only. Henderson strongly disagreed, arguing the discontinuity of data would be calamitous, diminishing the scientific value of previous records.[22] He prevailed and his department maintained all meteorological and flood warning work until January 1908 when, as part of Federation, the work transferred to the Commonwealth Bureau of Meteorology (BoM). The Queensland Government maintained control of river gauging as the data required to manage rivers was constitutionally determined to be a state responsibility. In order to meet their own professional needs for data and assist the state's development policies, Henderson and his colleagues monitored rainfall, run-off and streamflow, which, according to historical geographer Joseph Powell, steadily 'advanced the common stock of environmental information'.[23]

Henderson's Flood Solutions

Henderson's reports on water supply (1880), along with his two interim and final reports on the 1893 floods, provide the first significant studies of flood hydrology in South East Queensland. His reports collated known hydrographic and flood records after 1825 (excluding Indigenous knowledge) and substantially increased the environmental understanding of the Brisbane River catchment. These flood reports formed the basis of all further investigations on Brisbane flood mitigation. Henderson's 1895 interim report, *Floods, and the Mitigation of their Evil Effects*, reflected the economic reality that made expensive engineering solutions untenable. Consequently, Henderson recommended a cheap system of stream gauges and raised telegraph lines to provide timely flood warnings as used in France. This recommendation recognised both the cost and time to construct engineering works and reflected Henderson's personal belief in the need for hydrological knowledge to effectively manage water resources. Henderson concluded that there were no favourable sites for a dam and reiterated his recommendation for a flood warning system.[24]

However, the public wanted 'authoritative action', not just a flood warning system. The Brisbane Chamber of Commerce dismissed raising telegraph lines, erecting flood gauges, and the possibility of moving residents to higher ground or prohibiting the 'sale of flooded land for residential purposes' as 'palliatives'.[25] Vice-President George Fife accused the government of criminal negligence through its indifference, calling on them to employ a hydraulic engineer of 'large experience' to come to Queensland to find flood mitigation solutions.[26] Henderson's detailed final report, *Floods in Brisbane River and Schemes for Abatement of their Disastrous Effects*, recommended engineering strategies as a 'means to prevent or to mitigate the evil effects of floods'. This report's recommendations were more ambitious. Henderson reflected public sentiment, declaring that 'in view of the widespread distress and loss consequent on floods', actions 'to diminish, if not altogether prevent, their ruinous effects in future' were advisable. Although he considered these floods 'without parallel in the history of Queensland', Henderson knew that the 'excesses of Nature' could reoccur 'at any time', making 'some comprehensive scheme of protection' desirable.[27] Engineering would provide this protection.

Looking to traditional European engineering methods to control the river, Henderson considered canals, levees, cuttings, dredging and dams in his final report. He addressed the 'popular idea' of constructing a canal to divert the floodwaters to the sea, providing drawings of two possible canals, one leaving the river at Oxley and the other north of Yeronga, with both diverting the river to the sea at the mouth of Tingalpa Creek. Both would require extensive excavation, land reclamation, and construction of road and railway bridges, and would cost £9,523,194 and £7,138,000 respectively. This price alone made them, Henderson believed, 'out of the question'. Henderson also rejected the popular suggestion of a canal above Woodford, arguing that diversion canals provided minimal mitigation in a limited area, simply transferring floodwaters from one catchment to another at a prohibitive cost. Henderson had 'no hesitation in advising that their further consideration be abandoned'. He also dismissed levee banks as they required regular raising as the height of the riverbed increased through siltation. Levee banks, Henderson believed, were 'highly dangerous' and lulled people 'into a false sense of security'. They were expensive to build and maintain and were no longer in vogue with engineers.

Henderson considered a dam but with his estimated maximum daily discharge rate of 978,400 megalitres (a figure he and others later rethought) retention of this volume of water would require 'enormously massive' works. Based on his knowledge of dams in North America, Britain and France, he believed the size of the required fixed spillway dam for water storage would be prohibitively expensive and 'the idea ought to be abandoned'. He considered it 'extremely doubtful' that a suitable reservoir site could be found, including Henry Somerset's suggested site at Little Mount Brisbane on the Stanley River. Almost as an afterthought, Henderson suggested that a series of smaller and cheaper rubble-filled weirs may work for flood mitigation. However, engineer hydrologist Geoffrey Cossins later described these weirs as a more expensive and less effective solution.[28]

Henderson concluded that altering the river would be the most cost-effective solution, proposing three alternative schemes (A, B and C) for widening, deepening and regulating the river. These strategies would potentially reduce flood heights as they enabled rapid discharge of water, with the added benefit of improving navigation for large commercial vessels. Scheme A proposed truncating corners in the river at Gardens, Kangaroo, Norris and Bulimba points to form a wider channel from Victoria Bridge to the sea at a cost of £2,698,684. Approximately 21 kilometres of retaining walls would be built from the blasted rock and create 528 hectares of reclaimed land to offset the cost. Scheme B adopted the same plan for deepening and widening as Scheme A, but added a 'short cut' through Kangaroo Point and another through New Farm. The cuts would form two islands with the economic advantages of creating docks and 173 hectares of reclaimed land, a new government asset, which could be used for bulk stores and businesses. The scheme reduced the Brisbane River's length by approximately 3 kilometres between Victoria Bridge and Luggage Point. Scheme B, estimated at £3,374,891, would reduce floods in the city and South Brisbane by 0.6 metres more than Scheme A. Scheme C was effectively part one of Scheme A, to cost £2,047,360, with only the central 152 metres excavated to 8 metres, the remainder to be constructed later. An additional scheme (D), which outlined a series of training walls and cuttings, was to accompany any implemented plans. Henderson recommended Scheme B.

Recognising these major engineering schemes could take a decade to implement, towards the end of his 13-page report Henderson included a single paragraph that provided the only non-engineering solution to the issue of flood management. He 'strongly' advised that 'steps be immediately taken to prevent the erection, on low-lying flooded lands along the river banks below the city, of buildings of every kind, and also of all other structures that would retard the flow of flood waters'.[29] Although *The Brisbane Courier* published a thorough account of the report, this crucial paragraph drew little attention in the ensuing discussions.[30] If the government had found the courage to enforce this, future flood devastation would almost certainly have been reduced.

Henderson's report unleashed a flurry of opinions by self-professed experts. 'Lusta' informed *The Brisbane Courier* in 1898 that it required no expertise, only common sense, to realise river straightening by removing the corners would speed the passage of floodwater and increase the scour, reducing sedimentation. 'It does not require an engineer to tell us that a serpentine river is generally sluggish'. Lusta continued that the points were 'simply mud banks' with 'little or no commercial value', revealing a lack of consideration for their environmental role as part of the river.[31] The overtones of efficiency and economic progress were evident in the continuing desire for a straight river. Describing himself as a self-taught student of floods since 1890, Oxley resident Thomas O'Connor advocated training walls that would reclaim 'valuable wharfage frontages'. G. L. Lotz of Kangaroo Point dismissed the idea of employing a European expert and advocated a diversion channel at Redbank or Goodna, even offering to dig it himself. Henderson's scheme, Lotz argued, would 'spoil the city by unsightly walls, valuable property would be cut away, and the beauty of the river spoiled'. Lotz believed a 'proper flood prevention scheme', namely canals, was 'most urgently required to encourage people to build, and to improve the value of property'.[32] Francis Fuller, a civil engineer with 30 years of experience, recommended a dam with floodgates.[33] To these writers, riverside land had only real estate value. The consensus was that the bends should be removed to mitigate floods, improve navigation and increase available land.

While the public volunteered their views, the government left the report's recommendations in abeyance. Henderson anticipated this response. He noted that throughout the world 'scheme after scheme has been proposed by able engineers for averting the disastrous effects of floods, but often nothing has been done, and matters remain as before, possibly because of the great cost such works involve'.[34] With both Henderson and the government considering the cost prohibitive, the mitigation schemes did not proceed. Structural engineering advocates were unimpressed, especially when a 5.02-metre flood hit Brisbane in January 1898.

The 1898 flood brought a heightened interest in flood prevention and criticism of government inaction. Prominent citizen and political historian Charles Bernays expressed his disgust that 'absolutely nothing has been done either by the people or the Government towards preventing a recurrence' other than erecting flood gauges.

Rather than resort to 'apathy and short sightedness', he advocated through the Brisbane Chamber of Commerce that the government should hire the 'highest engineering authority' to find a solution.[35] In February 1898, the Brisbane Chamber of Commerce conference discussed the 'best method of minimising the effects of floods in Brisbane and districts', following up with a deputation to Treasurer Sir Robert Philp to demand the attainment of the 'highest expert opinion' on flood reduction and port improvements.[36] With local expertise limited beyond Henderson, an overseas expert had to be found. Politician Thomas Welsby suggested that 'India would be one of the best places' to look.[37]

Calling in the International Expert

In the late nineteenth century, Australia looked to British India for engineering expertise. According to historical geographer Joseph Powell, the country was 'becoming littered' with examples of the influence of Indian water engineering, including schemes for Coliban and Geelong (Victoria) in 1871 and Maitland (NSW) in 1877.[38] Many of the experts called in were British-Indian military engineers with decades of experience in irrigation, hydrology and large dam construction projects. These engineers also had relevant climatic knowledge as, like Queensland, Indian weather is influenced by monsoonal conditions. When the Queensland Government went looking for its international expert, Colonel John Pennycuick's credentials fitted the brief. Pennycuick was a former royal military engineer and consultant who had served in India from 1860 to 1896 in the Public Works Department as Chief Engineer and Draftsman. His main engineering project had been designing Periyar Dam in Madras, for which he received the Telford medal, a great honour from the Institution of Civil Engineers.

Philp received Pennycuick's *Report on Scheme for the Abatement of Floods in the Brisbane River* in November 1899. Pennycuick drew on his knowledge of Indian rivers but relied on Henderson's work as the basis of his report. He considered various schemes, largely by amateurs, but none, he wrote, deserved 'serious criticism'. Pennycuick dismissed levee banks and diversion canals as an enormously costly impediment to navigation and the river's natural flow. Canals would transfer the flood problem and provide little mitigation. Pennycuick also rejected Henderson's schemes A, B and C with their plans to widen, deepen and regulate the river, believing widening the river would bring relief but at a 'prohibitory' cost. He considered the effect of dredging minimal, and described training walls as a remedy 'worse than the disease'. Pennycuick supported cutting the points as 'sufficient relief to warrant the expense', although he considered the benefits exaggerated. Overall, he criticised that Henderson's schemes only dealt with mitigation around the city and did nothing to prevent flooding in the upper reaches. Any measures adopted, he maintained, should deal with the entire river. Applying Indian river hydrology, Pennycuick dismissed Henderson's estimated maximum discharge of 978,400 megalitres per day, calculating that it could not exceed 587,040 megalitres per day. These revised calculations substantially reduced the cost of a large dam, a strategy he recommended. Pennycuick declared a site at Middle Creek an 'admirable' location, 'singularly favourable for the construction of a dam of moderate height', and estimated land acquisition, engineering supervision and construction costs at £1,300,000.[39]

The Brisbane Chamber of Commerce challenged Pennycuick's report, as did community members. Drawing on his own 35 years of engineering experience, George Phillips wrote a letter to *The Brisbane Courier* on 10 January 1900 disputing Pennycuick's hydraulic estimates as conservative and declaring the proposed dam to be too small for the required flood storage. *The Brisbane Courier* believed Pennycuick had provided the answer and the city had to decide whether to accept his recommendation or 'admit that we were fools to call him in, and can get better advice among ourselves'.[40] The government had to evaluate Henderson's and Pennycuick's conflicting commissioned reports. With the cost of the dam close to Henderson's estimate of £1 million flood damage, the expense could not be justified. Engineer hydrologist Cossins argues that Henderson and Pennycuick both misinterpreted the flood hydrology and grossly over calculated the cost of a dam and that this delayed action.[41] While the economic benefit of flood mitigation could be disputed, the value of river improvements for navigation and trade could not. Southern colonies were luring commerce away from Queensland's inadequate ports, so income loss and navigational needs, rather than flood mitigation, motivated the first major engineering changes to the river.

Shaping the River

Navigational impediments restricted the river's use as the principal transportation route for large vessels. Siltation from the 1893 floods rendered much of the previous dredging useless; the depth of Hamilton Reach was reduced from 5 metres to 2.4 metres, and Eagle Farm Flats from 4.6 metres to 1.8 metres.[42] A deputation of businessmen to the Colonial Treasurer demanded immediate dredging to improve the riverbed. Portmaster Captain Thomas Michael Almond and Assistant Engineer and Nautical Surveyor Alexander Edward Cullen were adamant that the Brisbane River needed a greater suite of 'improvements'.[43] What followed was similar to the flood mitigation debate with a series of nineteenth-century engineering solutions advocated – dredging, cutting and training walls – as well as the strategy of consulting both local and international experts. Decades of dredging, the removal of bends in the river and the construction of training walls went ahead, all designed to 'improve' the river for efficient navigation.

Dredging reduced silt and gravel deposits, deepened the river channels and increased the river's natural scouring action. The dredges *Hydra*, *Groper* and *Playtypus* were employed and by June 1895 the channels between the river mouth and Hamilton reached a depth of almost 5 metres and a width of 91 metres. Dredging also continued in the Bremer River until the 1920s after the 1893 floods had obliterated all previous efforts. Almond and Cullen considered these actions inadequate and in 1898 recommended dredging the Brisbane River to a depth of 6 metres at low water, constructing a 2-metre training wall at Hamilton, and widening the river at Gardens, Kangaroo and Bulimba points. In their opinion, the removal of obstructive points, and widening, straightening and deepening the channels, improved navigation and would offer flood relief.[44]

In 1898, the Colonial Treasurer commissioned an international expert, New Zealand engineer Charles Napier Bell, to review Almond and Cullen's schemes. Bell also recommended dredging and constructing training walls at Hamilton and Parker Island. However, uncertain that removing the bends would have a 'material effect in lowering the height of high floods', he recommended another international expert be employed to complete a flood study.[45] Almond and Cullen were consulted and they again insisted on the Hamilton training wall, dredging to 6 metres and the removal of bends at Kangaroo and Bulimba points as 'a matter of utmost importance', citing concern about repeated shipping accidents. They recommended cuttings (in rounded figures) at Gardens Point (4 hectares), Kangaroo Point (2.4 hectares), Kinellan Point (5 hectares), Norris Point (0.4 hectare) and Bulimba Point (2 hectares).[46]

The Queensland Government invited Lindon W. Bates, an American dredging engineer with experience on the Mississippi, Volga, Scheldt and Hooghly rivers, to assess Almond and Cullen's scheme in 1898, which reflects a national shift away from Indian expertise and towards American knowledge at this time.[47] Bates recommended building training walls and cutting points, all of which required dredging. His business as the manufacturer of Lindon Bates Dredges, which were subsequently commissioned by the Queensland Government, appears to have raised no media concerns about a conflict of interest.[48] In 1911, Cullen, then Engineer for Harbours and Rivers, continued his campaign, advocating the removal of Gardens Point, the erection of training walls and cutting a 4.8 kilometre channel into the river, so the 'risk of trouble from flood will be seriously minimised'.[49] While solutions varied, the consensus remained that river regulation would solve flooding.

Training walls effectively converted the river to a canal, for many the ideal river, giving it definable and controllable boundaries, and preventing it from returning to its natural state in times of flood. Training walls were first constructed at Hamilton in 1900 (2,620 metres long), and later at Doughboy, Coxen Point, Lytton, Parker Island, Bulwer and the Botanic Gardens. Legislation in 1907 forced private citizens to build training walls on their riverfront land, with 3,048 metres of private walls built between South Brisbane and Bulimba by 1908.[50] By 1936, Pinkenba's training wall reached 2,606 metres in length.

Dredging proceeded apace. In 1906 alone, 1,848,545 tonnes of sediment were removed and by 1907 Cullen anticipated the river would be 7 metres deep and 91 metres wide at the river reach. By 1936 this was increased to 9 metres deep and 122 metres wide as far as Hamilton. The introduction of new technology – a rock drilling plant – enabled the blasting of steep rock walls to widen the channel to the width of two vessels. By 1901, 20,880 cubic metres of rock had been removed from Lytton Bar. River widening also created swinging basins at Pinkenba (1908), New Farm (1912), Hamilton (1914), Bulimba (1925) and Luggage Point (1932). Dredging of city reaches for navigation largely ceased after 1940 when construction of the Story Bridge limited the passage of large vessels, forcing wharves to move downstream to Hamilton.

Removing the river's bed had the additional benefit of creating more land. Soil and rock from the river dredging was used to form Bishop Island in 1910. Dredging of 300,000 tonnes after the 1928 flood helped 'reclaim', or more accurately 'appropriate', riverine land at the Parker Island reclamation area at Lytton. Spoil from the river's bed was deposited behind training walls, doubling their height to keep the river at bay. Millions of tons of dredged soil created the reclamation areas at Hamilton and Pinkenba in 1936 and 1937 and covered naturally tidal land to create industrial and navigational facilities. In 1954, a further 3,630 tonnes of silt pumped from the river created industrial land between Eagle Farm Road and the Brisbane River for wharf facilities. Approximately 162 hectares of swamps and mangrove land, the habitat of many riverine species, had been systematically reclaimed by 1927.[51]

The biggest river transformation was the cutting of Gardens, Kangaroo, Kinellan, Norris and Bulimba points, a strategy recommended by Henderson, Cullen and Almond, and Bates. This would, in the words of *The Brisbane Courier*, reduce the meandering nature of the river with its 'awkward bends' that posed navigational 'disabilities' and reduced the passage of floodwaters.[52] Initial work included removing Kangaroo Point's hairpin bend, and removing land from Gardens Point in 1900–01 and again in 1913. In the 1930s, the Bureau of Industry further 'regularized' the river, dredging 297,985 tonnes from the eastern side of Kangaroo Point and removing 38,405 cubic metres of rock from a projecting cliff behind the wharves.[53] Similar work occurred at all major river points as the river was reshaped. While economically driven to increase mercantile income through navigational improvements, with the secondary potential to minimise floods, these river modifications were underpinned by the persistent belief that humans were improving nature with engineering.

Adding Order to Natural Beauty

The notion of engineered improvements pervaded newspaper articles in the early 1900s. In 1927, *The Telegraph* declared that Brisbane boasted one of Australia's 'finest rivers': 'Nature gave the city the diamond in the rough, but the engineers of Brisbane can claim credit for having polished the rough stone, taken off its rough edges, and made it not only a thing of beauty, but a great commercial asset to the city.'[54] The same newspaper added: 'to the natural beauty of the river man has added the beauty of order'. Unsurprisingly, engineers agreed. Participants at the annual conference of the Institution of

Engineers, Australia in 1924 admired the engineering developments on the Brisbane River, with one speaker remarking, 'engineers made the Brisbane River what it is, and Nature made Sydney Harbour'.[55]

The enduring role of the river as an invaluable commercial asset was repeatedly expressed. University academic Dr Francis Cumbrae-Stewart believed it to be the 'greatest commercial river in Australia', and *The Brisbane Courier* labelled it a 'notable asset'.[56] Newspaper articles maintained it would be 'rash' to restrict development alongside the river, as this would reduce its full economic potential. *The Telegraph* stated, 'it is the function of government to see that the best is made of any opportunities which nature has provided for the commerce of the country'. If these 'opportunities' were found wanting, engineering skill was called on to improve nature and make it 'available for and capable of doing the business of the country'.[57] Prosperity, engineering and state interests were intertwined.

A few dissenting newspaper contributors lamented the consequent pollution from development and the encroachment on picturesque riverfront property by wharves and industry. But these concerns were tempered with economics. The pollution concerns about Hamilton wharves were linked with property devaluation, and *The Telegraph* regretted that cutting Gardens Point reduced useful and valuable land in the Botanic Gardens but found comfort that the needs of navigation and flood mitigation 'more than compensate for the encroachment on the people's recreation grounds'.[58]

Development made river modifications imperative and even justified the significant cost of resuming private land, unlike floodplain clearance. The ultimate hope remained that engineered river modifications would eliminate floods. *The Telegraph* clearly expressed this aspiration, declaring that with engineering 'the day will surely come when, free from fear of floods', the city could be built and the 'beauties of the river will be enhanced'.[59] Despite this ongoing faith in engineering works to prevent floods, plans to build dams languished as they were deemed prohibitively expensive. Also, not long after Pennycuick submitted his recommendation for Middle

Creek Dam in 1899, drought – Queensland's other competing water hazard – overshadowed the flood management deliberations.

Infrequent Floods and Rising Drought

Like floods themselves, the demand for flood mitigation proved episodic. As American geographer Gilbert Fowler White describes, 'flood hazard tends to wax and wane in the public mind in direct relation to the occurrence of high water'.[60] White argues that while flood protection is sought immediately after a flood, as years pass and flood memories fade, the population becomes increasingly indifferent to the issue as they focus on more visible and immediate needs. Infrequency allows people to forget or underestimate floods, or to assume they will never happen again.

Between 1899 and 1903 a nationwide drought, dubbed the Federation Drought, gripped the continent. As the Brisbane River threatened to run dry in 1902, floods left public consciousness. With the exception of a small flood in 1908, Queensland experienced a long dry period until January 1927 with droughts in 1915–16, 1918–19, 1923–24 and 1936–37. Dry years pushed floods into distant memory as water supply, not flood mitigation, became the government priority and focus of public debate. Engineer George Phillips re-entered discussions in 1905 advocating importing water from Stradbroke Island.[61] Again the Queensland Government looked to the overseas experts for a solution, commissioning distinguished American engineer Allen Hazen to investigate water supply in 1907. He charged an exorbitant fee, rejected the Stradbroke Island scheme and recommended construction of Lake Manchester Dam on Cabbage Tree Creek, a small tributary of the Brisbane River, and a dam on the Stanley River. Lake Manchester Dam was completed in 1916, but its flawed hydrology and design faults left it unable to play a major role in supplying Brisbane's water, and it could only be used for emergencies.[62]

Both the Ryan Labor Government (1915–19) and the Theodore Labor Government (1919–25) had other water priorities. Agrarian socialists, they regarded closer settlement as the means of developing the state and water provision and believed that dams and irrigation offered the key to success. Under the *Irrigation Act 1922*, administered by the new Queensland Irrigation Commission, water policy focused on agriculture. Throughout Queensland, many cities experienced flood and poor urban water supplies, and state money could not be concentrated in South East Queensland. Brisbane River floods were considered a local, urban issue that should be managed by the Metropolitan Water and Sewerage Board created by the state in 1909.

The Royal Commissioner from Melbourne

The questionable competency of the Metropolitan Water Supply and Sewerage Board (renamed in 1915) placed water supply under increasing political scrutiny. This board had spent £7 million in 17 years to little avail, leaving the city with an inadequate potable water supply, while actively investigating dam sites, a task beyond its mandate. The government, already dissatisfied with the board's inability to raise overseas loans, were less than impressed when a consortium of its members and associates personally purchased land around a proposed dam site at Little Nerang.[63] With suggestions of ineptitude and corruption abounding, the board came under scrutiny at a royal commission, led by eminent Melbourne engineer Alan Gordon Gutteridge, in 1927.

Although three decades had passed since Henderson and Pennycuick's reports, Gutteridge's brief had changed little from theirs – to determine the 'most efficient and economical methods' to provide and conserve Brisbane's water supply and flood prevention works.[64] The coupling of water supply and flood prevention remained. Gutteridge reviewed the reports of Henderson, Pennycuick, and Almond and Cullen, along with the hydrological records from major floods between 1887 and 1927, and called 58 witnesses (including engineers, farmers, labourers and water supply staff) before his inquiry. He reconsidered the hydrology and, with additional years of recorded data, found Henderson's calculations more reliable than Pennycuick assumed. Gutteridge allowed for a flood maximum daily discharge of 1,125,160 megalitres.

Gutteridge's report continued the dependence on engineering. He found that improvements in the lower Brisbane River (widening, straightening and training) would reduce the maximum flood heights by about 1.2 metres but would have no effect in the upper reaches or its tributaries. He also considered the proposed dams at Middle Creek on the Brisbane River (Pennycuick's recommended site) and Little Mount Brisbane on the Stanley River (Henderson's considered site). Gutteridge maintained that if the dam served the dual purpose of water supply and flood mitigation, the cost analysis significantly improved as a combined dam could be smaller and hence less expensive. A dual-purpose dam, although flagged as a possibility by Henderson in 1896, offered a significant departure in contemporary dam design. Dams were an expensive strategy and 'any gain was thought to be outweighed by the expense of the structure'.[65] However, in urban rather than rural areas, the flood damage bill can soon outweigh the price of a mitigation dam. The cost analysis increasingly skewed in favour of dam construction as Brisbane's population and urban footprint grew. If the dam could provide both flood mitigation and water supply, the ever-present dual challenges, the potential benefit would outweigh construction costs.

Gutteridge found that 'no one scheme would permit complete control of all floods', so he recommended that both the Middle Creek and Stanley River dams should be constructed, the latter first. He considered flood control measures urgent, warning that future floods would be more severe and cause 'inconceivable damage' estimated at £15 million.[66] He recognised that human activity such as deforestation and urbanisation could exacerbate floods, but upheld his brief, advocating engineering structures, rather than floodplain management, to address the city's dual environmental concerns. When his report received criticism, Gutteridge offered a response that was similar to Pennycuick's: 'I was consulted on how to protect Brisbane from flood damage. I have shown them how it can be done, and at what cost. It is for them, and the people whom they represent, to decide whether the game is worth the candle.'[67] Despite his pleas of urgency, the government did not act. Dam construction went into abeyance, delayed further by cost, administration and more investigation.

Shifting of Administrative Control

While dam construction did not proceed, the Gutteridge inquiry prompted the abolition of the Metropolitan Water Supply and Sewerage Board in April 1928, largely because of its own ineptitude. Administrative and executive control of South East Queensland's water supply transferred to the Brisbane City Council (BCC), a new local government authority created in 1925. Council appreciated the urgent need to expand both the storage and reticulation capacity of the city's water supply, although with limited funds it struggled to build a new reservoir at Eildon Hill and extend water mains. Council's Chief Engineer, William Bush, prepared a report on *Water Supply Extensions and Flood Mitigation* in 1930. Believing a dam to be the 'only reasonable method of controlling floods', Bush reiterated Guttridge's conclusions and recommended water supply and flood mitigation dams at Little Mount Brisbane and near Middle Creek.[68] However, economics again intervened as the Great Depression (1929–39) soon overwhelmed water supply issues.

By 1931 the Bureau of Economics and Statistics estimated that Queensland's unemployment exceeded 30 per cent of the workforce. Arthur Moore's Conservative Government, elected in 1929, had embraced deflationist policies, relying on private enterprise to stimulate the economy. When elected in 1932, William Forgan Smith's Labor Government inherited a £3,885,229 deficit and a 156 per cent increase in unemployment.[69] Forgan Smith championed John Maynard Keynes and Franklin D. Roosevelt's New Deal policies to improve employment through government work and established the Bureau of Industry to coordinate and manage a public works program, with high priority given to construction, electricity, sewerage and water resources.

The result was another water investigation, the *Brisbane Water Supply and Flood Prevention* report, which was completed in 1934 by the Special Committee of the Bureau of Inquiry, a committee comprised of highly qualified engineers. The chairman, civil engineer William (Bill) Nimmo, drew on his experience of water systems and management regimes in Queensland, New South Wales, Victoria and Tasmania. A fortunate choice, Nimmo's interest in hydrology was reflected in the 23 memos he submitted to the committee, including ground-breaking work on unit-hydrographs, flood probability studies and a floodplain map of Brisbane, all of which re-examined the work of Henderson, Pennycuick, Gutteridge and others. The report echoed the engineers of the past as recommendations included further 'regularising' of the concave bends opposite Kangaroo Point, Gardens Point and Newstead to remove obstructions, as well as cutting land at Kangaroo Point, New Farm and Seventeen Mile Rocks, and deepening the Town and South Brisbane reaches. The bureau's report also recommended construction of a dual-purpose dam to provide environmental security against 'all floods except the rarest and most calamitous known' and regulate the river flow. The estimated cost of under £2 million was less than the estimated damage of a major flood. The report concluded that finances compelled construction of only one dual-purpose dam until such a time as the two risks of flood and drought could be 'provided against separately', but the engineers also recognised the challenge of managing a multifunctional dam.[70]

Although the bureau considered Middle Creek a more effective dam site, giving 'almost complete protection', they rejected this more expensive option in favour of a dam at Little Mount Brisbane. Deemed the most cost-effective option to 'prevent all minor floods', reduce major floods and ensure adequate potable water until 1981, this scheme would dam the Stanley River, the major contributor to past floods. The bureau considered it 'probable' that Middle Creek Dam would be built in the future as both dams 'should give virtually complete protection' but 'for the present the community is spending what it can afford'.[71] A dam on the Stanley River, politicians agreed, would provide Brisbane's most affordable flood protection.

A 3.32-metre flood in central Brisbane in 1931 and the onset of drought in 1934 placed water on government agendas again and favoured the dam's construction. The need for employment relief altered the cost equation as the task required at least 1,500 men for four years, which would reduce unemployment by about 10 per cent.[72] The Stanley River Dam, engineers estimated, would remove £2,350,000 from the 1893 flood damage bill, which was less than the cost of the dam. With annual maintenance and interest equal to the annual risk of flood damage in Brisbane and Ipswich, Henry Wilbur Herbert, engineer and Bureau of Industry staff member, regarded the Little Mount Brisbane Dam as a wise 'insurance technique'.[73] The Bureau of Industry declared, 'there can be no doubt that the insurance basis justifies at least the river works and the cheaper dam' and 'in the meantime, and whatever the floods may be, the sense of security given to the community may be regarded as the profit on the investment'.[74]

The River is Dammed
After decades of consultation, climatic factors, unemployment relief, economics, risk analysis and engineering all converged, finally convincing the government to dam the Stanley River. The Stanley River Works Board, constituted under the *Bureau of Industry Amendment Act 1934*, commenced work on Somerset Dam in that year. World War II caused delays when labourers were relocated to Cairncross Dock between 1942 and 1948, after which the Office of the Coordinator General took responsibility for construction and completed the dam in 1959. The dam first supplemented Brisbane's water supply in 1941 (despite being incomplete) and supplied Brisbane with 154 megalitres of water daily by 1946. It also withheld heavy

rainfall in 1950.[75] On completion, Somerset Dam became BCC property under the *City of Brisbane (Water Supply) Act 1959*.

Public commentary reflected the belief that dams tamed floods. Visitors to Somerset Dam's construction site in 1934 were, according to *The Queensland Times*, 'awed by the imminence of the stupendous project', impressed by the 'fact that man was beginning the task of harnessing Nature'.[76] As gigantic engineering structures that are able to hold back megalitres of water, dams do inspire awe, especially when floodwaters rush through their gates. They are a massive physical manifestation of technology and human mastery of nature, described by historian David Nye as 'a technological sublime'.[77] These sentiments were clearly articulated in a celebratory brochure produced by the State Public Relations Bureau in the 1950s to commemorate the completion of Somerset Dam in which the government boasted of its 'lasting monument'. In the foreword, Premier Frank Nicklin wrote:

> nature was in a benevolent mood when the Stanley River Gorge was fashioned. Brisbane has been fortunate indeed in that such a remarkably good site has been available for a dam which could serve the dual purposes of safeguarding its water supply and taming a river which has had such a turbulent history in relation to past floods.[78]

In Nicklin's mind, human ingenuity – engineering – would improve upon nature to ensure human progress. Advocates maintained that the damming of the Stanley River should protect Brisbane from future flooding and guarantee water supply. Central to Nicklin's foreword lay the notion that the river had been tamed. After years of debate on appropriate flood mitigation methods, the path had been chosen – reliance on engineering and not floodplain management.

Somerset Dam, named in honour of Henry Plantagenet Somerset, was Australia's first dual-purpose flood mitigation and water supply dam. Designed to address the twin environmental concerns of drought and flood, the dam provided 40 per cent for water storage and 60 per cent for flood mitigation. At Full Supply Level (FSL at 99 metres) it had a storage capacity of approximately 200,000 megalitres, twice the volume of Sydney Harbour. Somerset Dam provided 90 per cent of Brisbane's water supply, with its storage capability calculated to meet the demands of the surrounding regions until 1981. This duality of purpose created an inbuilt tension that has plagued dam operators ever since and created competing priorities that cannot be entirely resolved.

Somerset Dam regulates the Stanley River catchment area. Although only 10 per cent of the total Brisbane River catchment, it is a major contributor to most Brisbane River floods because of its high rainfall, with 25 to 30 per cent of the total Stanley River floodwaters flowing through Somerset Dam. Hydrologists refer to 'favourable' and 'unfavourable' floods. When the rain falls in the headwaters and a large proportion of run-off comes from the Stanley River, the conditions are favourable and Somerset Dam is effective. In unfavourable floods, most flooding occurs downstream and cannot be managed. Nature determines the dam's effectiveness.

Using 1893 flood data, engineers calculated the mitigation effect of Somerset Dam. They found in the first 1893 flood's favourable conditions (where a large proportion of run-off came from the Stanley River) the dam would have reduced the flood by 3.5 to 4 metres at the Port Office. However, in the third 1893 flood most rain fell below the Stanley River. In these unfavourable conditions the dam would have reduced the flood by only 2 metres.[79] The temporal and spatial patterns of floods, with their inherent unpredictability, present difficulties for dam managers in knowing when to empty the flood storage. They must be guided by likely scenarios based on history and hydrological modelling. This flood hydrology remained a mystery to most of the population, for whom the very existence of the dam offered reassurance enough that floods could be prevented.

After decades of agitation, Brisbane finally had its water supply and flood mitigation dam. The Brisbane River had been tamed, its flow was regulated and floods could now be controlled or, better still, prevented. Water administrators, hydrologists and meteorologists were well aware of the remaining flood risk after Somerset Dam's completion and continually advocated their proffered solution – construction of a second dam. While a few dissenting voices recognised human contributions to the flood hazard, community consensus advocated the use of engineering measures to control the river.

Since 1893, public debate and government-commissioned engineering studies had focused almost entirely on finding an economically viable technocratic solution to address the twin hazards of drought and flood to provide the environmental security needed for the region to prosper. South East Queensland's future dependency on dams for flood mitigation was cemented. Further, construction of Somerset Dam created a false sense of security, the myth that the river was tamed and floods prevented. In 1974, the Coordinator General, Sir Charles Barton, aptly labelled this false hope the 'Somerset Dam Syndrome'.[80]

4

Encroaching on the Floodplain

AFTER 1959, THE Brisbane River system was regulated, its flow regime managed by Somerset Dam's gates. The ideology of controlling nature through engineering had prevailed as Somerset Dam had tamed the river. Or so many thought. Flood-free years, indeed drought, further nurtured this misconception. Political priorities, the unending pursuit of growth and the preservation of property rights outweighed the need for land management strategies to mitigate the flood hazard or preserve the river's floodplain and natural flow. Largely unrestricted by weak legislation and town planning regulations, South East Queensland enjoyed unfettered development of the floodplain.

After the 1893 floods, some individuals took matters into their own hands to manage areas liable to flooding. Businesses and settlers moved to the less-affected north side of the city, which marked South Brisbane's demise as an alternative city centre. Collective local action, rather than government initiative, prompted relocation in the Orleigh and Hill End estates. Thirty houses were washed away in 1893, all but one allotment in Orleigh Parade left vacant.[1] In 1914, 292 ratepayers and residents petitioned the South Brisbane Council and proposed they acquire the dormant allotments fronting the Brisbane River deemed 'unsuited for building purposes' for a public park or promenade. Negotiations on sale prices dragged on, despite the Hill End Progress Association persuading locals to accept a rate increase to fund acquisitions. Finally, in 1916 council resumed land for the formation of Orleigh Park. The 1885 boosters' promise of a doubling of investment went unfulfilled. Robert Burton valued his land at £150, less than he paid for it, but accepted £65. James MacMillan sold his five subdivisions for £5 each. Builder John Large fared even worse as he was forced to donate his three allotments gratis to the council in 1915.[2]

While council resumptions for flood protection proved to be a rare and lengthy procedure, mandatory resumptions occurred more readily for public works and council projects. The state showed reluctance to acquire flood-prone property to reduce the hazard, but had no difficulty compulsorily resuming 7,560 hectares of fertile farmland for the flood storage portion of Somerset Dam. Equally, the two Aboriginal stone axe heads found in the dam's excavations did not raise concerns about taking Indigenous land.[3] Compulsory acquisition was justified with the dam deemed to be in the state's interest.

National economic prosperity and the creation of the new municipality of Greater Brisbane in 1925 encouraged growth. BCC, formed through an amalgamation of 20 local authorities, controlled an area of 97,200 hectares, making it the second largest council in the world after Los Angeles. Today BCC remains Australia's largest council by population. Brisbane, historian John Cole argues, is a city-state, and many functions carried out by BCC are administered by state or statutory bodies in other Australian cities.[4] With a significant rates base, the first Lord Mayor, William Jolly, implemented a bold program of public works for Brisbane. Jolly, proud of the new city, produced a celebratory history booklet that included a marketing tag that persists today: 'Brisbane The River City'.[5]

Like other Queensland local governments, BCC's authority 'remains essentially limited by the sovereign prerogatives of the State'.[6] The state can, and does, intervene in planning matters. Municipal governments have the capacity to shape urban geographies, particularly through town planning, zoning and building approvals, powers granted to councils under state legislation. Hazard researchers have argued since 1942 that although land use planning and building controls cannot prevent flood losses, they can have a reductive effect. To do so, mandatory controls, created and enforced by government, are essential. Councils had some devolved powers of land resumption (largely intended for public works), but have been seemingly reluctant to use them.

Prior to the 1920s there were few planning controls in Brisbane, leaving development 'ramshackle' and 'uncoordinated'.[7] The growing town planning movement pushed for councils to be granted zoning, subdivision and drainage powers, which were successfully granted under the *Local Authorities Act 1923* and the *City of Brisbane Act 1924*. Yet, despite increased authority, South East Queensland local government planning largely ignored floods. Jolly's first proposed town plan progressed no further than a civic survey and city ordinances to guide development. Development constraints to reduce the flood hazard seemed unlikely as in 1926 Jolly stated a widely held belief: 'if we refused to allow buildings to be erected along the river banks we would damn the future of Brisbane'.[8] To Jolly, a successful future remained contingent on building on the floodplain and not 'locking up' land for flood mitigation, a belief shared by many ratepayers. Brisbane's riverside land was considered too valuable to not exploit.

The first regulations dealing with floodwaters, only introduced in 1956, reflected BCC's concerns with stormwater drainage and creek flooding, rather than riverine floods. Residential property could not be constructed in low-lying areas subject to flooding without council permission. Council had concessionary powers to override this regulation but no authority to remove the large number of existing houses. These ordinances also had no control over commercial construction on land prone to river flooding. Brisbane development proceeded without a town plan until 1965. When the long-awaited plan was finally ratified, it provided no further flood management tools than the previous drainage problem area ordinances.[9]

In Ipswich, floodplain management fared no better. The first by-laws, enacted in 1923 and updated in 1952, ignored floods and zoning. Master planning consultants in 1949 recognised that, like Brisbane, Ipswich had grown in an 'unguided' and 'haphazard' manner. Their report highlighted a need for regional flood prevention planning, especially as controls were still possible with over 121 hectares of flood-risk areas undeveloped. The report declared, 'it is within the possibility of sound finance to adopt a reclaiming scheme for this low part' and recommended an actuarial study to assess the costs of reclamation and the damage to 'stock, buildings and business spread over a number of years'. The consultants advocated creating riverside boulevards and raising or demolishing low-lying structures, along with an extensive riverbank tree planting scheme to reduce run-off and siltation.[10] Despite these sound recommendations, the 1949 Ipswich Town Plan did not address reclamation or prevent building on the floodplain. Similarly, there were no flooding provisions in the 1953 or 1957 Ipswich planning schemes, or the 1966–67 interim development by-laws – all lost opportunities to reduce flood vulnerability.

In Queensland, the state has exercised its authority to compulsorily resume land, most commonly to build roads and railways. States and councils are mandated by legislation to pay compensation to those affected by land reclamation. According to local government acts, a landowner adversely affected by changes to a planning scheme must be paid compensation as injurious affection, up to three years after any planning scheme comes into force.[11] This policy also applies to state acquisitions and reflects a cultural value that the government's main purpose is to protect the liberty and property of individuals. Land ownership was considered a right of citizenship, and restrictions on property development were politically unpalatable. This legal and fiscal constraint of compensation and rights of appeal has thwarted good decision-making and impedes flood mitigation planning to this day. Unlike the Federal Government of the United States, and the Australian state governments of New South Wales and Victoria, the Queensland Government remained slow to implement flood policies to shape urban development. New South Wales introduced a state-wide policy in 1977 that both removed and prevented urban development on floodplains. Victoria followed suit in 1978 with a floodplain management policy and guidelines.[12] Queensland's political climate impeded similar action.

Political scientist Colin Hughes says that development lies at the heart of Queensland politics; it is a state 'concerned with things and places, rather than people and ideas'.[13] Since the 1950s, Queensland state governments have promoted the property industry as the key to economic progress. Many have believed that Queensland's economic viability relies on continued population growth and urban expansion, so local and state governments have been reluctant to restrict development on the floodplain, preferring to control the river through engineering structures instead. This ideological stance served politically well connected businesses and construction companies that provided substantial economic stimulus in Queensland. These vested interests of government and developers were particularly apparent in Brisbane in the 1970s.

Conservative Premier Johannes (Joh) Bjelke-Petersen (1968–87) made his fortune clearing and farming the scrub around Kingaroy. With prominent developers listed among his friends and campaign supporters, Bjelke-Petersen informed parliament in his inaugural year (1947) that government had a clear role: expand and develop the state.[14] Bjelke-Petersen boasted of cranes on the horizon as his barometer of economic growth. Critics have characterised his ethos as 'rapacious development-at-any-cost'.[15] With this history, the Premier was unlikely to introduce legislative controls to restrict development on floodplains.

Similarly, Clem Jones, a former surveyor and Brisbane's Labor Lord Mayor from 1961 to 1975, had made sufficient wealth from land development and so refused his mayoral salary. His council's policies of building kilometres of kerbing and channelling, as well as sewerage and water reticulation services, throughout Brisbane were designed to catch up with suburban expansion and encourage further growth. Jones seemed equally unlikely to impede development. However, despite his policies and personal history, during the 1972 council election, Jones unsuccessfully appealed to the Premier to create stronger legislation to regulate the floodplains and leave flood areas 'as buffers against flash floods and tidal floods'.[16] Although only dealing with creek flooding and ignoring the river, this indicated a willingness to consider greater controls. But, without state authority, neither council's powers, nor the town plan, could be altered, and development on the floodplain flourished. Flood-free years, the growing faith in Somerset Dam to prevent floods, and poor town planning and state legislation joined a societal avarice for development that increased South East Queensland's flood hazard.

A Booming Hazard

Largely free from development constraints, Brisbane enjoyed a building boom in the 1920s. Record construction figures prompted *The Brisbane Courier* to report in 1926 that 'Brisbane is growing hourly in size before the eyes of its citizens', with over 3,000 dwellings constructed in that year.[17] Between 1925 and 1945 housing numbers increased from 50,000 to 76,000 and the population increased from 245,015 to 380,220. Most significantly, 88 per cent of ratepayers lived within 8 kilometres of the city centre in 1925, not far from the Brisbane River. The inner-city's urban density peaked in 1947 at 3,800 people per square kilometre. However, this density fell by more than a quarter in the period 1947–71 as the demographic spread changed with commercialisation, industrialisation and expanded public transport.[18] The completion of the Walter Taylor Bridge in 1936 gave motorists a river crossing at Indooroopilly and facilitated growth in the previously flooded Oxley/Chelmer region. Extended tramlines also opened up the southern suburbs of Moorooka in 1939 and Salisbury in 1941.

World War II stalled housing construction, as did the post-war shortages in building materials, but the baby boomers and post-war immigrants then increased Brisbane's population in two years by 18,000 people, reaching 420,000 in 1950. As Australia's fastest growing city, Brisbane's housing construction peaked in 1951 with 7,086 homes built, a trend easing state-wide after 1954. Records in 1954 showed that 28.8 per cent of the existing housing stock in Brisbane had been built after the war.[19] These new houses were constructed in previously undeveloped areas, many of which had been submerged in 1893. After 1950, extensive residential subdivision occurred in Oxley, Darra and Rocklea; these areas were among the worst affected in the moderate 1931 floods, with 50 families evacuated in the Rocklea and Oxley districts.[20] House numbers in Darra grew substantially from 690 in 1947 to 5,058 in 1971, and approximately 500 allotments were sold in Oxley between 1950 and 1953. This low-lying land had, the Bureau of Industry reported in 1933, acted as 'flood prevention dams for the benefit of Brisbane City'.[21] Building in a natural flood storage reservoir could only exacerbate the hazard, especially as impermeable surfaces reduced flood absorption and increased run-off. Once again the public risk was identified with *The Sunday Mail* predicting that 'Brisbane's suburban sprawl into what were once absorbing farmlands will be a prime contribution to further major floods'.[22] However, the pursuit of growth and post-war housing demands silenced these concerns.

Rocklea boomed with post-war industrial activity. State development led the way with the purchase of 66 Commonwealth wartime munitions buildings in 1949, an action designed to stimulate growth. The strategy worked with *The Courier-Mail* on 25 April declaring, 'Rocklea spells industry', as it was 'one of the busiest little suburbs in Brisbane'. Employment opportunities brought further residential and commercial growth to the area, the attraction increased by cheap land. In 1950, Rocklea offered 32 perch (809 square metre) blocks for between £100 and £150, a bargain when compared to the costs in nearby Tennyson of £150 to

£300, Moorooka of £200 to £500 and Annerley of £500 to £700.[23]
A 1950 government purchase of 324 hectares of land near Darra
for up to 3,000 Queensland Housing Commission homes in what
became Serviceton (later Inala), and the 1953 government purchase
of 144 hectares at Rocklea for the Department of Agriculture's
Animal Husbandry Research Station, may have encouraged new
residents to assume there was little flood risk if the state was
investing its money in the area.

Cheap land and housing commission activity also encouraged
floodplain development in the predominantly working-class city of
Ipswich. From 1948 to 1950, 50 new houses were constructed in the
suburb of Brassall, beside the Bremer River, with a further 30 housing
commission homes planned.[24] In 1950, Ipswich City Council (ICC)
approved 484 new houses, with an additional 552 approved in 1951.[25]
The cheaper land encouraged this residential development. In 1953,
a 24 perch (607 square metre) block cost £100 compared to £500
in Brisbane, and a new three-bedroom home could be purchased
for £2,000 rather than £2,500. The housing commission was
instrumental in developing the suburbs of Leichhardt and Riverview
on flood-vulnerable land. After 1957, large land subdivisions occurred
in the low-lying areas of Redbank and Riverview, and Goodna also
experienced growth with up to 60 houses constructed below the 1955
flood line (11.59 metres), despite the flooding of a dozen homes in
1931 when a flood reached 13.62 metres. By June 1973, Ipswich had
18,889 dwellings, many of them on the floodplain.[26]

Brisbane's settlement reached beyond public transport in the
1960s as car affordability enabled new suburban development
on riverside land. In 1960, BCC sacrificed its planned green
belt for progress and carved up hectares of land in the Kenmore
district, Moggill and Wacol, on both sides of the Brisbane River,
for residential estates. By 1971, 15 per cent of the population had
moved to these emerging suburbs, some 18 kilometres beyond the
city centre. In June 1973, Brisbane had 217,847 dwellings, mostly
single-storey owner-occupied houses on 32 perch (809 square metre)

blocks. Construction of multiple dwellings remained low-scale as it was limited to four storeys until 1964 when the 40-metre height restriction was removed. From the 1960s, commercial high-rise construction began in earnest and the urban density in flood-vulnerable areas substantially increased.[27] Table 4.1 shows the growth in population and occupied dwellings in Brisbane from 1891 to 1971.

Census Date	Population	Occupied Dwellings
1891	125,123	23,337
1901	145,384	26,124
1911	175,487	36,502
1921	257,905	53,648
1933	341,625	79,232
1947	457,462	113,797
1954	575,205	152,798
1961	692,634	187,147
1966	778,193	215,668
1971	867,784	251,036

Table 4.1: Summary of population growth within Brisbane Statistical Division.[28]

In the 1970s, many South East Queensland residents had no memory of the floods that had devastated their suburbs in the past. Newcomers and younger generations in Brisbane and Ipswich built their homes on the floodplain, unaware of the potential hazard. A survey in 1974 of 647 people flooded that year highlighted this lack of knowledge, with 65 per cent of respondents reporting that previous floods were beyond their personal experience. For 79 per cent of survey participants it was the first flood in their present dwelling. Over half (52.4 per cent) had no previous knowledge of floods in their area, with 67.1 per cent unaware of the likelihood of floods affecting their property.[29]

Many of the houses across Brisbane and Ipswich were constructed in flood-prone areas. Colonists originally settled near the river for water supply, transportation and access to fertile land. When cars became affordable the population could move beyond the tram and train lines and out of the floodplain but, despite this, most of the new suburbs were built in areas liable to flooding. Rather than restrict floodplain development, governments actively encouraged riverside residences with the growing population keen to spread onto the floodplain.

Some residents were prepared to accept the risk as they were attracted by riverside land, with suburbs like Chelmer, Fig Tree Pocket and St Lucia offering 'prestige' river views at bargain prices compared with Sydney. In December 1973, river frontage in Kenmore cost up to $38,750 compared with $150,000 in Vaucluse, Sydney. Rocklea and Oxley also offered affordability, with three-bedroom homes in Oxley available for $21,500.[30] Some moved to previously flooded areas hoping another flood would be decades away, confused by the hydrological terminology of a 1-in-100-year flood. Others were deluded into thinking that the river had been tamed by training, dredging and the construction of Somerset Dam.

Buoyed by the Somerset Dam Syndrome

After 1898, Brisbane remained largely flood-free with moderate floods in 1908 (3.59 metres) and 1931 (3.32 metres), and minor floods between 1927 and 1929. The mid-1930s were extreme drought years. September 1936 brought Brisbane's lowest rainfall since 1929. The river at Toogoolawah near the headwaters ceased to flow in October for the third successive season, with water levels lower than the 1902 drought.[31] In 1946, between May and August, Brisbane received the lowest rainfall on record for those months and 1953 saw the city's driest three-month period in 102 years.[32] These meteorological cycles confused local understanding as long dry periods allowed the memory of floods to fade and the delusion of immunity to flourish, the latter fortified by a human desire to believe that floods had been overcome by engineering ingenuity and relegated to the past.

Archibald Partridge, the Commissioner of Irrigation, identified this drought-induced complacency in 1928, noting that flood-free years had lulled the city's residents into 'a sense of false security'. He wrote, 'long exemption from floods has led to the close settlement of many areas which are in danger not only of submersion but of the effect of strong currents. In many cases the inhabitants are quite unaware of the possibility of danger.'[33] The opinion that climatic ignorance had encouraged floodplain development was shared by a writer to *The Queenslander* in 1927. Identified only as a 'highly practical man', the author wrote that in 'recent years the danger has been forgotten, and so the sale of allotments within the flood area, and building operations, have gone on at an unprecedented rate'.[34] In South East Queensland, construction continued to be the measure of progress, a culture upheld by vested interests of the government, developers and property owners. These groups had much to gain by perpetuating the myth of flood prevention. Hydrological complexities and cycles of flood and drought were simplified to support a misbelief that engineering had controlled the river.

The infrequency of floods, especially after Somerset Dam eliminated some small floods, reduced the social memory and environmental knowledge required to assess and manage the risk. Compounded with this is the tendency among amateurs and experts alike to assume the highest flood will never be exceeded. For many, the biggest possible flood is the last one they remember, and in South East Queensland these were the comparatively small 1931 and 1955 floods. *The Daily Standard* scathingly assessed the situation in 1933, arguing people have 'short memories or are too lazy to inquire as to flooding possibilities' and in the 40 years since 1893 'many thousands of homes have been erected in sites which were eight or ten feet under water at that time'.[35] People drew on their own experience, not historical data or, as Gilbert Fowler White maintains, 'eliminate[d] the hazard simply by ignoring it'.[36]

Journalists did little to dissuade the myth that Brisbane was flood-proof with newspapers declaring that the dam saved Brisbane every time heavy rain fell. In 1950, *Courier-Mail* writer Jack O'Callaghan fuelled the public's dream of a flood-proofed Brisbane with the headline 'Somerset Dam is city's wet weather safety-valve'. Even more audaciously he wrote, 'Brisbane is not yet unassailable by flood but whatever future drenching it may receive it will be mild in comparison with 1893.'[37] The Sunday Mail concurred, proclaiming 'Somerset Dam held and saved untold havoc', and The Queensland Times ran a headline that read 'Somerset Dam averted serious flood damage'.[38] Again in 1951, after 635 millimetres of rain fell in the Stanley River over five days, newspapers pronounced the dam had protected Brisbane with the headlines 'Somerset Dam Saves Serious Flooding' and 'Dam keeps flood from City'.[39] With these bold headlines and accompanying articles citing expert engineers, the public could be forgiven for thinking large floods were now controllable. When the Somerset Dam (Finance) Act was passed in 1954, the dam's cost having surpassed £3 million, The Courier-Mail justified the increasing cost as it would supply water for at least 20 years and 'could stop' £3 million flood damage, again implying environmental security against nature's extremes.[40]

Somerset Dam did withhold the 1950 and 1951 run-off with floods barely felt in Brisbane, but these events were relatively small. The myth of flood immunity matured during a larger flood in March 1955 when intense rain fell throughout Queensland. In Brisbane, floodwaters reached 2.36 metres at the Port Office Gauge, inundating low-lying properties. The newspapers had no doubt Somerset Dam had been Brisbane's saviour with The Courier-Mail announcing, 'wall at dam "saved city"'.[41] The favourable flood conditions, with much of the rain falling above Somerset Dam, meant the floodwaters could be withheld. Labor Premier Vince Gair praised the dam: 'Brisbane was now enjoying the benefit of the Government's long-range dual-purpose plan which was to ensure an adequate water supply [...] and at the same time, to mitigate the effect of disastrous floods similar to those which devastated Brisbane in the eighteen-nineties.'[42] Somerset Dam had successfully mitigated this moderate flood, reducing its height and saving thousands of properties from inundation.

In a 1950s promotional brochure, the State Public Relations Bureau suggested immunity while also declaring that Somerset Dam had delivered previously unattainable wealth, and linked the dam with nation building. The bureau boasted that 'since the dam was built, land flooded in 1893 but now capable of being reasonably safeguarded by the dam, has been used for homes and factory sites. The increased value of this land must now represent a very considerable national asset.'[43] *The Courier-Mail* in 1953 also coupled floodplain development and prosperity celebrating that 'there has been a great deal of building, both of homes and factories in relatively low-lying areas of Brisbane'. The newspaper continued, 'there is no doubt that Somerset Dam to-day [*sic*] represents a flood-prevention bargain. It was wisely started in times of unemployment and low costs, and its interest burden is light compared with the present value of the property which it now protects.'[44]

Not all were enamoured with the dam. Ecological concerns were raised by Country Party parliamentarian Walter Sparkes about dams constraining fish mobility, while a 'river expert' reported increased siltation in the river caused by averting floods. Others expressed apprehension about increased flooding above the dam, exacerbated by elevated water levels in the dam's lake that inundated upstream towns and low bridges.[45] Kilcoy in particular would pay the price for Brisbane's flood protection. Critics also argued that dam releases had caused the 1955 flood in Brisbane. Premier Vince Gair responded that heavy rainfall had caused significant run-off and by holding back water until the flood passed the junction of the Brisbane and Stanley rivers, these floodwaters were prevented from joining the Brisbane River's floodwaters. This strategy had reduced Brisbane's flood heights, although he conceded it added to the length of time areas downstream were inundated. As Gair accurately explained, this release strategy was 'in accordance with the accepted practice of flood mitigation and prevention',[46] his statement again implying immunity.

The criticism that the dam created the flood marked a cultural shift in attitudes. Adherence to an ideology of control through engineering shifted blame for floods from nature or God to the dam's failure, a phenomenon noted by historian Emily O'Gorman in the 1950s Murray River floods.[47] This new understanding of floods as human-created recognised the hybridity of floods as a state between nature and humans and would shape future responses to floods in South East Queensland. But engineers repeatedly warned that dams could only mitigate, and not prevent, flooding.

Warnings of Somerset's flood management limitations were issued periodically. On 8 March 1950, James Holt, Chief Engineer of the Coordinator General's Department and the engineer in charge of Somerset Dam, informed *The Courier-Mail* that the dam would prevent a minor flood, but, in engineering parlance, only take the 'top' off a serious flood. An article by Bureau of Industry staff member Henry Wilbur Herbert appeared in *The Courier-Mail* in 1953 with the unambiguous headline: 'If the rain is heavy enough Somerset Dam won't save Brisbane'.[48] He warned against complacency, maintaining that while the dam would reduce a minor (1931-sized) flood to a 'negligible size' it would only reduce a major flood by 10 feet (3 metres). Herbert further explained that if the rain fell in the Brisbane River (an 'unfavourable' flood) Somerset Dam would have no mitigating effect. A map included in the article revealed areas that could still be inundated after the construction of Somerset Dam, leaving no doubt of the flood risk. After the 1955 flood, the Coordinator General's Department informed *Courier-Mail* readers that although Somerset Dam could withhold Stanley River water, the Brisbane River alone could cause severe flooding and an upstream dam was incapable of stopping it.[49] In reality, Somerset Dam, a moderate-sized dam that managed only 10 per cent of the river catchment, had no capacity to withhold inflow downstream. With a finite flood storage capacity, controlled releases during floods were necessary.

Despite the warnings from Holt, Herbert and others, dubious

advertising perpetuated faith in Somerset Dam. In 1971, the Commissioner for Consumer Affairs received a complaint about a misleading advertisement by developer Alfred Grant, disputing the claim of 'high level' as the land in question had been inundated in 1893 and 1931. The Commissioner dismissed the complaint with a vague response suggesting Somerset Dam would reduce flooding by 10 feet (3 metres). According to the Commissioner, Alfred Grant had no case to answer, as the advertisement did not overtly promise flood immunity, nor had it contravened any council by-laws prohibiting development at this height. Development proceeded at a height below the 1931 flood level, which BCC considered a practical and economical compromise, despite its calculated flood frequency of 1 in 20 years.[50]

With the government supporting riverside development and approving subdivisions with lax development controls, and the belief that Somerset Dam would prevent floods, the populace continued to encroach on the floodplain. The development of the floodplain in the Centenary Estates, Yeronga and East Ipswich reveals the complex motivations for settling in vulnerable areas, as well as the roles of vested interests and local knowledge.

The Centenary Estates, Yeronga and East Ipswich

In 1959, L. J. Hooker Investment Corporation, Australia's largest real estate developers, acquired more than 1,214 hectares alongside the Brisbane River, extending 4 kilometres from Fig Tree Pocket to Darra. In 1893, *The Queenslander* had reported that 'pretty well the whole of the farms were submerged' in this area, but the houses, built on the high points, were 'free of water' with the exception of one.[51] The 1893 flood reached 17.9 metres at what is now Centenary Bridge at Jindalee. Given that much of Hooker's land had been flooded in 1893, how much consideration did the developers give to flooding?

In their planning report to BCC in 1960, Hooker's boosters promoted the land's first-class qualities for residential development with panoramic views and north-easterly breezes. Hooker formed the independent company, Centenary Estates, and council approved seven new suburbs in October 1961, with contracts already entered into. On 14 October 1964, Centenary Bridge opened, and with the completion of the Centenary Highway between Moggill and Ipswich in 1969 Brisbane's north-western and south-western suburbs were connected. There is barely a mention of the Brisbane River in the Centenary Estates' promotional brochure other than to reference its aesthetic beauty. The plan created 10,260 residential lots and 243 hectares of industrial and commercial development, delivering $1 million profit to Hooker and 1,376 kilometres of roads, water and sewerage reticulation, parks, and a golf course and swimming pool to the council, despite public objection.[52]

Geoffrey Cossins, council's flood engineer, met with the Centenary Estates developers in the 1960s to present flood-level data and flood maps that proved these new suburbs were a flood risk. Cossins recalls:

> they listened hard and went away and collected all the old people they could find who remembered the Big Flood and pointed out where it had come to. They carefully surveyed it, plotted it up, and triumphantly came to show me I was wrong. Because there had been nothing between 1898 and 1931, for those questioned, 1931 was the Big Flood.[53]

Correspondence supports Cossins's recollection. In April 1962, the BCC Chief Engineer's Office provided Hooker with flood data for the 1931 and 1955 floods. The company provided the Coordinator General with estimates of flood levels at eight points based on the 1955, 1931 and 19 February 1893 floods. Records show they included the 1893 data only for historical perspective, 'since it should now represent the worst historical flood conditions', not because they thought it could be repeated or surpassed. The developers dismissed the heights of the 1893 floods, estimating they would now be 2 or 2.5 metres lower because of Somerset Dam. Negotiations reached a compromise with a 1971 ruling that the minimum development control would be the height of the 1931 flood near the river, but reduced in the backwater area to midway between 1931 and 1955 flood heights, both considerably smaller than the 1893 flood.[54]

Town Clerk Tom McAulay supported this decision and articulated a commonly held view that it would be uneconomical to 'prohibit use of all land submerged by the 1893 flood line when it may be submerged for a few days (on a long-term average) every, say two hundred years'. Like Jolly in 1926, he resisted 'locking up' land. These development restrictions offered a compromise between the amount of time land would be flooded and the amount of damage caused. It would keep structures out of the path of more frequent floods to reduce obstruction and damage, but would still maximise land use.[55] This decision lies at the heart of Brisbane's flood problem. How much land do you keep clear from development for an infrequent flood event? Sixty years of flood immunity had diluted the perception of risk so protection below the 1931 flood level, a 1-in-20-year flood, seemed sufficient and fulfilled goals of prosperity.

In 1969, Beryl and Ken Wilson, a married couple with two children, were typical new residents of Centenary Estates. They were attracted to riverside land on Mount Ommaney Drive in Jindalee, especially as Ken, a keen sailor, appreciated its proximity to the Jindalee boat ramp. Like their neighbours, they attended a presentation by Peter Lightfoot, Managing Director of L. J. Hooker. Lightfoot extolled the virtues of the area and assured prospective buyers the land was clear of floods. Ken Wilson, raised beside the river at Corinda, had the benefit of local knowledge, as his father had told him about the 1893 floods. Further, the Sinnamon family, early settlers in Jindalee, showed the Wilsons a Moreton Bay fig tree that in 1893 had not been submerged above its roots. Ken, distrustful of Lightfoot, built his house in

1969 in line with the tree. In 1974, Ken's home stood above the floodwaters, although his neighbours were less fortunate.

Other residents in these new suburbs simply wanted to live on the river and took what precautions they could to minimise the risk, such as Jean and Graham Gahan, who purchased land in Diane Street, Yeronga, in 1958. Although the train had brought suburban development to Yeronga earlier, the western portion of the suburb remained agricultural until the late 1950s when it was sold for residential development. Graham, an electrical engineer, had experienced serious flooding in the Bundaberg region in 1942 and remembered 'being stopped by water' over Hyde Road, Yeronga, in 1955. Jean, a teacher, had also witnessed floods in her home town of Ipswich. Both considered floods when they bought land in Yeronga West but had a clear motivation for moving there. For the couple, riverside land offered an attractive place to live and raise a family. As Graham recalls:

> Diane Street had been a dairy when we got married and it was subdivided about the time we were looking to build a house [...] I realised this neck of the woods was a lovely little spot out by the river. I grew up by the river in a cane field area and I liked the idea of living by the river.[56]

With floods in mind, they took precautions. Graham 'consulted flood maps at the time and deemed the block safe'. Graham also benefitted from personal knowledge as an engineering colleague warned him not to rely on Somerset Dam. Jean explains, 'Our land was on a slope and we built up, with the garage underneath.' Graham adds, 'Unfortunately, when the 1974 flood came, the water came through my block but not into my house. So, I was half right.'

Many South East Queensland residents were newcomers to the region and were not privy to local knowledge. Between 1966 and 1971 the population in Brisbane had grown from 778,193 to 867,784. In 1971, only 48.5 per cent of residents had lived in the same dwelling since 1966 and many lacked experience of a major flood. Ipswich citizens also increased in number from 54,592 in 1966 to 61,582 in 1971, but they had more reason to be aware of flood risk.[57] With its low-lying pockets along the Bremer River, and without a dam to regulate the river's flow, Ipswich floods more frequently than Brisbane. Ipswich experienced six floods between 1927 and 1971, with the 1947 event reaching 15.19 metres in central Ipswich but going largely unnoticed in Brisbane.[58]

However, there were still purchasers who did not consider the flood risk in Ipswich. Robyn and Neal Flashman bought a house in Leslie Street, East Ipswich, in 1969. The street had been developed by Garth Llewellyn in the 1960s and was occupied by young families. Ipswich-raised, the Flashmans moved into the house closest to the Bremer River, attracted by affordability and the proximity to schools, hockey fields and the river itself. Neal's father warned them about swimming in floodwaters nearby during a 1930s flood, but this did not discourage them. As Robyn says, 'We liked the fact that the block backed on to the river or a gully that came up so we only had neighbours on two sides.' Floods were not mentioned in sales transactions, which Robyn attributed to 'there having been a long time between floods and we thought it won't happen again'.[59] Local knowledge, and even personal experience, proved no deterrent to building on the floodplain.

It seems incredible that developers and buyers ignored the flood risk in these areas when flood data was publicly available. In 1933, the Bureau of Industry published flood maps showing Brisbane areas most likely to be inundated at various flood heights. Newspapers also offered reminders, quoting engineers who warned of the risk of flood. In 1971, flood engineer and University of Queensland Professor Gordon McKay stated in *The Courier-Mail* that floods of the 1893 magnitude could be repeated. He said, 'Somerset Dam would only take off the peak of a major flood' and the situation would be 'far worse because of the high density building around creeks in Brisbane'.[60] Government-approved development of the floodplain had further intensified the hazard. In 1971, a report for the Coordinator General's Department on Brisbane's water supply and flooding concluded that Brisbane and Ipswich still faced a serious flood risk, and included a series of maps identifying the potential location and severity of flooding. Reputedly the Coordinator General considered the report too technical for public release.[61] The report exposed that a worse dynamic had been created in South East Queensland – an engineered river and an uncontrolled, more densely settled floodplain.

The 70-year reprieve from major flooding was, in the words of the Coordinator General's 1971 report, 'fortuitous', and a result of nature's decreased rainfall since 1909. Since 1931, only the 1955 flood had the potential to cause significant damage and Somerset Dam had played a mitigating role. Although the dam remained largely untested through flood infrequency, the misguided belief of flood prevention – the Somerset Dam Syndrome – flourished. This myth, which was 'freely used as a talking point by developers', had caused complacency, encouraged floodplain development and increased the risk of 'possible tragedy', leaving South East Queenslanders hopeful that the river had, as Premier Nicklin assured them in the 1950s, been tamed.[62]

The River Prevails: The 1974 Flood

IN JANUARY 1974, the river reclaimed its floodplain. Despite previous floods, Russell Hinze, the Member for South Coast since 1966, expressed his surprise, informing Parliament in March 1974 that 'We all believed that such a flood could never occur again [...] We honestly believed that, because of the dams we have built, we would never see a repetition of the 1893 flood.'[1] Although most likely referring to his fellow parliamentarians, the 'we' could easily have referred to many within the wider community who shared his faith that technocratic measures had eliminated extreme floods. Flood-free years and Somerset Dam (with its accompanying syndrome) had distorted the perception of risk. Although Somerset Dam had changed the hydrological dynamic and reduced flood levels, it had not made Brisbane immune to floods.

A Summer of Intense Rain

The summer of 1973–74 was one of Queensland's wettest summers in decades. Arch Shields, the Regional Director of the Bureau of Meteorology (BoM) at the time, estimated that roughly 900,000 million tonnes of rain fell over the state in January 1974, leaving most rivers in flood and large parts of Queensland submerged.[2] Cyclones Una, Vera and Wanda, and their accompanying monsoonal troughs, were major contributors to this rainfall. Cyclone Vera had moderated to a tropical low that then developed into Cyclone Wanda, crossing the coast near Gympie (170 kilometres north of Brisbane) on 24 January before moderating into a slow-moving rain depression lying in a large monsoonal trough. Despite daily newspaper and television accounts of floods elsewhere in Queensland, residents in the south-east seemed unaware of the impending threat. A high-pressure system over the Tasman Sea slowed the normal northward retreat of the monsoonal trough. As the deep low-pressure system oscillated above the Brisbane River catchment over the Australia Day weekend, the city experienced three separate periods of intense rainfall.

In January 1974, Brisbane received 872 millimetres of rain, second only to the 1,026 millimetres received in February 1893, and Ipswich received 780 millimetres, mostly over four days, a figure that exceeded the February 1893 rainfall of 737 millimetres. This rainfall was extremely intense, the factor most likely to cause flooding. Brisbane's 314 millimetres of rain on 26 January exceeded the average monthly rainfall and was the second highest rainfall amount since records were first kept. Ipswich received 340 millimetres on 27 January, the highest daily total ever recorded. New Beith, on Oxley Creek, recorded 683.4 millimetres in 48 hours, with 250 millimetres falling in six hours. Table 5.1 shows the rainfalls recorded in the catchment between 24 January and 31 January.

Intense rainfalls throughout the entire Brisbane River catchment made riverine flooding inevitable. As run-off increased in the Stanley River sub-catchment, Somerset Dam's floodwater storage (524,000 megalitres) lay empty ready to hold Stanley River floodwaters as its water supply compartment had already filled. As the rain continued, BCC dam managers Jack Clerke and Geoffrey Cossins mobilised at City Hall. Initially fearful of the safety of Brisbane's water supply dams at Enoggera and Gold Creek, their attention soon turned to Somerset Dam. The dam had not been operated in a major flood since 1955, and this flood was more akin to that in 1893 so it would test the capabilities of the dam and its operators.

	Ipswich (040101)	New Beith on Oxley Creek (040719)	Brisbane Regional Office (040214)
24 January	3.4	2	2.6
25 January	66.8	78.4	107
26 January	160.2	413.4	314
27 January	340	270	179.4
28 January	36	56	47.6
29 January	2	1.2	2.2
30 January	0.4	4.8	5.6
31 January	6	1	5.6
TOTAL	614.8	826.8	664

Table 5.1: Rainfall (millimetres) recorded in the lower Brisbane catchment for 24-hour periods, January 1974.
Compiled from BoM daily rainfall statistics for each station.

Testing the Somerset Dam Syndrome

Somerset Dam was designed to mitigate a major flood, but there was no official guide for how it would do this. Without a dam operations manual, Clerke and Cossins followed accepted practice for water retention and release modelled on the 1893 floods. On 25 January, BCC released water from Somerset Dam and planned to close the gates in time to stop the merge of floodwaters with the peak from the upper Brisbane River. With Lord Mayor Clem Jones at the Christchurch Commonwealth Games, Acting Lord Mayor Alderman Lynch publicly explained that this strategy would 'avoid any coincidence of flood peaks which could cause flooding along the Brisbane River'.[3] After the release, Somerset Dam's gates were shut to hold back incoming Stanley River floodwaters.

After the upper Brisbane River flood peak passed downstream of Stanley junction, the discharge from Somerset Dam recommenced to empty the flood storage compartment. Without knowledge of flood management practices, community consensus considered this action to be foolhardy – dams were designed to withhold floods not release them. When Clem Jones arrived back in Brisbane on 28 January, he chose to intervene in the flood management strategy.

With BCC officers working around the clock, Jones rang the office of Bernie O'Connell, BCC Chief Engineer, around midnight, demanding that Somerset Dam's gates be closed immediately to free Ipswich and Brisbane from the floodwaters. Council staff explained the release strategy, adding that gate closure would not assist Brisbane, risked Kilcoy flooding and jeopardised the safety of the dam. Heated arguments between council staff and Jones proceeded throughout the night. Jones pulled rank, insisting that as an elected lord mayor he must be obeyed and O'Connell conceded. The next morning at 11 am Jones called a press conference to announce the closure of the Somerset Dam gates at 2.30 pm on 29 January. He stated, 'I take full responsibility for the decision', admitting his decision had been made 'against the strong advice of senior Council officers'. But Jones believed that 'under the circumstances, we should take a calculated risk', adding, 'this is a tough decision, but if I held back on making this one I shouldn't be in office'.[4] Council officers reluctantly acquiesced and slowly closed the gates. By 2.15 am on 30 January all gates were fully closed, leaving Somerset Dam at full capacity for six days, with no mitigation capability, and causing Kilcoy to be badly inundated. Fortunately for Brisbane, another cyclone (Pam) with its load of monsoonal rain remained 300 kilometres off the coast.

At 3 pm on 29 January the flood level in Brisbane began dropping rapidly on the outgoing tide as hydrologists had predicted it would. Jones could cast himself as the strong leader, the hero for defying the bureaucrats to save Brisbane. The engineering fraternity, however, believed that Jones's actions were foolhardy, irresponsible, opportunistic and politically motivated, especially with Cyclone Pam's rain depression hovering nearby. Jones's behaviour was characteristic.[5] His admirers found him energetic, intellectually astute and decisive, and saw him as a visionary, an impressive media campaigner and a formidable debater, while his detractors labelled him arrogant, dictatorial and inflexible. He demanded unswerving loyalty from his caucus and staff, acted without consultation and, faced with dissension, could resort to volcanic outbursts of intimidation and abuse.[6] A solutions-driven politician, Jones wanted to be seen as effective in saving Brisbane from flooding. Fuelling existing tension between Brisbane and Kilcoy, Jones justified sacrificing Kilcoy: 'I took the risk – a small number of homes in Kilcoy could suffer when hundreds of homes would be helped in Brisbane.'[7] Geoffrey Cossins maintains that Jones was ill-advised by the state government's Commissioner of Irrigation and Water Supply, whose flood knowledge was limited. Another explanation is that Jones thought that flood heights would recede on the high tide and seized his moment to prove his strong leadership and 'gain some cheap political mileage'.[8] Jones's actions had no positive flood mitigation effect. As a direct consequence of the incident, a dam operations manual was written to ensure operational decisions were made by qualified engineers to avoid future political interference.

This response to the 1974 floods exposed the tension in dam management and highlighted a shift in public understanding towards a belief that human action could control floods and that any residual floods meant engineering failed to deliver flood immunity. Criticism soon fell on the operation of the dam. Jones's interference eroded public confidence in engineers, especially those who operated Somerset Dam. State parliamentarians sparring with local government further fuelled doubt, with Geoffrey Chinchen, Member for Mt Gravatt, implying the dam was mismanaged to ensure Brisbane's water supply.[9] Jones's comments nurtured Kilcoy residents' belief that their town had been sacrificed for Brisbane's safety and revealed another tension in dam operation: residents downstream need water withheld and those upstream demand release; both cannot be satisfied. Residents living below the dam also argued releases had increased flooding. In floods, rumours abound. Enoggera Dam was blamed for flooding even though it has no gates to control water releases and fears that Somerset Dam would collapse forced the evacuation of schools.

While the retention of water in Somerset Dam did increase

flooding above the dam, downstream the dam removed 1 metre from the flood height at the Port Office Gauge, 1.5 metres at Jindalee and 2 metres at Moggill. The total inflow to Somerset Dam was 646,125 megalitres, which exceeded the dam's temporary flood storage capacity. During the flood 204,850 megalitres had to be released, and, while the dam's operation secured the maximum mitigation possible and reduced the height of the flood, the release strategy increased its duration.[10] Rainfall patterns reduced the dam's mitigation potential as the heaviest rain fell downstream of Somerset Dam (an 'unfavourable' flood). A smaller flood than usual occurred in the Stanley River (above the dam) but a large flood occurred in the Brisbane River where it could not be withheld. Uniform rainfalls fell throughout the remainder of the catchment, flooding Lockyer Creek and the Bremer and Brisbane rivers. The large metropolitan rainfall and the unusually high flooding contributions of Lockyer Creek and the Bremer River were greater than in the second 1893 flood and significantly increased the flood levels downstream (Table 5.2).

Sub-catchment Floods	Stanley River	Upper Brisbane River	Lockyer Creek	Bremer River	Middle Reaches	City
1–4 Feb 1893	939	358	237	137	446	288
16–18 Feb 1893	430	252	266	260	414	406
4–6 Feb 1908	225	154	185	225	319	326
4–6 Feb 1931	452	219	192	163	337	433
27–28 Mar 1955	344	199	153	138	203	208
25–27 Jan 1974	410	252	297	446	417	593
25–29 Jan 1974	507	280	350	461	481	656

Table 5.2: Brisbane River sub-catchment rainfalls (millimetres) for various flood events.[11]

The Bureau of Industry had warned in the 1930s that the dam would mitigate 'all floods except the rarest and most calamitous known'; a caveat cited by generations of engineers.[12] Somerset Dam had a finite storage capacity and could not manage water in the other 90 per cent of the catchment. Yet in the popular mindset the term mitigation had morphed into the promise of prevention. Furthermore, there appeared to be little understanding that the 1974 flood was indeed this 'rare' and 'most calamitous' flood that engineers had forewarned would eventuate. In this scenario, releases were mandatory, with only limited mitigation possible. Similarly, in a major flood, decades of dredging, cutting and building retaining walls, all intended to minimise floods, had a negligible effect in the city and none upstream. Extreme floods provided indisputable evidence that the river had not been tamed. The faith in Somerset Dam and the passage of 70 largely flood-free years had created communal naivety about floods, and this complacency was reflected in how the authorities managed the crisis.

Crisis Management in a Record Flood
As the heavy rainfalls associated with Cyclone Wanda fell in the upper Stanley River on 24 January, BCC staff mobilised and BoM staff were on high alert as they issued their first flood warning at 10.30 pm that day for the upper Stanley River. By 11 am on 25 January warnings were issued that the upper Brisbane and Brisbane rivers and Lockyer Creek were rising. With moderate flooding predicted for the city reaches on the high tide, police began referring to a 'record flood' and braced themselves for imminent disaster. Brisbane's metropolitan creeks – the usual trouble spots of Moggill, Enoggera and Breakfast creeks and Kedron Brook – reached record heights causing three separate flash-flooding incidents on 25 and 26 January. Only Oxley Creek with its large, flat catchment could contain the water. However, creek flooding, a commonplace event in heavy rain, created little alarm about riverine flood.

Ipswich creeks were in extreme flood by late afternoon on 26 January when Bob Gamble, Deputy City Engineer of ICC, informed dam manager Jack Clerke that the Bremer River was rising at a 'fantastic rate' and had already exceeded the 1955 flood height. The Bremer River rose at 0.3 metres an hour, peaking at 20.7 metres at Ipswich on 27 January. Record discharge and run-off meant predicted flood heights were exceeded within hours. Ipswich experienced unusually heavy localised rain and the river recorded unprecedented velocity (6 to 7 metres per second).[13] Fortunately, the natural pondage between the Bremer River and Warrill Creek upstream from Ipswich around Amberley had reduced both flood levels and the discharge rate into the Bremer River downstream. While the initial peak at Ipswich had been caused by upstream run-off, as the water level in the Brisbane River started to rise floodwaters in the lower Bremer River were trapped. For 36 hours city flood levels maintained a height of 20.2 metres. Ipswich suffered three types of flooding: flash creek floods, Bremer River flooding and the backwater effect from the Brisbane River. Geoffrey Heatherwick, an engineer hydrologist in Brisbane BoM from 1969 to 1991, describes this as a 'rare' Bremer River flood.[14]

Meanwhile in Brisbane on 26 January the likelihood of a major flood was not yet apparent. The sun shone and Cossins, like many others, believed the flood threat had passed, unaware that the rain gauge at New Beith had topped 800 millimetres overnight. Fred Whitchurch, a keen member of the Indooroopilly District Estuary Association, took advantage of a dry Saturday and went canoeing with his son near Tennyson. They found Oxley Creek 'tumbling into the Brisbane River with a roar like a major jet plane taking off, with a huge whirlpool on either side' and were forced to paddle to safety. Engineer Geoffrey Cossins recalls that the next day at BCC offices 'all hell broke loose'. As the intertropical front returned from New South Wales, extreme floods were predicted and Cossins was summonsed to City Hall to relieve Clerke from his 31-hour shift. BCC officers went into emergency mode with shifts organised for the 36 staff members. Clerke and Cossins took shifts of 27 and 26 hours respectively to manage the dams. Staff from the Queensland Irrigation and Water Supply Commission joined the team to assist and procure food to enable a 24-hour flood response.

Direct telephone communications were established between BCC and BoM and a public information line was in constant use. Cossins describes the atmosphere in the office on 27 January as 'frantic with three telephones ringing continuously'.

Challenged by staff shortages, BoM was also under stress. The Regional Director, Arch Shields, had returned to his home at Upper Brookfield on 25 January for the weekend, only to be isolated by local flooding in Moggill Creek for the remainder of the floods. Malcolm Lamond, Deputy Regional Director, substituted for Shields. Engineer Gordon Macintosh, recovering from injuries sustained in a car accident a week earlier, worked his Friday shift of 15 hours in pain and was unable to return that weekend. Geoffrey Heatherwick soldiered on, calling on adrenalin as he worked a 60-hour shift between 7 am on Friday 25 January and 7 pm on Sunday 27 January, with two hours sleep snatched on an office stretcher on both nights. Finally, Alan Hall, supervising engineer of the Bureau's Flood Warning Programme, flew from Melbourne on Sunday night to relieve Heatherwick. An *Australian* journalist described the scene at the weather bureau where the staff were 'worn, tired and unshaven. Half-eaten sandwiches sit among myriad of charts and graphs of flood levels.' Officers endured enormous pressure as they monitored all Queensland rivers, issuing 102 flood warnings between 24 and 31 January throughout the state. Heatherwick and Cossins both experienced post-traumatic stress disorder in later years. Recalling the anxiety and tension during the floods, Heatherwick explains:

> most practicing hydrologists would be unaware of the soul searching and stress associated with flood forecasting in a big flood. There is enormous stress in handling all the things happening including continuous phone calls, seeking missing data, analysis of data and the need to get your forecast product out on time and you don't have too long to wait to see how good the forecast was.

The hydrologists were in uncharted territory as by 29 January all river gauges had peaked, revealing heights not seen since 1893, despite Somerset Dam (Table 5.3). They were aware that everyone was watching them and the possible dire consequences of an error.

Location	January 1893	February 1893	January 1974
Woodford*	11.73	10.05	8.6
Caboonbah*	22.63	n/a	16.32
Lowood*	26.39	n/a	22.02
Mount Crosby	32	31.28	26.74
Ipswich	24.5	23.6	20.7
Goodna	22.77	21.88	18.43
Centenary Bridge	17.9	16.6	8.09
Brisbane Port Office	8.35	8.09	5.45

Table 5.3: January 1974 flood peak heights compared with the two highest 1893 flood peaks in the Brisbane River catchment. Heights in metres on Australian Height Datum (AHD) unless marked *.

As flood warnings were issued, the rescue organisations mobilised. Central command for disaster management lay with the State Disaster Relief Organisation (SDRO), administered within the police department. Created in response to a 1968 storm in Killarney and first tested by Townsville's 1971 Cyclone Althea, the SDRO had yet to face floods or a state-wide crisis of this magnitude. An emergency operations room was established in police headquarters, with either the commissioner or assistant commissioner on duty at all times. Three police officers, telephonists, press liaison officers, and officers of the BCC, civil defence force and army were on hand, and the room was equipped with maps of flood areas and charts of available boats, aircraft and manpower. Despite these resources, Heatherwick maintains that they used existing information poorly, citing as an example the police rejection of the Bureau of Industry's 1933 flood map as 'old and obsolete' even though the 1974 floods proved them to be largely accurate.

Although the SDRO had held a two-hour hypothetical flood

practice exercise in October 1973, which they deemed a success, mistakes were made when the real event occurred. Cossins remains critical of policy decision-makers for not consulting the BCC or BoM hydrologists, those most abreast of the changing flood dynamics. Although BCC and BoM were in continual discussions, poor communication existed within and between other official organisations charged with disaster management. Jim Glynn, BCC liaison officer during the floods, described the situation at police headquarters as utter pandemonium as police ran about shouting, and yelling into and slamming down telephones, while the Police Commissioner, Ray Whitrod, calmly sat at his desk writing.[15] The lack of coordination hampered rescues and information dissemination.

The voluntary State Civil Defence Organisation (renamed the State Emergency Service in 1975) also assisted in the disaster management strategy. Formed in 1961, following New South Wales's lead, the organisation was also first deployed in 1971 after Cyclone Althea. The flood outstretched their capabilities as they were largely trained for a nuclear attack. Led by Director Colonel Kevin Whiting, civil defence officers doorknocked to organise evacuations; however, people refused to respond because they didn't recognise the uniform, and police had to be sent instead. In a history of the State Emergency Service (SES), the organisation conceded, 'some residents followed our recommendations, others didn't'.[16] Some refused to move. Jindalee resident Beryl Wilson recalls the civil defence ludicrously 'running up and down the streets with loud hailers ordering people to get out – where to was not stated – screaming that Somerset Dam was about to blow'.[17] Journalist Bob McDonald described how police or civil defence officers drove around Ipswich in cars using loud hailers to warn locals that Somerset Dam had been 'breached', an action that could only generate terror.[18] Civil defence members conceded they were 'poorly organised for this type of situation', but maintained they did a 'marvellous job with what resources and expertise were available'.[19] Perhaps their lack of boats best illustrates their poor preparedness.

These systemic and practical failings revealed a city unprepared for flooding. Insufficient rain gauges on the southern tributaries of the Bremer River and Oxley Creek made flood forecasting difficult. New Beith, shown to be a key rainfall gauge, only reported monthly, which was far too infrequent to be useful in flood forecasting. With telephone services above Somerset Dam cut and only two radios available, it proved difficult to manage dam releases. Communications steadily failed until only three gauges upstream of Mount Crosby could report, with ham radios used for communication. Just as the telegraph failed in 1893, demand crashed the telephone system in 1974, leaving no mechanism for mass distribution of information to the media.

In addition to newspaper articles, in 1974 vivid footage of the unfolding disaster was broadcast on television, but many people did not own televisions or even telephones. Beryl Wilson recalls people shouting messages across the flooded river at Jindalee, and public radio broadcasters were called on to disseminate information. Radio journalists repeatedly delivered personal messages, interspersed with news of flood heights, road closures and relief efforts. But in Ipswich flooded radio transmitters forced the local radio station, 4IP, off air. In Brisbane, Cossins and Heatherwick claim political intervention reduced warnings with the state issuing a directive 'at the highest level' to restrict radio broadcasts to avoid creating panic. They both consider the censorship irresponsible. Heatherwick recalls that while the commercial media complied, the Australian Broadcasting Commission defiantly issued regular warnings. Disseminating accurate and reliable information is essential as when communication breaks down rumour and hyperbole fill the void.

BoM found itself equally hamstrung by poor communication. With the formation of the national office in 1908, the bureau assumed responsibility for rainfall and river height recording. These duties increased to include national flood forecasting and warnings after the creation of a hydro-meteorological section in 1956. BoM's primary task was to disseminate warnings to radio and television broadcasters to reduce loss of life and property damage. In 1974, infrequent receipt of information delayed warnings. Heatherwick recalls staff having to travel by boat from the flooded BoM offices along Edward Street at 15-minute intervals to read makeshift emergency gauges erected on telephone poles.

While timely and accurate information is vital, it is equally important that facts are delivered in readily understood language. Heatherwick realised this need, and, despite the introduction of metric units on 1 January 1974, he provided forecasts in familiar imperial measurements to avoid confusion. But other information issues were harder to resolve. Flood terminology exposed a knowledge gulf between practitioners and the public and rendered flood height forecasts useless. Flood descriptions as 'minor', 'moderate' and 'major' are technical terms precisely defined by hydrologists and engineers, but they are largely meaningless to amateurs, causing misunderstanding. Malcolm Lamond conceded that the term 'moderate' had an unintended calming effect.[20] References to upper, middle or lower reaches of the river are even more obscure. Hydrologists sometimes refer to 'flood waves', as shown on a hydrograph to record a flood rise and fall, which, for non-experts, conjures up terrifying images of a tsunami racing towards the city. Media and police usage of terms such as 'wall of water' and 'surge' reinforced this image.

Many flood warnings depended on hydraulic knowledge for practical application. Riverbeds slope to ensure flow from the headwaters to the sea, unlike the horizontal surface of a lake, so during floods the water surface has a downstream incline. Consequently, while the Port Office experienced a flood height of 5.45 metres, Mount Crosby experienced a 26.74-metre flood. Hence a warning of a flood height in one location is meaningless in another. The translation of a central Brisbane flood height to a prediction for Moggill or Ipswich requires in-depth hydrological expertise. Similarly, comparisons with previous floods require knowledge of earlier flood heights. Jack Houston, Leader of the Opposition in 1974, critically commented that warnings were 'not related to people's homes' but a height at the Port Office, which was meaningless to many. John Herbert, Member for Sherwood, agreed and recommended readings against recognisable landmarks, such as bridges.[21] Towns in New South Wales had warning systems and flood levels linked to well-known locations; Brisbane did not. Without visible benchmarks and laymen's terminology, warnings were difficult to comprehend.

After the floods, BoM staff conceded their warnings were not readily understandable and should be given as a height below a landmark, rather than river height, and thereby not rely on historical or expert knowledge. Arch Shields admitted to 'problems of dissemination and interpretation of the warnings, coupled with some reluctance by the community to accept the gravity of the situation'. As a consequence, he felt the 'full value of the flood warning system was not achieved'. Yet he found 'some adverse criticism' directed at the bureau to be 'without justification'. Despite equipment failures and adverse working conditions, BoM managed to deliver remarkably accurate river height forecasts 21 hours in advance.[22] Dissemination, public understanding and response to the warnings were the problems, not forecast accuracy. As the public ignored or misunderstood warnings, opportunities to reduce loss of life and property were missed.

Many people, unconvinced of the severity of the approaching flood, did little to prepare. Journalist Bob McDonald claimed that on Saturday 26 January 1974 'most people still weren't taking it seriously. The Brisbane River would never flood.'[23] Cossins, revealing his frustration, agrees that 'people barely respond' to flood warnings. Heatherwick concurs, 'most people do not react to flood warnings, thinking it won't happen to them and it is not their problem'. Enid Robinson on the river at Chelmer proved a typical case. Mindful of floods, she and her husband, Kim, had built on the highest point of their block in 1956, withstanding minor floods and dry years. As the river rose in January 1974, Kim took to his boat to help those on lower ground already flooded. According to Enid's memoirs, it wasn't until they woke on Sunday that they realised 'the big flood had really come and we were already cut off by road'. Kim and Enid evacuated their children to family living nearby by boat and moved themselves and some furniture to the top storey to wait it out. As the waters subsided on Wednesday they had a 'nasty surprise – we were completely marooned by mud. Everything was coated in a thick, oozy, evil-smelling mess of brown mud; not just an inch or two, but anything up to three feet thick' (Figure 5.1). Her neighbours also adopted the common response of 'wait and see'.[24]

Figure 5.1: Chelmer in flood, 29 January 1974.
(State Library of Queensland API-084-0001-14-22)

Counting the Toll

Thanks to advances in technology, journalists could call on aerial photography, graphic colour photographs and television footage to convey news of the flood and its devastation, but the language and response in newspaper reports had changed little since 1893. Newspapers recounted people flocking to the river where, according to *The Australian*, on 'every bridge crowds stand fascinated by the angry version of their river', once a 'tranquil, winding waterway'. The sense of amazement and fascination at this 'angry' river prevailed once again. Newspapers reported that the spectators 'could not remember such savage turbulence', as 'houses were ripped off their stumps, steel walls of factories were torn open, and luxury craft were smashed to matchwood'.[25] In Ipswich, residents 'faced the flood threat grimly but calmly, with perhaps a touch of incredulity, that the Bremer River could actually attain such a height'.[26] Many expressed surprise at the extent of the floods, a response best exclaimed by a three-year-old in Gailes, who said, 'Mummy, the whole world is under water.'[27]

The media's language set a familiar agenda for the flood conversation. The language of conflict persisted with the phrases 'flood fighters', 'combat', 'battle', 'enemy' and 'war' used in reports following the floods. *The Queensland Times* also noted the awesome power of the floods: 'beds, chairs, tables, mattresses were seen smashing their way downstream and in the low-lying streets, roofs of partly submerged cars were further reminders of the might of nature at its fiercest'.[28] This language reaffirmed the perceived separation of humans and nature, and reinforced the concept that floods were abnormal, a hazard external to society. Once again, the underlying social, economic or political causes were not investigated. Societal leaders could concentrate on re-establishing order and progress, but first a flood toll had to be taken.

In Ipswich, floods inundated the older, low-lying areas of the inner city (Figures 5.2 and 5.3). Many homes in West Ipswich were washed away, the result of the Bremer River's high velocity. The newer suburbs of Leichhardt, One Mile, Booval, East Ipswich and Brassall joined the list of areas worst affected. Fourteen homes in Sydney Street, Brassall, were swept away leaving only stumps and a scene of 'utter devastation'.[29] In Leslie Street, East Ipswich, Robyn and Neal Flashman nervously witnessed floodwaters creeping up their backyard after breakfast, reaching their back door by 6 pm and the windows by 8 pm. By morning their roof was submerged, along with those of many neighbouring homes.

Figure 5.2: Floating debris in Brisbane Street, the main street of Ipswich, January 1974. (Picture Ipswich)

Figure 5.3: East Street, central Ipswich, January 1974. (Picture Ipswich)

An estimated 43 homes in Ipswich were destroyed and a further 1,674 had water encroach into living areas. Among these were dozens of government-provided housing commission homes in Leichhardt and One Mile. At Gailes more than 100 caravans were ripped from their berths and smashed against the bridge, leaving four people missing. Evacuations included 3,500 homes and approximately 15,000 people, which was substantial in a city of only 68,795 people. As the *Courier-Mail* editor accurately noted, Ipswich 'suffered more, proportionally, than Brisbane'.[30] Llewellyn Edwards, the State Member for Ipswich, lamented, 'my city was a devastated, destroyed city'.[31] With damage concentrated in the poorer areas, some families and businesses would never recover their losses.

By 28 January more than a third of Brisbane lay under water (Figures 5.4 and 5.5). The hardest hit suburbs in Brisbane were the affluent riverside suburbs of Chelmer, Sherwood, Graceville and Yeronga and the inexpensive land on the flats at Oxley and Rocklea. As in 1893, the floodwaters did not discriminate by wealth, drowning all houses in their path. Sherwood Member John Herbert informed Parliament that 'between Oxley Methodist Church on Oxley Road and the river (nearly a mile away), every house went under'. He estimated 75 per cent of Graceville State School children lived in flood-affected homes, 90 per cent of them in Rocklea.[32] Most of these homes were constructed after the 1930s bridge and rail expansion and when the government promoted settlement in the 1950s. All of these areas had flooded in 1893 and had been built in accordance with BCC and state regulations.

Homes along the Esplanade at Yeronga, on a relatively narrow section of the river, felt the full force of the floodwaters (Figure 5.6). Diane Street in Yeronga, home to the Gahan family, was one of the worst hit streets in Brisbane. Graham Gahan wrote to his mother of his 'shocking reality'. The 'raging muddy waters' had wreaked havoc and caused 'scenes of heartbreaking devastation and human suffering, leaving about seven homes seriously affected structurally.

Figure 5.4: LEFT – Edward Street, Brisbane City, January 1974. (BCC-B120-2387)

Figure 5.5: BELOW – Rescuing beer from the iconic XXXX Brewery at Milton, January 1974. (BCC-B120-2394)

Figure 5.6: ABOVE – Severe flooding at Yeronga, January 1974.
(State Library of Queensland 180258)

One disintegrated and another lies off its stumps in the backyard.
Two others are almost fit for demolition.'

Although the Gahan's house survived, their neighbours were
less fortunate. Shop owner Joe Rago living nearby on the Brisbane
Corso, Fairfield, found the walls and ceilings of his house ruined,
and the floorboards pushed up by the force of the water. Similarly,
bricklayer Javier Barrenechea described his home in Stimpson Street,
Fairfield, as drowned, with the floors, doors and windows warped
and buckled and plywood peeling off the kitchen cupboards. The
contents of many homes were destroyed, and, after the floodwaters
receded, damaged possessions could be found piled high on the
roadsides (Figure 5.7). Most of this area had been farmland in 1893
but by 1971 the local government area of Yeronga had a population
of 11,795 people occupying 3,871 dwellings.

Figure 5.7: Home contents reduced to rubbish in Orient Road, Yeronga.
(*Sunday Mail,* 3 February 1974. Courtesy of Newspix)

In Jindalee, one of the Centenary Estates suburbs developed in the 1960s, 268 houses sustained substantial inundation on the ground floor, with 207 of these reporting major flooding in their main living area. After the flood, a report claimed that the Jindalee developers had been demonised as this figure amounted to less than 20 per cent of houses.[33] However, the developers were aware of the flood risk but had only taken into account the 1931 floods, and the project had been approved by council. The Jindalee floodwaters reached Ken and Beryl Wilson's steps, stopping short of the 1893 flood height they had planned around. Houses on the street's river side were severely damaged, the water's velocity offering no match for timber or brick walls. While the Wilsons stayed for 10 years, counting on a flood-free decade and the appeal of riverside living justifying the risk, many other traumatised residents cleaned out their homes and moved on as they could not face another flood and did not believe Somerset Dam would save them in future.

The greatest loss was lives – 14 in Brisbane and 2 in Ipswich. Noel Stretton, an Ipswich chemist, drove through floodwaters to help staff empty his shop and drowned when his car was swept away, leaving behind his wife, Elizabeth, and five children. Aiden Sutton, a married clerk aged 50, returned to his home in St Lucia from his work at the city police headquarters for his reading glasses, swimming through swiftly swirling water that was 3 metres deep. Sutton's body was found wedged in a tree, his swimming ability no match for floodwaters travelling at 18 knots. The body of Frank Nester of Alderley, aged 39, was recovered downstream of Norman Bridge on Kelvin Grove Road. Some were found dead in flooded buildings, including Franz Nagy, a baker aged 52, of Gailey Road, St Lucia. Shane Patterson, aged two, was swept from his father's arms in a swollen creek after their car had been carried by floodwaters from Inala Avenue, Inala, and overturned into the surging river. Others died during attempted rescues, like Robert Adams, aged 56, who suffered a heart attack while being saved from Newmarket Caravan Park.[34] On 28 January a rescue mission in a LARC amphibious vehicle hit high-tension wires in Bellbowrie, with Major Risell (the Commanding Officer), Captain Ian Kerr (Australian Military Forces), Corporal Neville Barry Hourigan (Citizen Military Force), Bill Lickiss (Member for Mt Coot-tha) and 10 local residents on board, including an 86-year-old man, two children and a baby. Corporal Neville Hourigan died from electrocution, Captain Kerr was presumed dead as his body was never found, and three men were badly burned.[35]

Statistics hid the real human cost, with individual accounts conveying the personal impact. Left with only the stumps of his Keogh Street home in Ipswich, pensioner George Lawrence broke down and wept, 'it was everything I had [...] I have worked all my life and now this happens to me'.[36] Charles Amey of William Parade, Fairfield, aged 62, described his anguish in a letter to Premier Bjelke-Petersen: 'to return to a loved home, which has been completely submerged for three days, and find it covered and fouled by inches of evil smelling river silt, damaged and requiring large scale repairs [...] is a situation to daunt the stoutest heart'.[37] Three years short of retirement, he despaired of rebuilding his assets.

The Telegraph on 31 January reported, 'many were left with only the shells of their former homes, with all furnishings and household equipment left sodden useless wreckage by the floodwaters'. *The Courier-Mail* declared Brisbane 'a sombre city', with 'disbelief, hopelessness and defeat' etched in the faces of residents as they surveyed 'the wreckage that was, only a week ago, a lifetime's work'. The same paper declared, 'men and women wept unashamedly'.[38] Water containing chemical contaminants and raw sewage disgorged from the submerged Ipswich sewerage plant, domestic out-houses and septic systems, and flowed through houses. Floodwaters were littered with thousands of dead fowl, horses and cattle, mixed with debris and mud. Health warnings were issued for gastroenteritis and tetanus, and government officers provided free injections as disinfectant stocks ran out. As the waters receded, leaving layers of disease-carrying sludge and a trail of destroyed homes and possessions, the odour of effluent permeated the air – a smell people would never forget.

Assets throughout South East Queensland were destroyed as floodwaters indiscriminately inundated businesses and services. Ipswich, financially dependent on industry, suffered approximately $4 million in industrial losses and immediate unemployment of 500 people. Four Ipswich coal mines, significant employers of 300 people, closed permanently, and a quarter of the Ipswich retail and business district was damaged. Rail and roads to Brisbane and Toowoomba were cut and the city was left isolated. Floodwaters from Warrill and Purga creeks (tributaries of the Bremer River) rendered the RAAF Base Amberley inoperable as it was submerged by a 5.6 kilometre wide expanse of floodwater. Eighty-five per cent of residents were without power, some for seven days. The estimated damage to essential services in Ipswich was $4.5 million, with $3.22 million to council assets alone.[39]

With Brisbane's streets and train lines submerged, water craft became the transport of necessity. The Southeast Freeway, Bruce Highway, Gold Coast Highway and Ipswich Road, main routes out of the city, were cut. Only the Story Bridge was trafficable. On 27 January, a gravel barge crashed into the Centenary Bridge at Jindalee and it was feared the central girder had cracked, so the bridge was closed to all but police and rescue workers (Figure 5.8). Four charges of dynamite and a full load of water eventually sank the vessel. Damage reduced the bridge to one lane for 15 months. Another drama ensued on 28 January when the 66,000 tonne tanker *Robert Miller*, the biggest vessel ever constructed in Brisbane, swept out of control downstream from the Evans Deakin Shipyards and swung across the river, creating an obstruction to the floodwaters and threatening a block of luxury flats. It was held by the tug *Carlock* and its skipper, Leo Hartas, was hailed a hero. The port was closed and cross-river ferries ceased with many terminals wrecked.

Figure 5.8: A gravel barge crashed into the Centenary Bridge that had to be scuttled using dynamite. (*The Australian*, 26 January 1974. Courtesy of Newspix)

Around 30,000 telephones were rendered inoperable for weeks, and some mail services were suspended. Television was only available to those with electricity, which was a threatened commodity as floodwaters closed Tennyson Power Station, leaving only Bulimba and Swanbank power stations functioning. Floodwaters swamped 30 Brisbane inner-city and 70 suburban sub-stations, including

4 major sub-stations, leaving dozens of suburbs without power. Many suburbs were also without gas, and water supplies were compromised by the temporary closure of Mount Crosby Pumping Station.

The rural sector estimated state-wide losses of $50 million, with an indicative figure of $1.6 million wiped from the soya bean, lucerne and irrigated pastures in the Brisbane River catchment area. Small businesses lost conservatively $40 million, with some businesses left on the 'brink of collapse'.[40] The heavily promoted Rocklea industrial area was hit hard, with many businesses unable to resume production. Giant deep freezers at the Rocklea Markets were left full of rotting vegetables. One business alone, Tickle Wholesale Distributors, lost over $500,000 of stock in their South Brisbane, Fairfield and Ipswich warehouses.[41] The government sector also bore great expense with schools, railway lines, bridges and roads damaged, and the port rendered inoperable until millions of tonnes of silt were dredged from river channels. On 29 January, *The Courier-Mail* ominously and accurately recorded that 'the cost of restoration will far out-weigh anything else Queensland has ever known'.[42] This cost is directly attributed to development on the floodplain.

Damage estimates were $142 million direct damage (from Brisbane River inundation) and $178 million for indirect damage such as loss of income after flooding. These figures exclude other rivers and tributaries. Thirteen thousand residential, industrial and commercial buildings were affected.[43] Parliamentarian Bill Lickiss declared it 'a flood disaster that is unparalleled in the history of this State in terms of extent and effect'.[44] Commonwealth Treasurer Frank Crean described the state-wide floods as Queensland's 'greatest single disaster and probably the greatest in the history of Australia'.[45] Both statements could be contested with deaths surpassed in Gundagai (1852), Clermont (1916) and the Hunter Valley (1955), and the economic impact difficult to assess in real terms. But on a global scale they rated with Netherlands' 1953 storm surge ($84 million) and Chile's 1960 earthquake ($40 million).[46]

Brisbane's flood damage bill of $320 million had a significant impact on the economy, as it was 23 per cent of Queensland's 1972–73 consolidated revenue.[47]

Short-Term Actions Avoid Long-Term Solutions

Before reconstruction could occur, short-term responses were demanded of government. In times of crisis politicians need to be seen, especially by those affected. Populist Brisbane Lord Mayor Clem Jones knew this well, as he donned his gumboots to visit flooded parts of the city. Newspapers and television depicted Jones in a 'tinny' or wading in mud, offering comfort and promises of help. This reflected Jones's personality and style as a man of action and an excellent media campaigner. Premier Joh Bjelke-Petersen toured the state to visit flood-damaged areas, but he left the south-east corner largely to municipal leaders. He garnered public wrath by refusing to declare a state of emergency, which would have released funding and special state powers.

Unlike Jones who rushed home from the Christchurch Commonwealth Games, Prime Minister Gough Whitlam made a political error when, after the games, he continued on his Asian tour and only sent a message of concern from Kuala Lumpur. A *Courier-Mail* cartoon on 9 February captured the public anger in a scathing 'wish you were here' postcard from Brisbane. Federal ministers visited, but this did not satisfy flood-affected communities – the Prime Minister was missing in action. *The Courier-Mail* editorial unequivocally declared, 'the Brisbane floods are a national disaster. The nation's leader should be on hand.'[48] When Whitlam eventually visited Brisbane the mood turned ugly. On 14 February *The Australian* published a cartoon of Gough and Margaret Whitlam on aeroplane steps wearing life jackets, the sun shining and flowers growing. The tightly managed ensuing press conference went badly as the 30 journalists present, unimpressed by the Prime Minister's pile of briefing notes, accused Whitlam of remote-control leadership. When asked for a response to criticism for not visiting Brisbane sooner, Whitlam, nicknamed the 'dry foot PM', silently left the room.[49]

However, the government and its agencies were not inert and they, along with the community, focused on the short-term necessities of rescue, cleaning and aid. Over 500 people were rescued by a combination of local residents and police, civil defence, army and air force personnel in an event described by *The Sunday Mail* as 'Brisbane's Dunkirk'. Those flooded found accommodation in schools, churches and community halls, and accepted meals, clothing and supplies donated from interstate. Volunteers rescued possessions caked with vile mud and returned them clean. Private boats and helicopters from the isolated RAAF Base Amberley rescued stranded residents and provided relief. Public servants were granted leave to assist in the clean-up and tradesmen freely offered their services.

Over 1,500 army personnel were mobilised. Enid Robinson in Chelmer recalled how they 'moved in with clean-up equipment, willing and cheerful men and great efficiency. The whole world seemed to be coming to help – friends, people we hardly knew, the Salvation Army with hot meals, fruit and offers of assistance of every kind.' For over a week 'kind hands took away [...] dirty washing and returned piles of clean ironed clothing; volunteers came to scrub and shovel'.[50] Graham Gahan in Diane Street, Yeronga, recounts, 'there were people and trucks everywhere', strangers came from everywhere to help. He delighted in telling his mother, 'we're on Christian name terms with more people in Yeronga West now than we'd ever dreamed we would be'.[51] Human kindness and spirit shone through; heart-warming moments amid tragedy.

Councils opened makeshift dumps and damaged possessions were scooped up by front-end loaders and unceremoniously dumped in skips. As one volunteer noted, 'we're not just sweeping away the muck – we're sweeping away part of their life'.[52] The media extolled the selfless actions of assistance, and in doing so shaped the public narrative of floods. The dominant message became South East

Queenslanders' strength and resilience, community compassion and teamwork in the face of adversity. This skilfully diverted attention away from discussions of causality and responsibility.

The federal government offered relief payments, reimbursing the state for expenditure above $2 million and matching state personal hardship payments. Federal and state funds were distributed by the Government Flood Damaged Homes Committee for repairs or replacement of homes. These funds were means-tested. By 30 July 1974, this committee had made 7,864 payments totalling over $6 million. Thirty-eight substitute houses were purchased, providing a rare example of a long-term solution.[53] Businesses and the agricultural sector were given assistance, but sporting associations received no help. The distribution of government aid, a short-term solution to flood mitigation, became embroiled in political acrimony and arguments about equity.

A further inequity was flood insurance with policy owners discovering their policies included damage from rain but did not include floods. Flood cover required an expensive additional annual fee, an option not chosen by many. Some were insured, such as owners of Federal War Service Homes or Australian Government Defence Service Homes who automatically had Commonwealth Government flood insurance as standard cover and commercial properties were covered by insurance policies with underwriters overseas. Others, such as Queensland Housing Commission homes, did not. Unions, parliamentarians and affected home owners railed against these disparities. Underpinning the idea of insurance lay a popular belief that flood sufferers should receive compensation, along with the idea of assigning blame for flood damage.

Flood relief and insurance deals with symptoms rather than causes. Furthermore, they absolve town planners and individuals of responsibility and encourage irresponsible development on the floodplain. Development approvals in vulnerable areas, particularly as a result of the belief that Somerset Dam would reduce or even prevent floods, had greatly increased the flood hazard. But the 1974 floods exposed the fallacy of relying on Somerset Dam. South East Queensland was not flood proof. Although the dam had reduced the flood height, the 1974 flood damage was substantially greater than in 1893. *The Courier-Mail* acknowledged the problem of focusing on short-term solutions and the dam's mitigation capabilities, rather than systemic changes to floodplain management, declaring, 'one day it'll be worse [...] unless we can act'.[54] However, instead of addressing unregulated urban growth, the debate quickly dissolved into a recriminatory blame game. Instead of challenging the policy of relying solely on dams for flood mitigation, the 1974 floods ensured the government stuck more resolutely to its technocratic beliefs.

Dam Dependency

'BRISBANE SIMPLY CANNOT afford another flood as disastrous as this. Yet, if nothing is done, it certainly will suffer one', declared the *Courier-Mail* editor in the immediate aftermath of the 1974 floods.[1] The 1974 flood offered the opportunity to question the wisdom of dam dependency and alter the region's flood mitigation practices. Despite *The Courier-Mail*'s call for action, a new path was not chosen. Instead South East Queensland strengthened its reliance on dams by building a second flood mitigation dam, Wivenhoe Dam, completed in 1984. This created a stronger, more pervasive myth that South East Queensland had been flood-proofed, and the region's flood vulnerability increased.

The Blame Game

As the floodwaters receded and the clean-up began in 1974, those affected began questioning why they had been flooded. However, potential lessons for preventing future flood damage were lost as the debate degenerated and recrimination flourished. The shift in understanding that floods are natural but the hazard is human-created encouraged the attribution of blame. Many potential villains were identified, including developers, local and state governments, and floodplain dwellers. Arguments over flood damage culpability revealed the powerful influence of the development and building sectors and the popular misunderstandings of South East Queensland's enduring flood risk.

Developers were frequently cited in newspapers as the culprit for the flood. Jack Egerton, Queensland President of the Australian Labor Party, believed developers had 'reaped millions' by building on the floodplain and consciously ignoring earlier flood levels.[2] As a member of the Greater Brisbane Town Planning Committee, Egerton needed to deflect scrutiny from council regulations. He found support in the Labor Federal Science Minister, William Morrison, who claimed developers had filled in many natural watercourses and built homes or factories too close to the river or in areas with regular flooding.[3] Letters to the newspapers reflected the same sentiment. Mrs K. Thomas of Murarrie blamed unscrupulous developers selling land to 'young couples, to migrants or people from other parts of Australia who had no experience of Brisbane flood conditions'.[4] In her opinion, they knowingly exploited people who were unaware.

Developers refuted any culpability. Bill Bowden, State President of the Urban Development Institute of Australia, exonerated his profession, declaring they could not accept responsibility for a 'freak of nature'.[5] His colleague Allen Vogan, President of the Urban Development Institute of Australia, considered blaming developers 'absurd and immature' as floods were inevitable. He cavalierly argued that even if they built within prescribed flood levels and zoning constraints, a larger flood would make these precautions pointless.[6] John Hattrick, Queensland Director of L. J. Hooker, weighed in stating, 'no company develops any land without local-authority approval', and in doing so deftly shifted the blame onto councils for approving subdivisions and developments. Alexander Barr Yeates, Surveyor-General of Queensland, offered a strange defence when he declared, 'the developer is a human being. He wants to do the best for himself and his family by making profits. He is not restricted by the fine ethical principles of flooding in the future.'[7] Yeates justified profit and self-interest. After creating the hazard, developers could walk away.

For the community and the state government, local councils were a popular scapegoat, with their weak planning rules held responsible for the devastation of the floods. However, the state can, and does, intervene, in planning matters. In South East Queensland, floods exposed the commonly tense relationship between local and state politics, characterised by conflict and shifting responsibility.[8] By failing to devolve councils' authority to prevent floodplain development, the state had increased its culpability. As state and local governments fought to apportion or circumvent blame, neither took a firm lead on hazard reduction.

The limited powers of local government include zoning and development assessments, but Brisbane residents clearly considered BCC negligent in permitting development on flood-prone areas. Newspapers also maintained that the council had approved building construction in hazardous areas. The *Courier-Mail* editor cited evidence of creeks filled in and natural areas of flood mitigation altered to 'provide playing fields, industrial and housing estates, and other purposes'.[9] State politicians were happy to divert fault to councils, with the Member for Mount Gravatt, Geoffrey Chinchen, informing Parliament that BCC zoning had been badly executed, that the council had approved ill-advised zoning and issued building permits where they should have been prohibited, and saying that Brisbane had paid the price. Charles Porter, Member for Toowong, maintained that BCC had the 'worst record of any local authority in permitting what it knew should not be permitted'.[10] Certainly, substantial development had been permitted below the 1893 flood levels.

Unsurprisingly, Lord Mayor Clem Jones rebutted any criticism that BCC had wantonly allowed floodplain development, claiming, 'we have been doing all we can'. In his view, council had 'no control on industrial development on floodplains and it had little more control on residential development in these areas'. Deflecting blame, Jones claimed state legislation hamstrung councils and enshrined the rights of appeal and compensation, stating, 'we have taken some firms to court, unsuccessfully, in an effort to stop this development'.[11]

The courts protected an individual's alienable rights to develop their property and 'it was difficult to prevent people from building in low-lying areas', a charge supported by a 1974 Commonwealth investigation.[12] James (Jim) Cameron Slaughter, Jones's political ally and former town clerk, agreed that for many years 'we tried to keep people off the floodplains', but people successfully objected. He said, 'when we refused subdivision on low land at Sherwood, the first point of call for the buyers were the politicians and next thing we were interfering with the rights of private people'.[13] Council claimed powerlessness. Jack Egerton agreed with Jones, and said the Brisbane planning committee lacked 'power to prevent exploitation by developers'. He called on the state government 'to give the City Council power to stop building in danger areas' or 'resume flooded areas in Brisbane as parks and resettle residents in alternative housing to prevent a reoccurrence'.[14] Council wanted an amendment to the *City of Brisbane (Town Plan) Act of 1960* to grant them more authority to stop development.

As governments squabbled, jockeying to evade responsibility, some in the community identified a reliance on Somerset Dam to prevent floods as a root cause of the damage. The *Courier-Mail* editorial identified a prevalent 'it can't happen here' attitude, a belief encouraged by many dry years and faith that Somerset Dam prevented flooding.[15] As in other parts of the world, faith in technology had increased Brisbane's vulnerability.[16]

Despite the flood, the lure of attractive riverside or affordable low-lying land remained. As in the aftermath of the 1893 floods, the memory of floods receded and, with the aid of flood-free years, people returned to the floodplain. The real estate industry cynically believed people would forget the floods in six months and declared as early as 4 February that entrepreneurs were buying 'soggy' houses, hoping that when things dried out 'people would be rushing to buy land that was flooded back in January'.[17] For some it was worth the risk, a view clearly articulated by a local surveyor who intended to remain on the floodplain: 'How often do you have to suffer a flood like this? I'd live in one of these beautiful flood-prone suburbs and take my chances on having a flood every 50 years, or whatever it has to be.'[18] For some, restricting development for infrequent floods was foolish. *Sunday Mail* journalist John Bragg believed 'Brisbane has to live with floods', arguing that leaving the floodplain vacant was unviable and had that policy been implemented one-third of Brisbane would never have been built, including the CBD. Bragg cited Peter Lightfoot, general manager of the development company Centenary Estates, who claimed if the floodplains were cleared Brisbane would be an uneconomical 160 kilometre strip.[19] Capitalism and progress once again justified floodplain development.

Investigating the Causes

With conflicting views evident, as early as 31 January 1974, John Houston, Leader of the Opposition in the Queensland Parliament, supported the growing calls for a public flood inquiry, not 'to find a scapegoat' but to give people a 'chance to air their views and hear expert comment from a wide range of people'.[20] *The Courier-Mail* supported an inquiry, or royal commission, to make recommendations on future flood mitigation, stating the 'laws on land use of the city's floodplains, or the lack of laws, are an obvious term of reference. State and city authorities have been buck-passing on responsibility for residential development of flood-prone land.'[21]

Residents and community groups also placed development regulations in the spotlight. In a letter to Premier Joh Bjelke-Petersen, architect and ex–Australian Imperial Force engineer J. N. Allom requested an inquiry to urgently investigate council's failure 'to control the approval of construction projects on well-known flood prone land' with the hope of developing 'a more progressive policy on zoning standards and procedure'. Allom believed these 'faults of the past' – approvals on flood-prone land and poor zoning – could be 'identified and rectified' through legislation.[22] The Union of Australian Women maintained that a public inquiry would assure 'Queenslanders that all relevant experiences will be taken into consideration'. They added, 'We are convinced, like many other Queenslanders, that too many decisions about so-called development are made in the interest of profit for the "developers" rather than improvement of the quality of the lives of the people and the security and safety of their homes.'[23]

Over the early months of 1974 the groundswell for an inquiry grew. A Brisbane Flood Action Committee was formed, chaired by engineer Ernest Oliver, whose participation was prompted by his own vested interest as floodwaters had submerged his Fairfield home by 5 metres. He rallied support and on 28 July over 400 people gathered at Roma Street, demanding an inquiry to form a blueprint for future flood mitigation. They recommended six points worthy of investigation: engineering work, flood warning system, legislative change in flood-prone areas, a single water authority, operational emergency services, and standardised aid or insurance. Oliver informed *The Courier-Mail* that politicians had 'got away with a lot of promises and very little fulfilment' and said something needed to be done about flood mitigation.[24]

The inquiry received bureaucratic support. Jim Slaughter endorsed an inquiry to pinpoint flood-prone land and prohibit future construction. The Director of BoM, Arch Shields, agreed, saying, 'if flooding can't be stopped Brisbane has to plan to stop great public damage'. He found 'little real evidence, in the absence of an acceptable town plan, that floodplain management to avoid flood losses was given a very high priority, if indeed any at all', with public planning directed 'largely towards the provision of flood mitigation storages'.[25] Undoubtedly the state had relied on Somerset Dam for flood mitigation, a policy many believed warranted investigation.

Premier Bjelke-Petersen defiantly refused to hold a flood inquiry. He believed 'it is pointless to try and assign blame. No-one is blameless.' As he informed parliament, 'we know the cause'. Conservative Member Bill Lickiss told fellow parliamentarians that the floods were an act of God, and party colleague John Herbert stated the 'catastrophic rain' meant 'the flood was something that no Government could have avoided'. Labor Member Kevin Hooper agreed the main cause was the cyclone.[26] As politicians framed the flood as an unavoidable natural disaster, the fault of God or nature, as they had in 1893, they absolved themselves of responsibility for the damages and avoided an inquiry into land use legislation and regulations that might threaten the state government's lucrative land taxes and political donations from the development industry. Despite its complaints about lack of power to control floodplains, BCC did not give enthusiastic support to an inquiry. Increasing rates from new subdivisions were highly profitable, and upsetting constituents and unions could amount to political suicide. While newspapers gave initial attention to the need for an inquiry, the matter never gained the necessary public momentum or political support and another opportunity for systemic change was lost. Instead, the state remained committed to building Wivenhoe Dam, cementing the dependency on dams for flood mitigation.

Wivenhoe Dam – Brisbane's Flood Saviour

Although popular belief maintains that Wivenhoe Dam was built in response to the 1974 floods, in reality preliminary planning work commenced in the 1960s and gained momentum when the Coordinator General commissioned a feasibility study in 1971 by engineer and economist Trevor Grigg.[27] The dam's primary role was water supply, with growing demand expected to exceed supply by 1981. Flood mitigation remained a secondary concern, followed by a limited hydro-electricity capability. Cabinet approved Wivenhoe Dam in November 1971. Construction required total or partial acquisition of 238 properties and would inundate three Aboriginal Bora Rings, four burial areas, a campsite and a cave. The state considered acquisitions of land for a dam economically and political palatable, unlike repossessing properties on a floodplain. Land acquisitions began in 1973, contracts were let in 1977 and the first water was stored in Wivenhoe Dam in 1983, with the official opening in October 1985.

Wivenhoe Dam, 150 kilometres from the mouth of the
Brisbane River, has a 7,020 square kilometre catchment including
the Stanley River and the upper and middle reaches of the
Brisbane River. The dam's water supply storage (up to 67 metres)
can hold 1,165,200 megalitres at Full Supply Level (FSL). At
a cost of $75 million, the dam provided an annual yield of
230,000 megalitres and increased South East Queensland's water
supply by 80 per cent, storing five years' water supply. The design
allowed for a further 1,970,000 megalitres for temporary flood
storage (between 67 metres and the top of the embankment at
80.1 metres; Figure 6.1).[28] When full, Wivenhoe Dam's water supply
and flood mitigation capability is three times that of Somerset Dam
and together these dams manage 50 per cent of the catchment and
provide 60 per cent of South East Queensland's water.

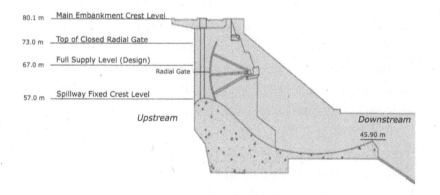

Figure 6.1: Cross-sectional diagram of Wivenhoe Dam looking east with
FSL at 67 metres and flood compartment (above FSL).
Drawing provided by Seqwater, modified.

Wivenhoe Dam, according to Grigg, would reduce both the
annual flood cost and a 1974 type flood from 7 metres (no dams) to
3.1 metres at the Port Office Gauge (post dams).[29] A Commonwealth
and state interdepartmental committee charged with reviewing
Brisbane's flood mitigation schemes in 1974 found the proposed

scheme offered the maximum protection available; only clearing the floodplain would prevent the hazard more effectively. Wivenhoe Dam would provide little protection for floods bigger than 1974, so the committee's report stated, 'it could be argued that there is no economic justification'. However, as the 1974 flood was the largest in 80 years and 'the kind against which the public is expecting protection', there was no 'politically acceptable alternative' other than building Wivenhoe Dam.[30] Experts understood the limited mitigating effect of dams on major floods, but equally recognised the political nature of floods. The Queensland Government could be seen to address floods with this engineering achievement and attract the essential political mileage.

Not everyone was enamoured with the Wivenhoe Dam flood solution. Engineers explained that Somerset Dam's caveats also applied to Wivenhoe Dam. Its efficacy would be determined by nature – the location, intensity and timing of rainfall. If floodwaters exceeded the dam's storage capacity, mandatory releases would reduce the mitigation effect. The likelihood of extreme floods remained and Wivenhoe Dam would not eliminate river flooding. Newspapers warned that floods could still occur, albeit tempered with the belief that dams would reduce them. Under the 1974 banner headline 'This could happen again', *The Courier-Mail* warned, 'don't be beguiled into false security: new dam or not at Wivenhoe, Brisbane and Ipswich will certainly be deluged with floods equally as severe as the Australia Day 1974 disasters'.[31]

Labor parliamentarian Edgar Baldwin maintained the proposed Wivenhoe Dam 'would have been filled several times' in 1974 and, while he supported its construction, he warned that the dam was not a long-term solution. He called on the government to stop protecting 'its friends the big housing monopolies, banks and insurance companies' and introduce legislation to stop floodplain development.[32] As engineering predecessors had done before him, Grigg advised in 1971 that Wivenhoe Dam should be accompanied by non-structural mitigation methods including acquisition of low-lying properties and preventing the reconstruction of damaged buildings. He definitively stated, 'if continuing encroachment onto the flood plain is not restrained, flood damage [...] will continue to increase', especially as flood awareness diminished and the community relied on the second dam.[33]

The Bjelke-Petersen government had found the desired technocratic solution to flooding. With the flood damage still clearly visible, on 19 February 1974 Bjelke-Petersen announced that the dam 'would be pushed ahead as quickly as possible for flood mitigation'. Community faith in Wivenhoe Dam to prevent floods was immediately apparent. *The Courier-Mail* supported this policy, stating, 'the dam would mean that Brisbane would not get another flood greater than 1931'.[34] *The Sunday Mail* pronounced with Wivenhoe Dam 'Brisbane should see an end to major floods'.[35] More blatantly, *The Telegraph* ran the headline 'It's our flood hope' with journalist Ted Crofts writing that although 'Nature will try to sink Brisbane again', next time 'Wivenhoe Dam may tame the river'; his rhetoric was reminiscent of the Somerset Dam Syndrome. In the smaller print within Croft's article, engineers warned that Wivenhoe Dam would reduce, but not eliminate, flooding. With seemingly no irony Crofts added, 'somehow one of those wild beliefs sprang up among some people that Somerset had removed all risk of serious flooding'.[36] Perhaps he did not realise that his own headlines would create the same myth about Wivenhoe Dam.

The dam opened with little fanfare on 18 October 1985. In the presence of 700 guests, Bjelke-Petersen declared he 'doubted if the 1974 flood could occur again because the dam would absorb an enormous quantity of water before any had to be released'.[37] *The Courier-Mail* was more definitive: 'Flood Threat Past: Sir Joh'. Overall the newspaper appeared underwhelmed by the occasion with the article relegated to page 18. Bjelke-Petersen felt compelled to contribute his own double-page article in *The Sunday Mail*, heralding his government's achievement. Clearly articulating notions of nation-building and progress, he declared the dam a '$460 million vital link in the State's continuing development', facilitating progress and expansion, to build a 'stronger State and a better life for all Queenslanders'. Major contractors funded advertisements heralding 'new growth' that reinforced the link with development. The project, described by Bjelke-Petersen as 'big by any standards',[38] reflected Australia's post–World War II preoccupation with large-scale engineering enterprises, best represented by the Snowy Mountains Scheme. This 'big engineering' trend peaked in Australia in the 1950s and globally in the 1970s.[39] The policy endured with the Queensland Water Resources Commission building 22 dams and 6 weirs between 1953 and 1985 to meet the imperative of water supply and irrigation for a growing population.

The construction of Wivenhoe Dam reflected the Bjelke-Petersen government's ideological framework that upheld development as the key to prosperity and growth, a stance that benefitted big property developers and construction companies. As a premier who later listed Wivenhoe Dam as one of the top ten achievements of his premiership, Bjelke-Petersen's commitment to the dam project was immutable.[40] He assured residents that the two dams – Somerset and Wivenhoe – would control the Brisbane River and protect the city from floods.

Despite Sir Joh's assurances, newspapers and engineers repeatedly warned that an over-reliance on Wivenhoe Dam could create a myth of protection. Large floods could not be prevented. In 1985, the Coordinator General warned that the mitigating potential of Wivenhoe Dam would be eroded through lack of town planning controls, just as Somerset Dam's 'effect was lost' owing to 'an over optimistic view in the reduction in height of large floods'.[41] The Premier's own department acknowledged the enduring risk in a briefing note for the dam's opening. Future floods were inevitable and the author 'hoped further movement onto the floodplain would not occur' after the dam's construction, advocating town planning measures to restrict development as in America and the United Kingdom.[42] Modern international floodplain management included flood plans and mapping, public education, acquisition of repeatedly flooded properties and federal insurance. But in Queensland these strategies were ignored; the state's flood response relied entirely on dams. Wivenhoe Dam fulfilled the state's flood obligations, leaving the remaining issues to local government town plans – the buck-passing continued.

Bjelke-Petersen declared Wivenhoe Dam the 'climax to 20 years of careful planning'.[43] However, its genesis was the 1893 floods when J. B. Henderson first considered a dam, a strategy further supported by generations of engineers and a community increasingly dependent on dams.

A Myopic Approach to Flood Mitigation

The state reliance on dams for flood mitigation further abrogated responsibility to local councils. This defied international and interstate trends that had been in place since the 1970s, which recognised the need for both structural and non-structural flood mitigation strategies, the latter designed to modify human behaviour. Hazards research identified that land use planning through appropriate development and building controls offered the most cost-effective way to manage the growth of future flood damage. In the mid-1970s, the Australian Water Resources Council adopted the 1930s American practice of using national benchmarks to compare floods and ascribed terms to measure floods in relation to floodplain development as a flood management tool. An average recurrence interval (ARI) was the average interval between floods of a comparable magnitude. The annual exceedance probability (AEP) was the probability of a flood of a similar size being equalled or exceeded in any one year. A flood that in size is likely to occur on average once every 100 years has a 1 per cent AEP and an ARI of 100 years. More simply, a flood of this size or larger has a 1 per cent chance of occurring in any year. But as this specialist terminology translated into popular understanding, the misconception developed that a flood of that magnitude would occur once every 100 years.[44] In reality, the 1974 flood was assessed as a 1-in-60-year event, with the probability of reoccurrence of 81 per cent in 100 years (Table 6.1). A flood of this size is likely to occur in a single lifetime. The 1893 floods, estimated to have both been 1-in-100-year events, occurred twice in one fortnight. There is no guaranteed interval, only a statistical probability.

ARI (Years) & Probability of Occurrence	Probability of Occurrence During Specified Period (%)			
	25 years	50 years	75 years	100 years
40 (2.5%)	47	72	85	92
60 (1.67%)	34	57	72	81
100 (1%)	22	39	53	63

Table 6.1: Probability of flood occurrence.

To guide planning and development policy, national guidelines and standards recommended local authorities adopt a modelled defined flood event (DFE) and a corresponding defined flood level (DFL). Both the DFE and DFL are hypothetical, based on historical floods and modelling, and are designed to discourage development below the DFL. Every mainland Australian state and territory, except Queensland, introduced state-wide floodplain management policies – the Australian Capital Territory in the early 1970s, New South Wales in 1977, Victoria in 1978, the Northern Territory in 1981, South Australia in 1983 and Western Australia in 1985. New South Wales implemented state-wide prescriptive and mandatory flood controls, not only preventing future development below the 1-in-100 level (1 per cent AEP) but also promoting the removal of earlier structures 'where practicable and appropriate' to reverse the legacy issues of path dependency.[45] Consequently New South Wales increased its towns' flood resilience and reduced flood damage. By contrast Queensland had no state policy on floods. The one-dimensional approach of relying on hard engineering to reduce flood hazard prevailed, with councils determining their own flood management strategies.

After the 1974 flood, water management remained a state

responsibility under the constitution with the state and local government managing land through legislation and regulation. The federal government's only flood role remained forecasting and warnings through BoM, and the provision of disaster relief. With the costs of flood relief escalating, the Whitlam government used cheque-book persuasion to intervene. The Queensland Government approached the Commonwealth for funding in the early 1970s after repeated creek flooding in Brisbane. Federal Minister and Ipswich resident William (Bill) Hayden wrote to Prime Minister Gough Whitlam expressing his reluctance to fund flood mitigation works on an ad hoc basis, as the hazard is the result of 'irresponsible urban planning' by both state and local government, and payment might be seen as condoning 'long-term dereliction of public duty'. Hayden recognised the political sensitivity of the issue, particularly as his Labor colleague faced a lord mayoral election and criticism of Clem Jones needed to be 'muted'.[46] Funding requests intensified after the 1974 floods and the Commonwealth acquiesced to fund a floods study by the Cities Commission, the first such study in Queensland. Subsidies were also provided for creek flood mitigation works in Brisbane and Wivenhoe Dam, but the generosity ended there. The federal government had a clear objective. They would minimise flood losses and disruption by providing BoM flood forecasting and warnings, as well as flood relief, while the states would produce comprehensive floodplain management strategies – both structural and non-structural. Further money for Queensland would be contingent on it producing a state-wide plan that compelled local government to regulate the floodplain.[47]

The Bjelke-Petersen government was unimpressed with this federal intervention. Since 1964, the Commonwealth had contributed millions to mitigation works on NSW rural rivers under special legislation and Queensland smelt injustice. But these funds had come from a National Water Resources Development Programme, which was designed to fulfil the federal government's political agenda to bolster urban areas and encourage decentralisation. According to the Commonwealth, urban flood mitigation was to be managed by rezoning and regulation to reduce the need for engineering works.[48] New South Wales's flood plan released cooperative federal, state and local government funding and construction arrangements. Reflecting his poor relationship with Canberra, Bjelke-Petersen questioned federal authority to intervene in state matters and repeatedly requested funding for public works, without the required state flood plan. He steadfastly insisted that any non-structural matters were local governments' responsibility, dismissing the need for state coordination. With a political stalemate reached, Queensland's refusal to design a state-wide flood plan denied the state access to federal funds.

The replacement of Bjelke-Petersen with Conservative premiers Michael Ahern (1987–89) and Russell Cooper (1989) did not alter Queensland's flood policy, nor did the election of Labor Premier Wayne Goss (1989–96). The political dynamics remained unchanged. In South East Queensland, governments still relied on growth, dependent on rates and land taxes and electorally buoyed by the perception of a strong economy. As the author of land legislation and arbiter of disputes in the courts, the state substantially influenced development. The residential property market remained the region's economic mainstay, with dwelling construction the largest source of capital investment since 1988. In 1995, Queensland's development industry was valued at $5.5 billion, with property developers listed in the state's top 20 registered companies. For international corporations, Brisbane had branch office status, creating a power vacuum able to be filled by a local land-based elite – developers, property owners and land professionals – that became the city's lead actors, the core of its growth lobby, motivated by self-seeking profit. Their access to government power remained both informal and official, including developers being represented on the State Council for Economic Development and the BCC Development Advisory Committee.[49] The property industry and associated unions constituted the political parties' greatest electoral funders.

Long-term hazard-reduction strategies would frustrate development and annoy land-owning constituents, and thereby risk political suicide in a three-year electoral cycle. With a development-focused economy that supported the political and social elite, restrictive floodplain management legislation remained unacceptable.

The introduction of the *Local Government (Planning and Environment) Act 1990* offered an ideal opportunity to implement state-wide flood management, but instead failed to redress planning problems and protected lawful non-conforming uses. Worse still, councils continued to be liable for up to three years' compensation to owners if development rules changed, and now appeals could be held in a Planning and Environment Court established by the state.[50] The rights of the individual property owner continued to overrule mandatory flood planning. Although the act stipulated council must consider flooding when rezoning, the final decision rested with the state. The conservative Borbidge government (1996–98) made construction a priority, with the *Integrated Planning Act 1997* designed to streamline development.

The state's steadfast refusal to introduce a flood plan, focusing instead on capital works, denied Queensland millions of dollars of federal flood mitigation funding. Much of the $7 million spent annually on flood mitigation went to New South Wales, although Queensland had the highest exposure to flood damage nationally. In the early 1990s, NSW governments invested $10 million on flood studies matched by the Commonwealth, and structural measures were accompanied by land use and building controls. In Queensland, a state-wide policy to guide local governments' floodplain management was sorely needed as few councils had floodplain management policies that met national standards. From the mid-1990s, the Commonwealth Government steadily reduced its disaster payments that were contingent on evidence of floodplain management. Between 1989 and 2011, Queensland's flood damage averaged over $50 million per year, and in excess of $100 million in 2000–01.[51] Despite increasing political and economic pressure, the state government remained slow to act.

A major change in South East Queensland's flood policy occurred at a bureaucratic and not political level. BoM led a Queensland Flood Warning Consultative Committee in 1987 to advise on flood warnings and mitigation measures. Another step occurred in 1998 when the government formed a State Disaster Mitigation Committee to provide advice and facilitate action on disasters. The committee recommended preparation of a discussion paper on a state flood risk management policy and a State Planning Policy (SPP) for natural disaster mitigation. The matter reached a climax in 2002 when the Department of Emergency Services, in consultation with the Department of Local Government and Planning, commenced work on an SPP that would include flood mitigation. The Department of Natural Resources and Mines (whose responsibilities included water), in consultation with BoM, prepared the *State Flood Risk Management Policy Discussion Paper*. This paper criticised the 'current fragmented approach' and recognised that councils had insufficient statutory powers, resources and knowledge to implement mandatory planning and floodplain control measures. The proposed SPP on natural disasters was insufficient, the paper argued, and would 'not offer an exhaustive approach to floodplain management'. Nor would it have legislative power.[52] The discussion paper was published, stamped 'Not Government Policy' and sent to Cabinet, only to be rejected. Instead SPP 1/03 *Mitigating the Adverse Impacts of Flood, Bushfire and Landslide* was introduced in 2003, but this was a much weaker policy than the discussion paper advocated.

More than 20 years after the 1974 floods and the introduction of state-wide flood policies in New South Wales and Victoria, Queensland's Labor Government under Peter Beattie (1998–2007) finally introduced a flood policy, bowing to economic pressure and accepted hazard-management practice, yet this policy was weaker than its interstate counterparts. The policy stated that 'the Queensland Government considers that development should minimise the potential adverse impacts of flood, bushfire and landslide on people, property, economic activity and the environment'. Councils were to adopt the 1-in-100-year flood level (known as Q100) and use land regulations to reduce communities' vulnerability to natural hazards. The rhetoric suggested a move away from a total reliance on dams, yet little changed. In reality, floodplain management had been reduced to one of a number of natural hazards in a brief policy document, rather than a legislatively binding state flood risk management policy as in New South Wales. It did not mitigate existing risk and only managed future risk up to Q100. It also continued the disincentive for proactive planning by maintaining two years' compensation for changed development applications. Years of best practice and interstate success in minimising flood hazard were reduced in Queensland to a multifaceted broad set of guidelines.

Under the *Sustainable Planning Act 2009* (SPA), introduced by the Anna Bligh Labor Government (2007–12), councils were encouraged to adopt SPP 1/03, undertake a flood study with mapping and establish a modelled DFE. Although indicating overt state involvement in flood management, these requirements were not mandatory and were full of loopholes. For example, lower habitable heights were permitted in six Brisbane localities where a 'risk management approach' could be used if implementation of the DFL created 'an undesirable outcome'. If a development met a particular need it could 'override some aspects of risk associated with the natural hazard'.[53] Councils utilised flexibility in the system to allow development below the accepted DFL. The underlying policy was clear – development controls should not, to quote SPP 1/03, reduce the 'capacity to use the land within the floodplain'. The SPA allowed negotiation, rather than prohibition of development below the DFL, and retained the rights of appeal and one year's compensation. The legislation also introduced other legacy problems. A building removed from a site, with no material change of use, could be replaced within two years providing it maintained the same footprint, with little change to design or building materials, despite both being recognised hazard-reduction strategies. Private certifiers could grant approvals, with local and state governments powerless to stop them.

Filling a State Government Vacuum

In the absence of state leadership, councils took limited action on floodplain management. Both Brisbane and Ipswich city councils adopted the DFE and DFL that reached an acceptable balance between economic progress and flood hazard. In 1976, Brisbane adopted a 1 per cent AEP as its DFE with the corresponding DFL, even though the 1974 flood was considered a more frequent 1-in-60-year event.[54] Under the 1978 City of Brisbane Town Plan, the DFL was reduced to 3.7 metres at the Port Office Gauge, a height lower than the 1974 flood (5.45 metres).[55] When approving development applications, all habitable floors had to be above this reduced DFL, with other levels, most commonly a storage room, garage or lobby, allowed to be below this level.[56] These heights were based on the calculated 3 metres future mitigating effect of Wivenhoe Dam. Council rejected a higher DFL, believing restrictions above the 1974 flood would have 'high consequences on the city's urban, social and economic fabric'. Although a higher DFL would reduce risk and potential damage, council argued the 'costs could outweigh the benefits'.[57] These DFL restrictions applied only to new structures as retrospective building codes could not be introduced without triggering compensation. With 90 per cent of Brisbane's houses built before the implementation of this policy in 1978, generations of older houses built on the floodplain had to rely on the region's historical practices, and in Brisbane this meant a continued over-reliance on dams.

The refusal to adequately manage the floodplain had left Brisbane with a legacy of vulnerability. After the 1974 floods, BCC utilised the few options available to them to reduce flood damage. Its primary concern, however, was the more frequent creek flooding, with riverine flooding neglected. Council maintained acquiring 'all land affected by floodwaters' was 'impractical' as this would amount to a 'third of Brisbane', with the possibility that 'another flood could be higher again'. As a senior government engineer informed *The Sunday Mail*, 'We can't move whole suburbs because the cost would be prohibitive.'[58] Clem Jones informed *The Australian* that 'resettling thousands of people' from flood-prone areas 'just will not work', listing cost and residents' reluctance to move as the main reasons.[59] Repossessing houses, BCC maintained, would have a minimal impact and vast expense. In 1974, a land-exchange scheme was introduced with state and council funds used to relocate flood-damaged homes to council land; however, only 35 home owners satisfied the strict qualifications.[60] Expense limited the scheme's scope. A similar scheme, the Voluntary Home Purchase Scheme, introduced by Lord Mayor Campbell Newman in 2006, himself an engineer, offered purchase of frequently flooded properties (those flooded every two years), where there was 'no viable infrastructure solution to eliminate the flood risk'.[61] The dependence on technical solutions permeated council decisions.

In Ipswich, floodplain management was even more lenient than in Brisbane. In 1976, the Ipswich Town Plan adopted a 1-in-20-year flood height as the DFL, allowing development well below the 1974 flood height. Further, Ipswich only comprehensively implemented the recommended Q100 DFL in 2004, but exceptions were again made for existing buildings.[62] Ipswich could little afford this weak policy as hydrologists describe the Bremer River as Queensland's second most dangerous river, probably the most 'complex hydrological/ hydraulic problem in the context of flood forecasting that the Bureau has in Australia'. Flood warnings are hard to determine with the period between heavy rainfall and flood as little as six to nine hours. The Bremer River remained largely unregulated and Wivenhoe Dam would provide little or no protection against a 1974-type flood.[63] Here, land management offered the only viable flood solution.

Experts regularly warned BCC that relying on Wivenhoe Dam

for flood management was flawed; a substantial flood risk remained. Engineering flood modelling calculated that the estimated mitigating effect of the dam was too high and the DFL too low. In 1988, the BCC commissioned engineering firm Sinclair Knight Merz (SKM) to assess Brisbane's flood risk. The subsequent report estimated a 1-in-100 peak flow would produce a flood of 5.7 metres at the Port Office, a height 1.9 metres above the permitted development levels. This put thousands of properties at risk and exposed council to liability.[64] Council disputed SKM's data and produced its own flood study in 1999, which estimated a flood height of 5 metres. As the SKM report was challenged, it remained a draft, and BCC deemed it inappropriate to release possibly inaccurate information while further studies were underway. Professor Russell Mein, a Monash University expert, was commissioned to independently assess the report and found that the stated flood magnitude was an overestimate.[65]

The Queensland Department of Natural Resources, Mines and Energy produced its own study in 2003, the same year an independent panel recommended that BCC maintain 3.3 metres as the 1 per cent AEP. A media leak prompted a Crime and Misconduct Commission (CMC) investigation, which cleared BCC officers but recommended better transparency for ratepayers.[66] Liberal Alderman and Lord Mayor aspirant Campbell Newman campaigned against the Labor Council's secrecy over the flood study and promised to radically overhaul policies if elected. Yet when elected in 2004 his administrative changes did little more than increase ratepayer access to flood information.

After 2003, council automated its flood information system and improved the accuracy of Q100 mapping on individual properties. From 2005, FloodWise Property Reports that showed flood corridors and heights and minimum habitable floor levels were freely available to all. These reports were launched free online in July 2008, along with fact sheets and articles on council's website. Between 2004/5 and 2011 BCC spent $481.6 million on creek flood planning, mitigation, and awareness and response initiatives.[67] However, for many people flood maps and tables of flood heights and development levels require interpretation. This was the province of local government, yet neither BCC nor ICC executed a public education role. While providing data addressed CMC concerns about public education and seemingly addressed flood hazard, it largely deflected council culpability.

Having diluted the risk by providing information, the Brisbane City Plan 2000 reaffirmed the DFL of 3.7 metres plus an additional 500-millimetres for habitable areas to 'allow for a factor of safety, uncertainties and localised effects'. Commercial and industrial development could be lower at 300 millimetres above the DFL. Alternatively, a 'risk management approach' could be utilised, which indicated flexibility in approvals.[68] Ipswich continued to rely on the relatively higher Q100 level. In both councils, implementation of the DFL allowed discretion and development below this level was not prohibited. Both DFLs remained lower than the 1974 flood, hereby relying on the mitigating effects of Wivenhoe Dam and following the historical path of dam dependence and vulnerability.

Intensifying the Urban Flood Hazard
The flood hazard grew at a rapid pace. Between 1995 and 2006 Brisbane became Australia's fastest growing city. Between 2004 and 2009, the growth rate was 2.3 per cent, compared to Melbourne's 2 per cent and Sydney's 1.3 per cent. The South East Queensland Regional Plan 2005–2026 identified the need for an additional 156,000 dwellings in Brisbane by 2031. Redevelopment and infill in existing urban areas would provide at least 138,000 additional dwellings, with flood-prone suburbs identified as potential development areas.[69] The federal Building Better Cities Program encouraged urban renewal and, after 1992, medium- to high-density residential accommodation replaced numerous freestanding houses in inner-city suburbs, often those in high flood-risk areas. The Urban Renewal Taskforce, charged with 'revitalising derelict industrial suburbs in Brisbane', concentrated

their efforts in the inner (and low-lying) suburbs with plans to replace industrial and warehouse sites with over 6,500 new homes. Under the urban renewal schemes BCC constructed a continuous 14 kilometre Riverwalk in the inner city, built 17 river ferry terminals and redeveloped 120 hectares of waterfront land.[70] All of these schemes were vulnerable to flood damage, and by blocking the path of floodwaters these developments potentially reduced flow and increased flood height. Between 2005 and 2011, BCC approved 1,811 development applications within the 1974 flood footprint. Since that flood, Brisbane and Ipswich grew substantially and the urban density in low-lying areas intensified. Brisbane's population grew from 712,500 in 1973 to 2,065,998 in 2011, and the dwelling numbers grew from 217,847 to 822,174. Over the same years, the population of Ipswich grew from 65,000 to 166,908, with the dwelling numbers increasing from 18,889 to 63,136.

With urban gentrification in the 1980s came the South Brisbane cultural centre precinct, boosted by Expo 88 and the resultant South Bank development. Tennyson, St Lucia, West End and Toowong, all flooded in 1974, became home to luxury residences and multistorey units. As the wharves moved downstream of the city centre and industries and wool stores closed, the riverbank became a developer's dream. The Dockside apartment complex and hospitality precinct replaced Evans Deakin Shipyards at Kangaroo Point in the 1990s. Those approving new developments could not blame legacy issues. Land clearance and the construction of impermeable surfaces reduced the land's capacity to absorb water and increased run-off, in turn increasing the future flood hazard.

Decades without major floods fostered the myth that the river had been tamed by Wivenhoe Dam, and comparatively minor floods upstream of Moggill in the 1980s, and in Brisbane in 1991 and 1996, allowed floods to recede in the public consciousness. Again, South East Queensland entered the other half of its other climatic cycle: drought. With it, the community became preoccupied with water supply. Climate scientists describe this trend as the 'hydro-illogical cycle', whereby drought creates awareness of water supply, followed by concern and panic, only to be relieved by rain after which apathy sets in until the drought returns and the cyclical pattern continues.[71]

Between 2001 and 2009, South East Queensland endured the longest drought since British settlement. The fear of water shortage loomed as the population and consumption increased, with worrying estimates of Wivenhoe Dam plummeting to 5 per cent by 2009. Labelled the 'Millennium Drought', its longevity meant that stronger flood mitigation strategies seemed redundant, with Liberal National Member Jeffrey Seeney advocating the reduction of Wivenhoe Dam's flood storage capacity by 2 metres for 228,000 megalitres of extra water storage, an idea flagged in a draft South East Queensland Water Strategy in 2009. In Seeney's opinion, 'you'd have to be a duffer, not to use the flood buffer'.[72]

As Wivenhoe Dam dried to its lowest point at 15 per cent in July 2007, draconian measures were required to curb usage from 300 litres per person each day to 140 litres. Water prices increased, reflecting a user-pays mentality, and average local area consumptions were published to shame residents into water conservation. With sprinklers banned and tanks and water-saving devices installed through government subsidies, water usage met the 140-litre target. South East Queensland residents became the nation's most frugal water users, among the lowest in the developed world. Water managers investigated a water grid, a desalination plant, water recycling and raising of Wivenhoe Dam's wall to increase water supply storage. Community obsession became saving water, not mitigating its excesses.

Wivenhoe Dam, drought and complacency fuelled the myth of flood immunity. The flood hazard and development flourished, largely untrammelled. If more rain fell than the dam could hold, or it fell downstream, the mitigation capacity would be greatly curtailed. South East Queensland's dam dependency had left the capital at great risk once again.

The Untameable Torrent: The 2011 Flood

WITH FLOODWATERS SURGING towards the capital, Brisbane's Lord Mayor, Campbell Newman, held a press conference on 11 January 2011 to warn his constituents of imminent flood. He declared, 'unfortunately, the big shock absorber that is [Wivenhoe Dam] was now full [...] We are in uncharted territory.' He warned the water was 'going to come down the river in Brisbane and there's not much dam managers can do about it'.[1] South East Queensland's dependency on dams to manage floods, as well as Wivenhoe Dam and its operators, faced the greatest test since the dam's completion.

The years 2010 and 2011 were a La Niña period throughout Australia. Further, the Southern Oscillation Index (SOI) was the highest December value on record and highest monthly value since 1973, indicating heavy rain but not necessarily floods. Two months in 2010 were unseasonably wet with September and December the wettest of those months on record in Queensland. The Brisbane metropolitan area received 479.8 millimetres of rain in December 2010, three times the long-term average rainfall. With the catchment soaked, the rainfall to run-off ratio for each new rainfall event increased and the flood potential grew.

Between 28 November 2010 and 12 January 2011, South East Queensland experienced four distinctive weather events. The first saw extensive rain fall across the state from 28 November to 22 December 2010, compounded by a second event of extreme rain brought with Cyclone Tasha. By 5 January 2011, more than 78 per cent of Queensland, over 1 million square kilometres (greater than the area of France and Germany combined), was flooded and had been declared a disaster area, leaving 40 towns and over 2.5 million people affected.[2] The third event brought intense rainfall over three days (10 to 12 January 2011) directly over the Brisbane River catchment that resulted in flooding in Ipswich and Brisbane. Up to 300 millimetres of rain had fallen in the catchment in the 24 hours prior to 9 am on 10 January, with over 700 millimetres estimated across the same area in the following 24 hours.[3]

The fourth, and most extraordinary, event occurred on the afternoon of 10 January 2011 when a thunderstorm dumped up to 94 millimetres of rain in one hour over Toowoomba, causing flash flooding in Toowoomba and the upper Lockyer Valley. Described by Police Commissioner Bob Atkinson as an 'inland tsunami', the floodwaters rose with extraordinary speed and inundated central Toowoomba. Extremely heavy rainfall over the upper and middle reaches of Lockyer Creek brought flash floods surging towards Grantham. With limited gauges in the region, it is estimated that the water was rising at 12 metres per hour, moving at a rate of 2 to 3 metres per second, the intensity sufficient to rip houses from their foundations. The world watched television footage in horror as a 'wave of water' obliterated townships, taking at least 21 lives with it.[4]

The major contributor to flooding is rain intensity, rather than total rainfall; 100 millimetres in one hour will cause greater flooding than if the same amount of rain is spread over 24 hours. January's heavy rainfall, although significantly less than December's, arrived in three days rather than over a month. Official readings between 9 and 13 January recorded rainfall of 480 millimetres at Wivenhoe Dam and 370 millimetres at Somerset Dam. As some rain gauges failed, quantitative assessments of rainfall rely on personal accounts.[5] Retrospective accounts by Queensland Rail staff from 10 January recorded 93 millimetres in one hour near Spring Bluff and 107 millimetres in two hours at Postmans Ridge (at the base of the Toowoomba Range). Nearby, a home owner recorded 210 millimetres in 30 minutes before her gauge washed away. Although these readings were higher than those recorded by BoM, Peter Baddiley, a hydrologist in the Flood Warning Centre with 30 years of experience, asserts the localised rainfall reached 300 millimetres in one hour, much higher than official readings.[6] Between 9 and 13 January, the four day average for Wivenhoe and Somerset dams were 315 millimetres and 515 millimetres respectively, and 263 millimetres and 213 millimetres for Lockyer Creek and the Bremer River. The floodwaters from the Brisbane River tributaries added to the massive flow heading towards Brisbane. This rainfall, neither forecast nor obvious on the radar, had an estimated ARI of 1 in 2,000 years for durations between 6 and 48 hours.[7]

On 12 January the sun shone in Brisbane, as it did before the arrival of the flood peak in 1974, creating an eerie calm as people waited for, or ignored, the inevitable flood. Describing the day as 'very surreal', and an 'almost perfect Queensland summer day', Premier Anna Bligh cautioned, 'we can take no comfort from that blue sky. The water and rain have already done their damage, they are in the catchment and they are on their way down our river system.'[8] The lower-lying suburbs of Jindalee, Milton/Toowong and South Brisbane/Yeronga were already experiencing flooding. With a major flood imminent, authorities warned of flood heights equalling 1974, and encouraged evacuations. Prepare for the worst, they counselled. But many ignored the warnings, pinning their hopes on 'mighty Wivenhoe Dam', perceived as 'the great protector', to save Brisbane.[9]

Wivenhoe Will Save Us

The dams did mitigate the flood, but they had not flood-proofed the region. The perception of safety was an illusion. Wivenhoe Dam and its operators were called on to manage the flood, but with the intensity, timing and location of the rainfall, total flood prevention could not be achieved.

As early as 2010, flood managers recognised the warning signs for potential flooding, with the Ipswich Local Disaster Management Group warning the 'ingredients were in place for a deluge similar to the unforgettable '74 floods'.[10] Advancements in forecasting and greater scientific understanding of La Niña and the SOI since the 1974 floods enabled BoM to forecast the potential for higher rainfall and possible flooding, and to brief Cabinet and agencies as early as September 2010.[11]

Pressure mounted on the government to reduce the water supply portion of Wivenhoe Dam in anticipation of flooding. On 25 October 2010, Stephen Robertson, Minister for Energy and Water Utilities, took the unprecedented ministerial step of seeking formal advice about pre-emptive water releases to increase the flood storage capacity. State water managers advised reducing water supply storage to 95 per cent would have 'negligible benefits'.[12] Anything more could not be countenanced. Only months after the Millennium Drought had ended, fears of water shortage strongly permeated South East Queensland's water management strategies. On Christmas Eve 2010, Premier Anna Bligh met with Jim Davidson (the Regional Director of BoM since 2002) and Bob Atkinson (Police Commissioner) and was warned that the 'weather patterns were building to treacherous levels'.[13] Authorities were on alert.

Wivenhoe Dam management is mandated by legislation that the water supply compartment is preserved until the dam level reaches 67.25 metres; water *cannot* be released in anticipation of heavy rain. The temporary flood storage (up to 80 metres) is left empty for management of floodwaters. The dam cannot be utilised for flood management until the dam levels reach 67.2 metres. The *Manual of Operational Procedures for Flood Mitigation at Wivenhoe Dam and Somerset Dam* (the *Manual*) defines the procedures for dam operation during a flood.[14] Developed in 1968, with subsequent revisions, the *Manual* articulates the objectives of flood management in ascending order of importance: minimising impacts to riparian flora and fauna during the drain-down phase after a flood (reducing dam to FSL); retention of FSL in the dam after a flood; minimising disruption to rural life in the Brisbane and Stanley river valleys; optimum protection of urbanised areas from inundation; and, ultimately, the structural safety of the dam. The *Manual* provides four strategies (W1 to W4) designed to achieve these objectives (Table 7.1). As no two floods are alike, the *Manual* covers the most common eventualities, leaving the senior engineer in charge of operations to seek departmental approval for 'reasonable discretion' to depart from the *Manual* to cope with 'unusual occurrences' based on their 'professional experience'.

Strategy	Water Level (metres AHD) at Wivenhoe Dam	Maximum Allowable Release Rate (cubic metres per second)	Aim
W1	Up to 68.5	1,900	Primary consideration is to minimise disruption to downstream rural life
W2	68.5–74	<3,500	Transition strategy from minimising impact on rural life to protecting urban areas from inundation
W3	68.5–74	<4,000	Primary consideration is to protect urban areas from inundation
W4	74	No limit	Primary consideration is to protect structural safety of the dam

Table 7.1: Wivenhoe Dam water release strategies according to the *Manual*.

Three strategies were implemented in 2011 as events overtook the need to use W2, and strategy W4 was used for the first time. The operators were in untested territory. Under strategy W3, once Wivenhoe Dam storage reached between 68.5 metres and 74 metres water had to be released, at a rate no greater than a flow of 4,000 cubic metres per second. This flow was the calculated upper limit of non-damaging floods at Moggill and downstream, thereby fulfilling the objective of protecting urban areas. Strategy W4 *must* be implemented if predicted dam levels exceed 74 metres in order to protect the dam's structural safety. Water at 75.5 metres would trigger the dam's fuse plug (a hydrological safety valve to preserve the integrity of the dam) and automatically release uncontrolled water. Dam operators had discretionary powers to commence early implementation of strategy W4 with no limits on release rates as the entire strategy is based on preventing the catastrophic effects of the dam overtopping. The implementation of W4 would inundate houses downstream; hence, according to Flood Operations Engineer John Tibaldi, it 'is not a step you would take lightly', and requires a large degree of certainty.[15]

Four flood operations engineers, Robert (Rob) Ayre, Terrence (Terry) Malone, John Tibaldi and John Ruffini were charged with the task of managing floods at Wivenhoe Dam. Permanent government employees since the 1980s, their skills were called on during floods as an extra duty. Combined, they had 100 years of experience in the specialised field of flood management and were experts among a small group of 25 peers nationally, half of whom worked for BoM.[16] They were assisted by nine flood officers operating within the Seqwater Flood Operations Centre. This group managed three flood events between 16 December 2010 and 2 January 2011 (Table 7.2). Each event prompted dam releases with approximately 690,000 megalitres released from Wivenhoe Dam in that period. After each event, the dam returned to FSL and the catchment remained soaked.

Event Start Date	Event End Date	Volume Released (megalitres)
13/12/2010	16/12/2010	70,000
17/12/2010	24/12/2010	150,000
26/12/2010	02/01/2011	470,000

Table 7.2: Wivenhoe Dam water releases in December 2010 and January 2011.[17]

The dams then experienced another two substantial inflows over just 30 hours. Wivenhoe Dam's peak inflow rate reached 10,000 cubic metres per second early on 10 January and a second peak reached approximately 11,500 cubic metres per second late on 11 January. By contrast there were 16 days between the two major floods in 1893. Both 2011 peaks were comparable in both nature and flow to the single 1974 flood. In total, Wivenhoe Dam received 2.65 million megalitres, almost double the 1974 volumes and rivalling those of 1893. This quantity is hard to comprehend, but, as a rough comparison, it would fill 1,000,000 Olympic swimming pools. The dam reached a maximum height of 74.97 metres AHD rapidly after the second peak.[18] The flood storage almost reached capacity. Maximum water releases under W4 were essential to protect the dam's structure, and soon after the second peak the dam reached its maximum outflow. When these unprecedented releases joined the substantial contributions from the uncontrolled Lockyer Creek and Bremer River racing towards the capital, the city faced a major flood risk. Fortunately, rainfall in the downstream urban areas was just 166 millimetres compared with 600 millimetres in 1974, resulting in a much lower contribution from Brisbane creeks than experienced in 1974.

Floods Don't Follow Manuals

Dam operations manuals are based on historical precedent and modelled hydrological events to determine flood management strategies. They are based on likely flood scenarios that reduce the vagaries of nature to typical or standard events and cannot pre-empt every possible meteorological or hydrological event. They are also designed as a tool to alleviate the stress and fatigue experienced by those forced to make decisions in ever-changing situations and prevent external intervention similar to that by Lord Mayor Clem Jones in 1974.

Minor rainfall and accompanying dam releases had occurred between 6 January and 8 January 2011, causing only minor flooding and some bridge inundation. By late afternoon on 10 January, the flood engineers were hopeful they had managed the situation and none thought a major flood likely. Forecast rainfall did not justify additional releases but, as Malone recalls, when he reported for work at 7 am on 11 January 'all hell was breaking loose' with 'rainfalls of 50, 60, 70 mm per hour' recorded, requiring further dam releases.

By mid-morning the upper Brisbane and Bremer rivers were in flood, with Ipswich likely to be flooded the next day and Brisbane in two days. This flood was now expected to match 1974 levels, and was predicted to inundate 9,000 properties and damage a further 30,000, about 10 per cent of the 400,000 buildings and homes in Brisbane. The Premier briefed Ipswich Mayor Paul Pisasale and Lord Mayor Campbell Newman and convened a media conference to warn the cities to brace for major flooding.

From 10 to 13 January, the four flood engineers mostly remained at work, while flood officers came and went if they could get home, relying on support staff to bring food and other supplies. Dam operators were permanently at the dam sites. Constant communication was maintained between the operations centre and BoM for updated rainfall forecasts. Unlike in 1974, the flood operations centre received frequent rainfall and water level data from the Automated Local Evaluation in Real Time (ALERT) system, which was relayed by radio. The Brisbane River had between 120 and 150 rain gauges in operation, making it the best real-time instrumented catchment in Australia.[19] The data received were constantly changing, with Malone estimating they received 20,000 gauge recordings every day at the peak of the flood. River level gauging stations reported every 50 millimetres, so dozens arrived each hour. Malone recalls, 'things were happening so quickly. I would run a model and it would be out of date [...] We'd be on the phone constantly to the Bureau of Meteorology asking, "How much rain are we going to get?"' Malone acknowledges another dilemma that was facing the engineers: 'We didn't really know how much water was coming down the Lockyer and to a lesser extent the Bremer River.' Both the unregulated Lockyer Creek and the Bremer River are difficult to quantify hydrologically in models and this unpredictability hampered the release strategy.

Fortunately, a partial shutdown of the CBD power grid did not affect the flood operation centre in Turbot Street. Senior management dealt with the media and general inquiries, minimising phone calls and allowing the officers to concentrate on dam operation. Somerset and Wivenhoe dams required constant monitoring as did the rapidly filling North Pine Dam. Staff ran on adrenalin and the stress levels were high. The situation deteriorated further on 11 January when Wivenhoe Dam reached 190 per cent (the maximum capacity is 200 per cent). As its peak inflow reached almost 10,300 cubic metres per second on 11 January dam releases were increased to just under 7,500 cubic metres per second for two hours.[20]

Although fears arose on 12 January that the floods would be 'worse than 1974', the actual flood height was smaller. The Bremer River peaked at 19.25 metres in Ipswich, compared with 20.7 metres in 1974, and 24.5 metres and 23.6 metres in 1893. The Brisbane River peaked at 4.46 metres at the Port Office Gauge, compared with 5.45 metres in 1974, and 8.35 metres and 8.09 metres in 1893 (Table 7.3). Seqwater estimates that without the dams the peak flood height would have been approximately 2 metres higher with a further 14,000 properties impacted. The dams had reduced the flood flow in the lower Brisbane River by approximately 40 per cent.[21]

Year	Bremer at Ipswich	Goodna	Centenary Bridge	Brisbane Port Office
1893	24.5	22.7	17.90	8.35
1893	23.6	21.88	16.6	8.09
1974	20.7	18.43	14.1	5.45
2011	19.25	16.4	12.07	4.46

Table 7.3: Heights in metres of the floods of 1893, 1974 and 2011 at key urban locations.

Escaping the River's Path

Despite the months of rainfall and warnings of major flooding from BoM, politicians and the media, many people waited to see what would happen. Some decided to stay as long as possible before evacuating, instead hoping to wait it out. Petta Savage told *The Queensland Times* that her family sought refuge on the second floor of her Basin Pocket home in Ipswich, with the water lapping the ceiling of the first floor and depositing fish on the stairs. Rodney Ash stayed in his family's Moores Pocket home on the Bremer River, saving as many possessions as possible. As he backed out of his driveway on 11 January at 10.30 pm the house went under. Seeking refuge at Karalee, Rodney and his family watched the Brisbane River rise the next day. Rodney's wife, Vicki, recalls, 'shipping containers, cutlery, outdoor furniture settings – you name it, it went past', while floodwaters rose to 1.57 metres in their home. Her neighbour opposite, Margaret Pawson, had only lived in temperate countries where, in her words, she 'never thought anything about flooding'.[22] Margaret's daughter insisted she leave and on the next day, 12 January, the river reached her windows, 1.1 metres above ground. Some relied on 1974 flood heights, believing the water would go no higher and ignoring the reality of flood variations. Community worker Christine MacDonald remembers a resident informing her that they were fine in 1974. Two hours later 'the house was gone'.[23] As in 1974, flood knowledge proved to be a liability for some, but it was an asset for others.

Arie van den Ende remembered the 1974 floods. He joined the SES when it formed in 1975 and had served as the controller of the Ipswich unit since 1984. With many locals on his team, 1974 was a valuable template. His officers were flat out, especially as the water came up 'very fast', 'too fast'[24]. His staff doorknocked trying to persuade people to evacuate, and moved to full rescue operations as the rising floodwaters caught people unprepared. SES officers sandbagged properties, rescued people and pets, closed roads, chased boats and pontoons down the river to avert disaster, organised power generators for the evacuation centres, distributed essential medicines and much more. SES officers also coordinated their activities with police, defence personnel and other emergency services.

With 25 per cent of Ipswich under water, more than 1,100 people fled to the safety of evacuation centres at the showground, schools and halls. A further 3,000 sought refuge with family and friends. There were four official evacuation centres, but ad hoc centres sprung up as more residents were flooded and demand for help increased. With electrical power cut in nearby homes, residents delivered the contents of their freezers to Avon Hall, where dozens of Leichhardt residents sheltered, including frozen chickens, hams and prawns. Local supermarkets also delivered truckloads to evacuation centres. Ipswich City Councillor Charlie Pisasale recalls the scene at the hall, where volunteers 'baked dinners and goodness knows what else. Some of the community hadn't eaten so well for a long time.'[25] With One Mile Bridge cut, many were unable to reach Leichhardt. Both grammar schools rallied, offering their boarding facilities and assembly halls to those seeking refuge. St Joseph's Primary School in North Ipswich took this a step further, opening their buildings to both humans and animals. Councillor Cheryl Bromage said that by 4 am on 12 January the school hall bulged with 140 people, as well as pet cats, rats, birds and dogs, almost as many animals as people. A local chef volunteered his services, 'took over the kitchen' and, according to Bromage, cooked 'the most amazing meals, roast meals, roast vegetables' for those sheltering there.

With Ipswich flooded, Brisbane residents soon mobilised. Campbell Newman warned that 13 January would be 'D-Day' – Deluge Day – and encouraged anyone who lived near the river to prepare for the worst-case scenario. Police Deputy Commissioner Ian Stewart warned *Courier-Mail* readers on 12 January that 'Ipswich and Brisbane are now facing their greatest threat and toughest test in 35 years'. Council and SES distributed an estimated 90,000 sandbags in one day. Residents frantically sandbagged their properties, even robbing the fake beach at South Bank of its sand (Figure 7.1). Doorways were piled high with sandbags, and toilets, sinks and showers were plugged to stop sewage backing up.

City workers fled the CBD. Arterial roads and bridges became gridlocked car parks as the floodwater began to rise in the lower-lying suburbs. On the afternoon of 12 January central Brisbane was a ghost town, occupied largely by flood voyeurs. Photographer Lyle Radford recalled his city view from a helicopter: normally 'wall to wall' people and cars, 'you could count the cars on one hand. There was just the eerie, eerie sensation.' With 30 suburbs deemed high risk and roads flooded, many could not get home. Others, more than 45,000 people, were forced to flee their homes, most heading to the safety of evacuation centres, their new residences for the next few nights. Some relocated to higher ground, sheltered by family, friends or strangers. Those with boats became instant saviours.

Figure 7.1: Frantic sandbagging at Kodak Beach, South Bank.
(Courtesy of Jackie Ryan)

As in 1974, many expressed a reluctance to move, impeded by a lack of understanding of what was happening. Consequently, throughout the evening of 13 January the SES dealt with more than 3,000 desperate calls for help. Sean Keniry and Steven Lewis, both 22, were disinclined to leave their Jindalee home. Only after seeing their neighbour's 1974 photo of their house submerged to roof level did they change their minds. When they returned, their beds and couch were floating, while unknown furniture and rubbish had also assumed residency. Numerous people left insufficient time to save possessions or vital medications, surprised by the speed of the rising water. Newspapers reported the cry across the suburbs: 'the water just came up too quickly'. Greg Kelly from Breakfast Creek watched the water rise a foot in his backyard before an SES member told him to get out. He fled to the RNA Showgrounds after packing whatever he could into his car.

Gerard and Gwendoline Johnston, living in their newly renovated riverside Chelmer home, devised an evacuation plan. But, as they later informed the *Gold Coast Bulletin*, they ended up swimming 'for their lives with just the clothes on their backs'. With floodwaters rising rapidly, they grabbed essential personal papers and the dog, then waded through chest-deep water and climbed fences to seek safety with a relative. However, 'the water chased them'. Four hours later they fled to the train station bound for the RNA Showgrounds. Sitting on the train looking out at whole suburbs under water, Gwendoline described the situation as 'surreal. I couldn't believe it was happening to us.' Gerard, suffering from post-cancer reduced lung capacity, required oxygen and was left 'distressed, anxious and close to collapse'. Realising his dream home would probably be condemned he vowed not to rebuild on the same block, explaining, 'I couldn't go through this again.'[26]

A Raging River

As the Brisbane River floodwaters raced downstream, Sheila Wyldbore at her home in Lather Road, Bellbowrie, recorded her impression of the river:

> The river is three times as wide as usual, it has broken its banks and is moving tremendously fast, with huge trees, pontoons, boats and general flotsam rushing past. A moment ago a pile of stuff, the size of a small island went by [...] with a portaloo perched, magnificently, if somewhat incongruously on top!

Sheila and her husband, Ron, sadly watched their pontoon disappear under water. The neighbour's pontoon, with boat attached, was washed away. Patrice Shaw lived on Birkin Road, Bellbowrie,

150 metres from the river and normally 19 metres above it. She considered it 'unfathomable to think that the river could ever rise enough to break the bank'.[27] Yet it did.

The Moggill Ferry broke free of its guide hawsers on the Riverview slipway, threatening to rush downstream. To ensure the safety of the vessel, Greg Mole, master of the ferry, remained on board throughout the flood. Together with former skipper Frank Dobias, he reconnected the hawsers and fixed eight lines to the riverbank to secure the barge. They hoisted two Queensland State of Origin flags, defying anyone to destroy the vessel, a deed they would consider sacrilege.[28]

Restaurants moored in the river alongside Coronation Drive at Milton proved little match for the river. One, a popular venue for 22 years known as Oxley's on the River, had recently reopened in 2010. Its new name, Drift, became ironic as a large section was ripped from its moorings, crashing into the Go Between Bridge before heading to Moreton Bay and washing up at Sandgate, 30 kilometres north. The sight of Drift as its sails sunk into the river became a defining moment of the flood, as thousands watched footage of its tables and chairs spilling into the water. The iconic party boat, The Island, a 52-metre steel barge that had traversed the river since 1966, threatened to break its moorings. Authorities devised a plan to sink it until navy divers declared it safe.

The much celebrated $17 million Riverwalk, built to give better public access to the river, broke up as it was battered by floodwaters and debris. Pieces slammed into moored boats as projectiles at up to 22 kilometres per hour as they hurtled towards Moreton Bay (Figure 7.2). Hearing the news on the radio at 4.15 am that a 150-metre, 300-tonne chunk was careering towards the Gateway Bridge, tugboat skipper Doug Hislop and engineer Peter Fenton jumped on board the tug *Mavis* hoping to avert disaster. Drawing on their 40 years of experience, they straightened the boardwalk so that it passed safely under the bridge then followed it downstream nudging it occasionally until it reached Nudgee Beach. On

14 January, 65-year-old Doug Hislop informed a *Courier-Mail* journalist that when he saw the boardwalk under construction he knew one day he would see it float past his depot. Hailed heroes, the men chuckled that they were just doing their jobs.

Figure 7.2: The Riverwalk broke into pieces and washed away in the 2011 flood. (BCC-DVD11-1100)

Looking at the normally slow-flowing Brisbane river, it is hard to imagine it in flood. It is even more difficult to appreciate its energy and dynamism as it flowed with the strength to rip out trees and carry walkways, livestock, shipping containers, houses and caravans. 'Boaties clocked' the river's peak at over 20 knots, 'ten times its normal sleepy progress'.[29] Journalist Lisa Millar, having recorded a piece for ABC television during the flood, reflected, 'I thought the river would be powerful but silent. It is loud. And furious. Ferry pontoons, truck tyres, concrete slabs are racing past me. The river is roaring out its intention to wreak damage: it's demanding our attention and fear.'[30] *Courier-Mail* journalist Matthew Condon noted, 'the river now had a distinct smell – it reeked of soil. And, more disturbingly, it had a sound. A gentle, relentless hiss.'[31] On 13 January he stood at the rail on the William Jolly Bridge watching as the swollen river passed:

Its cargo – broken window frames, tyres, plastic bottles, even a fleet of half a dozen navy couch cushions – was, I understood, the sad detritus of people's lives. Our own people's lives, after yet another catastrophic flooding on the Brisbane River.[32]

Spectators frequently referred to the river as angry. The water raged past, undeterred by the human debris in its wake, as it reclaimed its floodplain. Floodwaters subsumed the suburbs, rendering streets and landmarks unrecognisable (Figure 7.3). In Fairfield and West End, people in water craft passed over the top of bus shelters, street signs and basketball hoops (Figure 7.4). Canoes could be launched from balconies and were able to cruise through open windows.[33] Television antennas, rooftops of two-storey houses and the tip of the McDonald's arches at Milton peaked out from the floodwaters. Rocklea, with its factories and markets, lay fully submerged. In Goodna, resident Lyle Radford recalls a boat trailer stuck in the fork of a gumtree, about 15 metres in the air.

Figure 7.3: The 2011 floodwaters rendered motorways useless and made road signs redundant. (BCC-DVD11-110142)

Figure 7.4: Houses submerged in Crutchley Street, Fairfield.
(Courtesy of John Doody and State Library of Queensland 28585-0001-0047)

Where the floodwaters rose and flowed from proved difficult for many to comprehend. Brisbane's tangled streets and gentle slopes hide flood vulnerability, the river's shape leaving pockets spared from the desolation. On visiting Brisbane after the floods, journalist Simon Marnie remarked that only smell did not respect boundaries, 'wafting across roads' where water could not go.[34]

Facing the Damage

In most areas, the flood path was all too familiar. The Bremer and Brisbane river floodwaters covered much of the land subsumed by the 1893 and 1974 events. By 12 January, 7,221 buildings in Ipswich, including 3,000 homes, were flood affected, some to roof height. The worst hit suburbs were Basin Pocket where 230 homes were inundated and Karalee/Barellan Point where 206 homes went under. In Ipswich, almost 500 businesses closed, including a Coles supermarket. Destroyed in the 1974 floods and rebuilt on the same site, the Coles was submerged to its roof. *Courier-Mail* journalist Paul Syvret reported that determining where the river began and the city ended proved 'impossible to tell', the scene a 'sea of muddy water swirling around treetops and the roofs of homes and businesses'.[35] Main roads and 43 local roads were cut, and the cross-river David Trumpy Bridge was closed to all but essential traffic. Floodwaters inundated eastern Ipswich suburbs with approximately 600 homes and units submerged. As the water reached 8 metres high, Goodna's St Ives Shopping Centre became a swimming pool for bull sharks.

After the flood, Rodney and Vicki Ash returned to their Moores Pocket home, opening the front door to be assaulted by the 'incredible stench of stinking mud' and waist-deep water. Prawns, previously in the freezer, were strewn throughout the house, squatting in the pool table pockets. Live fish had also taken up residence, and flood debris had punched holes in the walls. Tearfully, Vicki recalls, 'everything we owned was totalled'.

In Goodna, one of the worst affected suburbs, water covered Dorothy Reddaway's unit well over the roof. Her ceilings fell in, the cupboards were ripped off the walls, and other people's chairs and tables were dumped on her roof. Floodwaters and Goodna's sewage poured into the Gailes caravan park, destroying 95 vans and leaving the 100 permanent residents homeless and largely destitute. Steve Tunny described the horror to journalist Trent Dalton. With residents on disability pensions and others with mental health issues, evacuation over five hours proved challenging but essential as permanent homes were lifted and carried 50 metres through the park, ungraciously dumped on other caravans. Tunny's home was left 'a maze of wreckage'. When Dalton apologised for putting his foot through the floor, once the eastern wall of his caravan, Tunny drily responded, 'Don't worry mate, you can't break anything.' The shocking stench turned away kind-hearted volunteers.[36]

With Moggill Road submerged, Brisbane's western suburbs were marooned for days. After 2 metres of water swept through Bellbowrie Shopping Plaza all food supplies were destroyed, and the rest was left rotting in fridges and freezers without electricity. The Moggill Uniting Church congregation rallied, not only offering shelter, food and comfort but also organising a helicopter for an emergency food drop. Defence personnel delivered pallets of food, using 26 heavy-duty vehicles to distribute the supplies to local residents (Figure 7.5). Joined by the Country Women's Association, the Rotary Club, the Lions Club and other community members (including local medical practitioners), a vital Flood Relief Centre was created to relieve those who had been without power and food supplies.

Figure 7.5: Pallets of food delivered to the isolated residents of Moggill.
(Courtesy of Catherine Solomon)

The floods reduced Brisbane's CBD to an archipelago with 22 streets and hundreds of buildings inundated. Some businesses closed for five days, which unsettled the local economy. In total, 14,100 Brisbane properties were affected across 94 suburbs, with 1,203 houses flooded, along with 1,879 businesses partly inundated and 557 completely submerged.[37] Phone lines failed and more than 127,000 homes across South East Queensland lost electricity, as did Brisbane's CBD. Sewerage treatment plants overflowed and pumping stations failed. Transport routes were greatly affected with highways to the north and west cut, inner-city bridges closed, and the Riverside Expressway reduced to one lane. Public transport was also affected with some train lines cut off by floodwaters, bus services suspended, ferry terminals destroyed and the port closed.

In Rosalie, Jan Dalton returned to her home to find her life records – family photo albums, personal journals and tax records – floating past. In the words of Trent Dalton, 'she howled at the magnitude of her misfortune'.[38] Nearby, the owners of Cold Rock Ice Creamery were confronted with a shop 'full of sour, melted ice-cream; grown men were retching almost vomiting out the back'. The XXXX Brewery in Milton sat filled with 2.5 metres of water for almost three days. At Graceville, David Keers returned to his home to find the water had reached his roof: 'Some ceilings were sagging, others had fallen in.' Damage was minimised as he had stripped the house before the floods after being warned by a neighbour who was flooded in 1974. Further upstream in Rocklea, Chris Angelos lost the books he had been collecting for 30 years as four bookcases were soaked by the water. He had moved his possessions to a storage facility, but it too went under. The water reached almost ceiling height in his home. He recalled, 'the house was just trashed; all the furniture basically lifted up and dropped where it was, so we had a fridge sitting over on its side, lounge suites were pointing up in the air'.[39]

Once again, floods had devastated Brisbane costing BCC in excess of $440 million in damages, one-fifth of its annual revenue. Flood damage totalled $120 million for ICC. Damage across South East Queensland amounted to $3 billion.[40] Lives were also lost. Along with the 24 people who perished in the Toowoomba region and the Lockyer Valley, Vietnamese national Van Toan Giang, aged 25, drowned after being sucked into a storm drain when checking on his father's inundated property at Durack.[41] *The Sydney Morning Herald* banner headline encapsulated the devastation: 'The drowned city Brisbane 13-1-2011'.

Responding to the Flood

The flood response echoed that of 1893 and 1974 with emergency and financial resources mobilised for rescue, relief and recovery. The community responded with compassion as people were relocated to evacuation centres and many donated time and finances to help with the clean-up. While the volunteers earned praise, political leaders received mixed reviews, and insurers and government relief programs earned scorn for their inequities. As in earlier floods, the media shaped the rhetoric, drawing on language that echoed 1893 and 1974, and reinforcing notions of battling nature rather than engaging in debate on the human causes of the flood damage.

The Disaster Management Group assembled at the emergency headquarters at Kelvin Grove. This group comprised the Premier, senior ministers, departmental directors general, and personnel from relevant government and non-government agencies. Having learned lessons from America's Hurricane Katrina just years before and recognising the need for a whole-of-government response, the group's role was to coordinate resources and expertise and make high-level decisions including evacuations and shutting down power and public transport throughout South East Queensland. Compared with 1974, resources were better utilised and coordinated. As information dissemination remained key, television and radio switched to a 24-hour news cycle as the Premier and others issued frequent updates.

Newspaper reports were less detailed than they were in 1893, with television and social media drawing on graphic photographs and video to convey the ensuing drama and devastation internationally. Facebook reportedly conveyed official information to 4.5 million people while an estimated 8 million people followed the flood reports on Twitter. Informal groups were established with 8,000 people signing up to the Ipswich Flooding Community Reports Facebook page. Unlike Brisbane's previous floods, the internet could distribute real-time footage globally, uncensored and raw. News of 'the killer floods down under' was circulated by almost 6,000 media outlets.[42] The BoM website received 9.4

billion hits in December 2010 and January 2011. Councils used SMS messages and leaflet drops to keep residents up to date. The BCC call centre and website were in high demand, the latter crashing under pressure. In the era of digital cameras and mobile phones, the 2011 floods became the most photographed incident in Australian history.[43]

The media environment in which natural disasters were documented had changed, but the emotive language had not. *The Courier-Mail* described 'deluge day' when the 'brutal', 'frightening' river became a 'wild sea of flotsam' as the 'murky tide seeped into the suburbs'.[44] Journalist Matthew Condon echoed his 1893 counterparts: 'Locals gathered along its banks simply to stand and watch. They observed silently, mesmerised, in awe of this show of power. It moved faster than anyone could ever remember, and carried flotsam and jetsam that rushed past like broken pieces of tragedies that may have occurred upstream.'[45] *The Courier-Mail* quoted Campbell Newman: 'I am feeling a sense of horror and awe about the power of the river [...] livelihoods are going down that river in front of our eyes.'[46] Floods still evoked emotions of wonder, spectacle and amazement.

The power of Mother Nature also still featured in the accounts: 'Mother Nature seemed to be winning the war'; 'we know how dangerous Mother Nature has been'; 'Mother Nature's cruel hand'; and 'Mother Nature has unleashed a fury like never before'.[47] God too attracted blame once again as an 'act of God struck a capital city with such force'.[48] This language reaffirmed artificial separations of humans and nature. The language of warfare also reappeared. Journalist Mike Colman likened inundated suburbs to 'wartime battlefields as the enemy pushed inexorably forward – and what a fearsome enemy she was'.[49] His colleagues referred to a city and homes 'under siege', 'besieged by floods of the century' and a 'war zone'.[50] Locals suggested 'an act of betrayal' as 'their beloved river' had let Brisbane down, failing to fulfil its perceived aesthetic and economic role in the unending pursuit of prosperity.[51] They forgot that the river had made no such bargain.

The language about the floods remained underpinned by notions of power, especially humans versus nature. This was exemplified by Premier Anna Bligh at a press conference on 10 January when she declared, 'it felt like a wrestling-back of control from nature'.[52] In her 2013 autobiography, with two chapters dedicated to the floods, Bligh described the Toowoomba events as:

> simply beyond our comprehension and our vocabulary. They introduced a threatening air of unpredictability. For the first time in all those unsettling weeks of trouble, it seemed that we had truly lost control. That we could not even know what would happen next. Worse, it felt that all our knowledge, our science, our preparation and experience might be useless in the face of Mother Nature's new and incomprehensible behaviour.[53]

What such observations overlooked was that 'we' had never had the control to lose – that was a delusion. The narrative remained unchanged from 1893, dominated by the ideals of control and human superiority, and intensified by the faith in engineering and dams, rather than an environmental awareness of the inevitability of floodplain inundation.

As the initial shock subsided, a pervasive rhetoric emerged that emphasised strength and resilience, and human triumph in the face of adversity wrought by nature. Media reporting highlighted courage, stamina and community mobilisation in the face of tragedy and destruction. *The Courier-Mail*'s editorial policy was to focus on rebuilding, not blame, running the headline on 14 January: 'Defiance. As the flood of 2011 recedes, the fightback begins'. Similarly, *The Sunday Mail* editor claimed that 'climatic adversities' had forged Queensland, where 'extreme conditions become commonplace, and where the forces of nature are able to rear up and defy man's best efforts at any time. That has created a strength of character, a unique spirit. Queenslanders are resilient people.'[54] The language tapped into a long tradition of parochialism, extolling virtues and behaviours critical to being a 'Queenslander', a strategy designed to encourage locals to rebuild.

Bligh epitomised this narrative as she faced the media on 11 January after floods destroyed the Lockyer Valley with the statement: 'This [...] may be breaking our hearts [...] but it will not break our will.' A deliberate, powerful rallying cry, it became a banner headline in *The Australian* the next day. At the height of the crisis, two days later, Bligh mobilised Queensland residents in her heartfelt, personally written 'We are Queenslanders' speech. Choking back tears she declared, 'We're the people they breed tough north of the border. We're the ones that they knock down and we get up again [...] Together, we can pull through this and that's what I am determined to do and with your help, we can achieve that.'[54] While this speech touched a chord with many, offering hope and comfort, its focus on improving morale was short term and therefore undermined deeper understandings of the environment and the need to modify human behaviour to increase resilience.

For the government, recovery was paramount and demanded visible leadership. Bligh became a 'symbol of Queensland unity', reminding people that their leaders 'understood their pain' and were actively working to fix the problem.[56] Looking at times very human – exhausted, teary and 'haggard', slightly dishevelled with rain-soaked hair – Bligh was 'one of us, for us' as one Queenslander informed *The Australian*. Twitter users regarded Bligh's information as reliable; her presence reassuring, sincere and inspiring; her character strong, empathetic, inspirational and charismatic.[57] The floods boosted Bligh's flagging electoral popularity, albeit briefly.

Campbell Newman worked tirelessly to address Brisbane's problems, his military engineering training rising to the fore. Ipswich Mayor Paul Pisasale, well-tuned to the power of popular opinion, remained constantly visible on the streets and global television screens. Prime Minister Julia Gillard fared less well than local politicians. Although Gillard managed the situation better than Gough Whitlam had in 1974, critics described her as cold, her words 'clunky' and full of platitudes, her actions 'stilted', 'robotic and rehearsed'.[58] Photographs of her predecessor, former prime minister Kevin Rudd (a Brisbane resident himself), at ease wading through water and pitching in further eroded Gillard's standing in Queensland.

Bligh's appeal to Queensland's parochialism succeeded. Queenslanders opened their hearts and wallets and donations of money, clothing and food supplies poured in. On the weekend of 15 and 16 January kindness spilled onto the streets as thousands of strangers, armed with brooms, shovels and food, volunteered to help. The media labelled them the 'mud army', 'broom brigade' and 'gumboot army', the battle now a 'war on mud' (Figure 7.6). Volunteers came from throughout Queensland and interstate; 62,000 people registered with BCC as volunteers with a further 180,000 unregistered volunteers and over 800 defence personnel joining in the clean-up. In Ipswich, 4,000 registered people volunteered. These helpers came to personify resilience, community spirit and notions of being Australian.

Figure 7.6: The Mud Army in action in Oxley, 16 January 2011.
(BCC-DVD11-110150)

Busloads of volunteers poured into the suburbs. Irene Comstive, aged 88, watched speechlessly in Rosalie as 50 strangers hauled 'her entire life's possessions on to her front lawn'. Journalist Trent Dalton described the 'surreal scene' as 'like some twisted, medieval yard sale. Few items looked salvageable, most tossed on vehicles and awaited destruction.' Nearby, shop manager Wadad Aoude stood stunned as trucks and bulldozers carried away what she described as '16 years, seven days a week, of hard work'. She added, 'you're staring at my lifetime right there in the rubbish'.[59] The streets were crowded with trucks, bulldozers, high-pressure hoses and volunteers removing rubbish. Chipboard and timber veneer proved no match for floodwater and mud, and only hardwood furniture escaped the ignominy of the skip.

People's generosity seemed as overwhelming as the damage. Many expressed gratitude for the hordes of helpers bearing food and drinks for both those flooded and the Mud Army. Margaret Pawson in Moores Pocket, Ipswich, recalled how, as her children cleaned her house, strangers 'arrived with scones and sandwiches', and set up barbecues. She described it as 'akin' to when she was a World War II evacuee in England, a time when 'people banded together and helped each other, and had street parties to keep your morale up'.

The Mud Army worked tirelessly in good humour, surrounded by the reek of dead animals, decaying vegetation, glutinous mud and rancid sewage that created a foul-smelling miasma that permeated nostrils, clothing and memory. Possessions were discarded and streets hoarded rubbish, baking in 35-degree heat (Figures 7.7 and 7.8). The piles were so high and wide they obscured street signs and impeded access to properties. Carpets, floors, walls and ceilings were stripped, and the suburban streets were lined with house carcasses. By 3 March, 338,494 tonnes of destroyed property and possessions had been added to Brisbane's landfill, more than half of the 600,000 tonnes dumped in the entire previous year.[60]

Figure 7.7: Possessions ready for the dump in Melbourne Street, Brassall, Ipswich. (Courtesy of Sally Hetherington)

Figure 7.8: A loved library destined for landfill in Gladstone Street, Oxley. (BCC-DVD11-110149)

The mood was sombre. People stood in the wreckage of their homes, all they owned sheathed in stinking mud. Yet the human spirit and good humour shone through. One local wag adorned the statue of football hero Wally Lewis outside the flooded Suncorp Stadium with floaties, goggles and a snorkel (Figure 7.9). A sign appeared in Ipswich outside a community hall: 'Aquatic bingo only today. See ya next week.' Another outside the North Ipswich Leagues Club read: 'Snr football club training as usual bring swimmers.' Outside a normally land-bound home in Rosalie a sign read: 'For sale – waterfront property, 0410 HELP.'

Figure 7.9: Statue of Wally Lewis at Suncorp Stadium adorned with floaties, goggles and a snorkel. (Photographer: Gary Ramage, *The Australian*, 1 February 2011. Courtesy of Newspix)

People desperately needed help, with many overwhelmed as to how to begin rebuilding their homes, much less their lives. The Premier's Flood Relief Appeal collected public donations and delivered direct financial aid, distributing $55 million in Brisbane and $34 million in Ipswich. The fund was means-tested and not available to those with incomes above $150,000 or to renters or investors, leaving many without assistance. The Commonwealth Government made available $1,000 relief payments for adults and $400 for children, with a total of $18.5 million distributed to 14,647 Queensland residents between 31 December 2011 and 12 January 2012. Centrelink provided up to 13 weeks of income for flood-induced unemployment. Essential Household Contents Grants were given to low-income families, along with Structural Assistance Grants and grants and loans to small businesses and primary producers. Tension arose over inequities in the system, but this was not even close to the extent of the wrath over insurance.

Residents and businesses combined submitted 38,000 insurance claims, totalling $1.5 billion, but, as in 1974, many found they were uninsured.[61] Most household policies excluded riverine flood. Suncorp, with automatic flood coverage since 2008, was the exception, and consequently the South East Queensland floods cost Suncorp almost $90 million. Many of those flooded railed against insurers, frustrated that they could not be compensated for their losses. Bowing to community pressure, Commonwealth Bank distributed a compassionate fund of $50 million to CommInsure customers and RACQ gave $10 million. The state too had uninsured assets, with disaster-prone Queensland the 'only major Australian state economy' without insurance, deeming it not 'good value for money', according to *The Australian* on 3 February, and relying on the Commonwealth Government to pay 75 per cent of the damages.[62] Australian taxpayers were slugged a one-off levy to recoup $1.8 billion, effectively meaning the country financed the cost of Queensland's escalating flood hazard. The Opposition Government and economists objected, preferring to use budget surplus rather than hit consumers. While the human suffering was palpable, focus on contested insurance claims avoided questioning the efficacy of insurance as a flood relief strategy. Insurance treats the symptom of living on the floodplain. It does not address the cause – irresponsible land use and poor hazard planning – and it absolves government and individual responsibility in favour of compensation.

The Increased Hazard

While legacy issues in older suburbs contributed to the number of flooded houses in 2011, thousands of new homes had been built on the floodplains since 1974. The myth of flood immunity, dependence on dams to mitigate floods, poor land-use practices, and policies of urban renewal, growth and consolidation meant that when the next inevitable major flood did occur, the damage was significantly greater. On 12 January, Bligh acknowledged that damage could exceed previous floods as 'the city was much bigger, much more populated and has many parts under flood that didn't even exist in 1974'.[63] Brisbane's population of over two million people in 2011 dwarfed the 700,000 residents in 1974. BCC estimated that 10 per cent of the residential properties affected by the 2011 floods were built after 1978.[64]

In some flooded areas, for example the Moggill and Bellbowrie district, settlement had been sparse in 1974, offering the opportunity for greater flood regulation for subsequent development. When Clem Jones named the suburb and opened the Bellbowrie Shopping Plaza in November 1973, fewer than 20 homes stood nearby in an area earmarked as a 2,000-lot housing estate. In 2011, Bellbowrie's population had swelled from its 1976 population of 771 to 5,413. Moggill's population had also grown, from 707 to 3,606. Although Moggill's 1974 flood peak was 2 metres higher, in 2011 many of the new homes were submerged, as well as the shopping plaza to 0.3 metres below the roofline.[65] Despite repeated flooding in the Jindalee and Seventeen Mile Rocks region, new estates of luxury riverside homes, including Windermere and Edenbrook estates, were carved out after 1974 only to be inundated in 2011. Similarly, prior to 1991, Graceville Park, a multi-level complex of 90 townhouses, had been a paddock traversed by a creek. In 2011, 81 townhouses were flooded at the complex, with 60 totally inundated.[66]

Urban densification also increased flood damage. Subdividing suburban blocks for a second dwelling doubled the flood hazard per unit area, and the post-1974 trend of converting single-storey dwellings to multi-storey dwellings also swelled the number of people who were flood affected. While habitable areas may have been above the water level, basement car parks, including storage and electrical services, were submerged, leaving entire buildings uninhabitable. Luxury apartments had been built at Tennyson Reach on 11.9 hectares of the riverside site of the decommissioned Tennyson Power Station, land that had substantially flooded in 1974. A deal between the state and Tennis Queensland in 2002 had given property developer Mirvac land to construct an international tennis centre and 400 apartments. Several apartment owners reported receiving assurances from Mirvac that floods were an unlikely event with Wivenhoe Dam.[67] Development approval had been granted by BCC on a site provided by the state, so property owners felt that the development had received governmental endorsement. The 2011 floods reached 9.05 metres at Tennyson Reach, which was less than the 10.8 metres reached in 1974 but 0.65 metres higher than the DFL. Two of the three towers flooded on the lower floors, creating damage totalling $6 million. In June 2011, Mirvac persuaded BCC to acquire its now unviable land for $9 million, well above market value, plus pay Mirvac $6 million to redevelop the site as parkland.[68]

Ipswich had also increased its vulnerability through floodplain development. Goodna, devastated in 1974, boasted 1,000 new homes by 1994, and the size of St Ives Shopping Centre tripled. With approvals granted at a 'rapid rate', the suburb had 'bounced back', making it hard, according to Councillor Paul Tully in 1994, to guess 'the area had suffered a flood'.[69] A large portion of Goodna's 2011 population of 8,777, especially the 41 per cent born overseas, would have been unaware of the flood risk. Brand new homes in a 2010 North Booval estate were also devastated, an event Rachel Nolan, the State Member for Ipswich in 2011, considers 'incredibly distressing and utterly shocking – a terrible failure of planning'. Council policies had focused on rebuilding after the 1974 floods and development had intensified the hazard.

In 2005, Bremer Waters, an over-50s resort, opened on the banks of the Bremer River at Moores Pocket, Ipswich. Designed in three stages, advertisements offered 183 homes on 12 hectares beside the 'serene' and 'picturesque' river. Although a legal development, built with ICC approval, 100 of the 175 homes in the estate flooded and the community centre was submerged to 1.7 metres on the top floor. Residents were left battling insurance companies and forced to return to work, their retirement plans abandoned. Along with the aged-care facilities Suncare Lakes at Brassall and Cabanda Care in Rosewood, Bremer Waters' occupants had to be evacuated, highlighting a questionable practice of accommodating the most vulnerable on floodplains, a problem internationally acknowledged in hazard scholarship.[70]

Brisbane and Ipswich councils had implemented a modelled DFL to guide development that was lower than the 1974 flood, based on the perceived mitigating effect of Wivenhoe Dam. The inherent variability in rainfall, with the resultant uncertainty in flood behaviour, cannot follow a predictable solution that allows a perfect model, DFL and manual to control a natural event. Reducing hydrological complexity to a 'one case fits all' approach is doomed to failure. As described in Chapter 6, council planning regimes left loopholes open for development below the DFLs. State interests could also override local policy to permit development. Rules governing building after the 1974 floods were hamstrung by the need to compensate developers should the planning regulations change (under the rule of injurious affection). Structures could be rebuilt on the same site with no design modifications, such as Bunnings on Oxley's floodplain, which used commercial insurance funds to rebuild after 2011, with council powerless to stop it as it was unwilling to pay compensation. The loopholes in legislation and town plans had been exposed.

All peak flood levels recorded in the 2011 flood were higher than the existing DFLs. Between the modelled DFL and the 2011 flood height were 9,767 structures (Table 7.4). If councils had adopted the

1974 flood height as the DFL, and not relied on Wivenhoe Dam, many buildings would have been saved from inundation. Wivenhoe Dam had reduced the flood peak by 2 metres, rather than the calculated 3 metres. Refusal to adopt a multidimensional approach that included tougher building codes, development restrictions in vulnerable areas and public education (all internationally accepted hazard management tools) had substantially increased the potential damage of floods. A lack of political courage between the 1974 and 2011 floods created policies that had intensified the hazard. The public questioned the accuracy of the DFL, with critics recalling previous studies that had suggested the application of higher levels.

	Current Q100	Current DFL	Jan 2011	1974 Flood (5.54 metres)	Jan 2011 Minus DFL
Commercial	1,171	1,178	2,759	2,907	1,581
Industrial	783	1,589	2,000	2,482	411
Community	24	34	46	48	12
Multi-Dwelling Residential	6,814	10,756	15,834	18,025	5,078
Single-Dwelling Residential	4,666	7,543	10,228	12,306	2,685
Total	13,458	21,100	30,867	35,768	9,767

Table 7.4: Number of BCC properties affected by the differing flood scenarios.[71]

People searched for answers as to why their properties were flooded; they were keen to assign blame for their losses. Wivenhoe Dam, long regarded as Brisbane's saviour, had seemingly failed to prevent flooding. It had not delivered on the myth of flood immunity and the community demanded an explanation. The spotlight shifted to the operation of the dam, its beam firmly directed on the flood engineers.

Flood Management with Hindsight

BEFORE THE JANUARY 2011 floodwaters had receded, media debate on dam operations began, exposing varying community responses. The water conservation obsession was quickly forgotten as attention returned to floods. Some recognised that extreme, intense rainfall and run-off rates caused severe floods; however, the dominant rhetoric focused on the dams, reflecting the persistence in the faith in engineering to control nature. On 15–16 January, *Australian* journalist Hedley Thomas posed the question 'How much did releasing huge volumes of water contribute to the catastrophe?' The first scenario in this article suggested the Wivenhoe Dam operators did an exceptional job in extenuating circumstances. His 'gravely serious' alternative scenario suggested years of drought had conditioned 'political masters' and bureaucrats to withhold more water than necessary, ignoring the repeated BoM warnings of impending extreme rain. Through inaction, dam operators were 'compelled in a crisis situation to release thousands of megalitres quickly turning what would have been a moderate flood in Brisbane into a natural disaster'.[1] *Courier-Mail* cartoonist Sean Leahy encapsulated the debate on water retention or release on 8 March 2011: 'Wivenhoe Release ... Damned if they did ... Damned if they didn't.'

In the face of the flood devastation and public debate, on 17 January 2011 the Queensland Government established the

Queensland Floods Commission of Inquiry (QFCI) on the state-wide floods to examine the preparation, planning and response by three tiers of government, early warning and forecasting, dam operations (release strategies), performance of insurance companies, and local planning/construction in flood-prone areas. The QFCI was headed by Commissioner and Supreme Court judge Catherine Holmes and two deputy commissioners – former police commissioner Jim O'Sullivan and engineer Phil Cummins. Their interim report was to be completed within the year, in advance of the next storm season. In announcing the QFCI, the Premier declared, 'this is not a criticism of what we have done. It will identify what we did well and what we can do better.'[2] Hence, when the QFCI was announced, Terry Malone, one of the four dam engineers named in the media, felt relief that he would be heard and he believed 'the truth would set [him] free'.

Premier Anna Bligh vowed when announcing the inquiry that 'no question will be left unexamined'.[3] The editor of *The Australian* expressed a popular aspiration: 'we need an inquiry not to lay blame but to recommend new ways to protect life and property'.[4] In his opening remarks to the QFCI, Peter Callaghan SC, as counsel assisting the QFCI, suggested that, as the lessons of 1974 were lost, the commission afforded an opportunity to ensure these lessons were 'learned' and 'recorded for the future'. He hoped Queenslanders would not be 'condemned to the fate of those who cannot remember the past, nor left vulnerable at the hands of those who might choose to forget it'.[5] The QFCI offered an opportunity to redress past errors and change the path dependency on dams for hazard reduction.

The lessons should have exposed poor land use practices, but Callaghan quickly diverted the QFCI towards his key issues, which focused on the Brisbane River – the wisdom of maintaining FSL, the operation of the dams, compliance with the *Manual* and the impact of dam releases. These issues almost solely concentrated on water management. The government justified this narrow approach, arguing that the interim report must focus on short-term problems including flood warnings and dam management in case of another flood. Longer term problems of land use and insurance could be addressed later.

Any inquiry is only as effective as the questions it addresses. Inquiry outcomes are also dependent on receiving and understanding expert commentary. As indicated by Callaghan, rather than a search for answers, the QFCI soon became an adversarial environment more focused on finding fault than finding solutions. The four flood engineers – Ayre, Malone, Tibaldi and Ruffini – became key witnesses at the QFCI as their actions came under scrutiny. When the QFCI was announced, they were preparing an event report, required by the *Manual* within six weeks of flood. This report, the *Manual* and documents generated during the floods became evidence. A concentration on procedural adherence and blame detracted from the commission's potential to expose systemic problems in pursuit of flood resilience.

With the QFCI established, Seqwater hydrological data were embargoed and government departments silenced. While Commonwealth-employed meteorologists and hydrologists could address the media about the science, state employees could not. Journalists were left to rely on limited information to fill the news vacuum. Newspapers recirculated the same information, naming and criticising the dam engineers, but the state denied them the right of reply. For some journalists, the silence became the story as it suggested a cover-up or conspiracy. Retired engineers, not gagged by conditions of employment, were quoted. Self-professed, or media-labelled, experts, some hiding behind anonymity, came forward. Chemical engineer Michael O'Brien, described by *The Australian* as a dam expert, entered the knowledge void and became the quoted authority. He condemned the dam management, although he later conceded that his analysis had been based on the 'very limited' public information, notably from BoM.[6] This concession was unreported in the media. A 24-hour media cycle leaves little opportunity for analysis or fact-checking, or retraction of inaccuracies. The spurious use of self-professed 'experts' fanned unfounded media speculation and misinformation as an economics professor, a lawyer and farmers were cited to challenge hydrologists.

Dissenting viewpoints were also covered by the media, reflecting the division in public opinion. Some journalists argued that the dam managers should be praised, with Bligh and Newman offering the defence that the unprecedented rain left few alternatives.[7] However, the opposite view – that the flood was largely the product of water released from the dam, either too early or too late – prevailed.[8] With each iteration the belief grew more entrenched. The flood became framed as the 'great avoidable catastrophe' caused by dam mismanagement.[9] Hedley Thomas wrote that the community 'increasingly' viewed Wivenhoe Dam 'as the chief culprit behind the Brisbane flood'.[10] This view gained credibility when a report funded by the Insurance Council of Australia stated the dam created the flood peak, causing a 'dam release flood'.[11]

Rather than challenge faith in engineering to control floods, the public debate shifted to blaming individuals. O'Brien, the chemical engineer, promulgated the view of 'an avoidable disaster', exonerating the dam and claiming that 'prudent operation would have prevented most of the flooding'.[12] The operators, he maintained, had caused the flood.

'A Dam Release Flood'

In 1896, J. B. Henderson had highlighted the inherent problem of dual-purpose dams for managers. His words proved to be prophetic:

> by whom and how is it to be decided whether the water should be retained or released? If it be retained, and a second or third flood takes place, the valley, with reservoirs designed for a single flood, will be devastated exactly as if no reservoirs existed, and the officer in charge will be greatly blamed; if, on the other hand, the waters are released, and no second flood takes place, there will be no water for irrigation purposes. Crops may then suffer, and

the consequences may be disastrous, and the controlling officer will be censured. In either event the outlay incurred in forming the reservoirs will have been of no avail.[13]

As the QFCI and media commentary progressed, Minister Stephen Robertson and flood officers were indeed censured.

The first issue raised was the minister's and dam engineers' perceived failure to reduce dam levels to 75 per cent with the prediction of heavy rain. Mark Babister, a hydrologist employed as an expert by the QFCI, expressed the view that the effect would have been minimal. The torrential rain negated the impact and floods would have occurred regardless.[14] Furthermore, if the dam had been reduced to 75 per cent and the forecast rainfall did not arrive or fell downstream, water supply would have been compromised.

The option of earlier dam releases received microscopic attention. The *Australian* editorial on 13 April 2011 expressed a view that Robertson and the dam managers 'failed to address hard questions' and use 'common sense' to address the accurate forecasts of a wet La Niña summer. Early releases, the editor claimed, would have reduced flood levels. The accuracy of the forecasts can only be determined with hindsight. Analysts subsequently calculated that actual precipitation during the event varied as much as 200 per cent from predictions. The *Manual* stipulated the timing of the releases with strategies W1 to W4 (see Table 7.1 in Chapter 7) and significant variation constituted a *Manual* violation. Even without the *Manual*'s constraints, flood operations engineers argued early releases defied sound practice, a gamble in Tibaldi's opinion. Although early release on the night of 9 January may have reduced the flood peak, it would have caused unnecessary urban inundation had the 11 January rain not occurred. Had the rain fallen farther downstream, an early release strategy would have increased Brisbane's flood peak.[15] The QFCI interim report concurred that early release may have increased downstream flooding.[16]

Some journalists became increasingly convinced of the engineers' culpability. Hedley Thomas at *The Australian* argued that if the dam levels had been lower, the rainfall event 'could have been comfortably managed'. Instead, it 'turned into a major flood that would devastate thousands of homes'.[17] But hydrological evidence showed the first event had been 'comfortably managed', significantly reducing flood levels in Brisbane.[18] Before the dam could be reduced to the desired FSL, a second, equally large rainfall event occurred. That water could not be withheld.

The dam operators were not only criticised for withholding water, but also for releasing it. Journalists Hedley Thomas and David Uren declared the flood 'the direct result of the release from Wivenhoe, the city's flood shield'. They maintained that data showed that 'without the unprecedented and massive release at a peak rate of 645,000 ML' on 11 January 'the floods would have been minimal'.[19] Critics implied ineptitude, but the reality was clear: the dam had reached capacity. The water level peaked at 74.97 metres AHD, just 0.53 metres below the fuse plug. At that level, large releases were essential under strategy W4. The QFCI interim report recognised that 'the ability of operators to manage a flood is very limited when the volume of rainfall run-off greatly exceeds the volume of the available flood storage within the dam'.[20] The dam's finite capacity for water storage mandated releases, which contributed to flooding downstream.

Engineers and hydrologists appearing before the QFCI expressed frustration at its process. To them the QFCI was a technical debate based on hydrological and hydraulic data and modelling. Yet they found themselves hamstrung by an instruction not to use tables and diagrams, their tools of trade, instead having to reduce all data to words in order to be understood by legal teams. The QFCI's recommendations were determined by lawyers after the only engineer, Deputy Commissioner Phil Cummins, was stood down through a challenge of conflict of interest.[21] Lawyers are wordsmiths, engineers are technocrats – throughout the QFCI their different ways of thinking and explaining situations clashed. The QFCI forensically scrutinised the *Manual* and the application of W1 to W4 strategies, rather than the quality of the decision-making. The flood engineers testified that the terms W1 to W4 were 'seldom referred to by engineers, who rarely called them by their technical names'. This terminology codified objectives and strategies but was not routinely used in flood operations, with engineers focused on data, releases and consequences, not the nomenclature of their actions. Robert Ayre explained that 'strategy labels are generally only attributed after the event as part of the reporting process'.[22] Engineers testified the correct strategies were employed, while Callaghan accused them of fixing the report and writing 'fiction'.[23] Journalists wrote of a conspiracy, a manufactured cover-up to hide the implementation of the wrong strategies. Failure to use terminology W1 to W4 was regarded as failure to follow the *Manual*, although three independent reviews and Babister all found the engineers had complied with the *Manual*.

This focus on the *Manual* reflected the arrogance of human belief that the complexities of nature could be made predictable, and be reduced to guidelines and codified strategies. Engineers felt professionally slighted. Steven Goh, the President of Engineers Australia – Queensland, defended his colleagues, explaining how engineers rely on extensive training and experience 'when making decisions in time of crisis [and] do not just blindly follow manuals'.[24] Further, as each flood differs from designed flood scenarios, Goh asserted that blind adherence to a manual 'may deliver a detrimental outcome'.[25] The *Manual* allowed reasonable discretion. Many professions, including surgeons and pilots, acknowledge that there is a gap between manuals and practice. This may be where the genius lies. But a bad outcome can see professionals plummet from hero to villain.

The QFCI interim report was issued in August 2011 with 175 recommendations concentrated on short-term issues. It found the engineers 'diligent and competent' and said they had 'acted in good faith throughout the flood event'.[26] A final report would address longer term issues including floodplain management, emergency response and insurance. Hedley Thomas rejected the interim report findings and in January 2012 claimed in *The Australian* that the flood engineers had not correctly implemented the W1 to W4 strategies and hence breached the *Manual*, citing 'unearthed emails' by the engineers as proof of a cover-up.[27] As a direct consequence of these allegations and claims by Thomas that the engineers had misled the QFCI, additional documents were sought. The QFCI reopened for 10 days, placing the flood engineers firmly in the spotlight to determine if they had lied to the inquiry, falsified documents and not complied with the *Manual*. The media offered a blunt assessment, expressed by the *Brisbane Times* in February 2012 that the inquiry would 'investigate allegations that the four engineers who controlled Wivenhoe Dam botched the water releases, caused unnecessary flooding and misled the Inquiry over what water release strategies they were working under'.[28]

Business as Usual

The QFCI's final report, issued on 16 March 2012, did look beyond dam operations and determined Queensland's 'attention to flood risk has been ad hoc' and devoid of a 'coherent approach to floodplain management'. Yet, compared with the flood engineers, the state and councils were left largely unscathed. Poor planning decisions were blamed on science as the report claimed a lack of information about previous floods to determine appropriate DFLs had impeded flood planning as good decisions require 'accurate data'.[29] Identifying another scapegoat further exonerated governments and developers. Past development decisions and practices were largely relegated to history, with all recommendations looking to the future. The report's major recommendations included the completion of a flood study of the Brisbane River catchment, flood maps and local government floodplain management plans. Decisions about appropriate development control levels, Q100 heights and flow rates were not to be promulgated until the recommended flood studies were completed. So it was business as usual for floodplain developers.

The QFCI upheld the existing State Planning Policy on floods instead of a stronger approach and honoured previous development commitments and rules of compensation. The commission recommended that uniform development controls for vulnerable areas should be added to existing local planning schemes, and suggested a state-wide policy. It also recommended that if the state government chose not to create a state-wide policy, councils should accept responsibility for floodplain management. The aim, according to the QFCI, was for 'Queensland's planning framework to encourage the consideration of flooding in the assessment of development applications'. Again, this language allowed flexibility not compulsion. The state 'should' provide guidance, and councils 'should consider' implementation, not 'must'. Like the Henderson, Pennycuick and Gutteridge inquiries before them, the QFCI was restricted by financial and political realities as its terms of reference were to make 'appropriate, feasible and cost effective' recommendations to improve future response to floods. Commissioner Catherine Holmes's preface to the final QFCI report echoed the concerns of Henderson, Pennycuick and Gutteridge about subsequent inaction. She warned, 'there is a risk that the [QFCI's recommendations] will be enthusiastically taken up in the short term, but, absent another flood disaster in the next few years, priorities will drift and the lessons will be forgotten'.[30]

After 13 months and a cost of $15 million, the QFCI's recommendations largely allowed the retention of the status quo for floodplain planning. For the state and local councils, the loopholes and development compensation remained. The obfuscation on flood responsibility also endured as the state abrogated flood studies and management plans to councils. Local government pleaded lack of resources and requested state coordination, funding and technical assistance, not least because catchments cross local government boundaries. The state government was exonerated from both past and future responsibility. Although the commissioner had argued that floodplain management lay at the heart of the QFCI, these issues received very little media attention. In the court of public opinion, the issue remained dam management.

The QFCI disputed the correct application of the W1 to W4 strategies, especially in the documentation, and found the flood engineers were in technical breach of the *Manual*. The commission recommended the matter be referred to the CMC to investigate if Ayre, Malone and Tibaldi's preparation of documents and oral testimony constituted crimes or misconduct (Holmes did not refer Ruffini). On 20 August 2012, the CMC investigation concluded that there was no case to answer as there was no evidence of criminal offences or official misconduct.[31] The CMC also judged the confusing *Manual* at fault. A report by the Department of the Interior and the US Army Corps of Engineers, commissioned by the state government, further exonerated the engineers and it too blamed the *Manual*.[32] Despite these findings, the flood engineers still face further scrutiny as witnesses in a class action against Seqwater, SunWater and the State of Queensland by those seeking compensation for financial loss and damage caused by the inferred negligent operation of the dams. This case is predicated on a human's ability to predict weather and, implausibly, control floods.

While *The Courier-Mail* offered more balanced reporting and largely focused on human stories of suffering and resilience, *The Australian* concentrated on allegations of wrongdoing and prevented analysis of the current systems that had increased the flood hazard. This has deterred communal discussion on ways to decrease future risk. Issues of development in vulnerable areas raised by the QFCI were addressed in part, but deficiencies in past practices and land laws, and the need for systemic changes, were postponed by a perceived need for future flood studies. Little was done to address these legacy issues, and South East Queensland rebuilt property on its floodplain, with governmental approvals and without mandatory change to location, design or building materials.

Although Deputy Premier Andrew Fraser asserted the QFCI was about the 'truth' and never about politics, Commissioner Phil Cummins claimed the inquiry had been 'a very political process', limited greatly by the terms of reference.[33] The selected and selective key issues, media debate and use of technical experts had certainly shaped the outcome. Discrediting the government's 'non-political' claim, Bligh delayed both state and local council elections until the release of the final QFCI report. Bligh's government suffered a landslide defeat in March 2012. Although he had expressed flood concerns while Lord Mayor, the new Premier, Campbell Newman, hardly embraced the commission's recommendations with just over half of the recommendations (76 of 123) applicable to state government still outstanding in January 2013.[34]

Despite the prevailing rhetoric that blamed dams and engineers for flooding, some journalists recognised other causes. *The Courier-Mail* considered floods 'the vagaries of nature', the hazard increased by 'decades of planning decisions that have seen parts of Brisbane once considered flood-prone become prime real estate'.[35] The fallacy of relying entirely on dams had been exposed, but the community did not want to hear this and politicians were keen to divert attention from their lack of action over floodplain development. For those with vested interests in preserving floodplain development, the stakes were too high. A public call for a moratorium on floodplain development was opposed by both the Planning Institute of Australia and local government, with Mayor Paul Pisasale maintaining Ipswich 'needed to grow'.[36] The real estate industry became the most vocal campaigner, with fears of property prices plummeting.

Real estate agents were keen to resume floodplain development and wanted to be able to buy and sell existing residential and commercial properties on the floodplain. Johnston Dixon, specialists in selling riverside property, stated that the dam and river should be exonerated:

> If the Class Action goes the way it should, it will be confirmed that
> neither the Brisbane nor the Bremer River caused the devastating
> 2011 Brisbane Floods; that neither did Wivenhoe nor Somerset
> Dam cause the 2011 Brisbane Floods, that the blame lay squarely
> as has been so long suspected at the feet of those charged with
> their [the dams'] management.

The agents said the class action would 're-instate our dams as saviours
not sinners' and time would 're-instate our river as Brisbane's only
one true real estate royalty'. Johnston Dixon, although not confident
that those responsible would be held accountable for their 'mind-
numbing incompetence', surmised the industry had 'weathered the
storm', including the 'man-made floods'. Their 2013 *River Report*
concluded, 'as ever we will commit to doing whatever is in our
power to uphold and promote the value of what to us is held dear,
riverfront property'.[37]

Other real estate agencies joined the cause. Brian White, chair
of the agency Ray White, maintained that the 'Wivenhoe promise'
brought market assurance that 'Brisbane was now flood proof'.
'Confidence that there will be a different outcome to a similar
weather event will be the key' to market recovery, announced
White.[38] The government could offer no such guarantee, and
instead allowed the myth of a 'man-made flood' to flourish, fuelling
the delusion of flood immunity with silence. Riverside dwellers
supported White's view, well aware of the risk to their economic
prospects. John Grant, a Chelmer resident, informed *The Courier-
Mail* if the flood was a 'stuff up' then property prices would be
restored, otherwise 'Brisbane will be cast into an economic and
investment backwater as we are forced to close large parts of the
city and riverside areas and move to higher ground'.[39] The link with
property and prosperity remained firmly entrenched.

Engineer Trevor Grigg recognised the inherent risk of blaming
the bureaucrat, arguing it reinforced a dangerous view that 'if only
we get the operation of the dam right, we won't have any flooding

of this river'.[40] Shaping the flood as a bureaucratic error allowed the myth to endure, upholding current land use policies and practices. The strategy seemed successful. In 2012, Johnston Dixon reported that property market recovery was quicker than in 1974 as 'there's a perception that the flood was caused by bad management of Wivenhoe [Dam] and if that can be fixed up, then waterfront living is fine again'.[41]

Journalist Paul Syvret recognised the fallacy of depending on Wivenhoe Dam and underestimating nature. As he wrote in *The Courier-Mail* in January 2012, 'the dam had absorbed all nature could throw at it; done its job. But', as he explained to readers, 'the deadly rain storm that hit the catchment that Monday was supposed to miss Wivenhoe. It didn't, instead hovering there for hours, helping to dump what was the equivalent of two Sydney Harbours worth of water into the already swollen dam every 24 hours.' The dam had to cope with more water than had flowed during the 1974 floods. This, as Syvret noted, was a 1-in-2,000-year event.[42] As always, the flood was caused by heavy rain, this time more than the dam could withhold. The combination of two inflow peaks, dam releases and flood contributions from tributaries downstream of the dam made flooding inevitable. Governments had determined an acceptable level of risk, a modelled DFE with its corresponding DFL. There was an ever-present risk of flood, but popular opinion ignored this. Instead, an increasingly risk-averse society searched for someone to blame rather than accept the reality of the flood hazard that human actions had created.

In its final report, the QFCI acknowledged that:

> contemporary society does not countenance a fatalistic approach to such inevitabilities, even if their occurrence is unpredictable. There is an expectation that government will act to protect its citizens from disaster, and that all available science should be applied so that nature and extent of the risk is known and appropriate action taken to ameliorate it.[43]

What society wanted was for science and government to remove the risk altogether, an unattainable goal. Interstate newspapers expressed what many Queenslanders were unwilling to hear. 'The drama has proven once again that forces of nature in Australia respect little, if any, human intervention', deduced the *Sydney Morning Herald* editor on 14 January 2011.[44] *Australian* journalist Stephen Lunn described the Brisbane River in flood as 'an untamable torrent', explaining, 'as the deadly Queensland floods once again so shockingly show, thousands of years of human ingenuity and endeavour, of trial and error, and in more recent times of great technological advancement still sees us unable to bend nature to our will'. Premier Bligh reminded Queenslanders that 'dams do not stop floods'; they can only mitigate and minimise the impact, a fact many refused to accept.[45]

For floodplain dwellers, Wivenhoe Dam remains a talisman if operated correctly. If human error could be proven, then the myth that a river can be controlled with technology could be upheld. Rainfall can exceed a dam's capacity and can fall downstream, factors that only nature can determine.

No Two Floods Are the Same: The 2022 Flood

As the Brisbane River rose to 3.11 metres in the city on the morning of Sunday 27 February 2022, Lord Mayor Adrian Schrinner fronted the media to warn residents that this was a very different weather event to what Brisbane had seen in the past. 'This is a unique event, there is no doubt about that,' Schrinner told reporters. 'In 2011 we saw the rain had stopped while the river continued to rise. Right now, we're seeing rain bucketing down. We have a rain bomb above south-east Queensland and it continues to come down.'[1] Premier Annastacia Palaszcuk urged residents to be prepared, saying, 'It's literally a rain bomb sitting over the entire south-east Queensland' and describing the system as 'unrelenting' and 'unpredictable'.[2]

Although meteorologists dismissed the term 'rain bomb', instead describing it as an 'atmospheric river'[3], the phrase took hold in the media and in the popular imagination as the way to explain the torrential and incessant rain. Others referred to the ominous red mass indicating extreme rainfall on the Bureau of Meteorology (BoM) radar images as a 'tsunami from the sky'.[4] Whatever the nomenclature, it was clear that South East Queensland was again in flood.

The 2022 'Rain Bomb'

In late November 2021, BoM declared a La Niña event in the Pacific Ocean for the 2021–22 summer, a climate phase that usually brings above-average rain. This was the second year of a rare triple La Niña event, with only three such events declared since Australian record collection began in 1900 (the others were in 1954–57, 1973–76 and 1998–2001). After months of higher than average rainfall, ex-Tropical Cyclone Seth brought heavy rain to the region between 29 December 2021 and 10 January 2022, making the ground saturated and waterways full, the perfect catchment conditions for increased run-off and flooding. As well as a La Niña event, after 22 February 2022 there were additional climatic factors that increased the chance of heavy rain: a positive Southern Annular Mode, a negative Indian Ocean Dipole, a low-pressure trough in the Coral Sea, a 'blocking' high pressure system in the Tasman Sea over New Zealand and an 'unusually cold upper atmosphere weather system across the Great Australian Bight'.[5] A coastal trough also fed a large volume of moist tropical air into eastern Australia.[6] The stage was set for an extreme weather event.

On 25 February 2022, *The Courier-Mail* reported 'astronomical' amounts of rain were falling to the north around Maryborough as a weather system sitting off the coast dumped more than 420 millimetres of rain overnight.[7] Initial modelling indicated that the upper low-pressure system would move quickly east off the coast, but instead the 'rain bomb' or atmospheric river formed and moved very slowly south.

In Ipswich, as early as 24 February, localised flooding was inundating roads as warnings were issued for creek flooding. Over four days (25 to 28 February inclusive), Ipswich received 682 millimetres of rain.[8] The 224 millimetres recorded on 26 February was the highest daily total since 1974, when 340 millimetres fell in one day. Wivenhoe Dam received 314 millimetres on 26 February, a new daily rainfall record and 66 millimetres higher than the previous record attained in the 2011 flood. The Amberley gauge recorded

936 millimetres over the summer, which was 111 millimetres higher than the 2011 record and more than twice the location's average summer rainfall.[9] This rainfall exceeded all previous records.[10]

In Brisbane, the recorded rainfall between 25 and 28 February vastly exceeded forecasts. On 26 February, BoM warned there was a higher than 10 per cent chance of rain exceeding 240 millimetres on average in Brisbane the next day, but the four official automated Brisbane stations recorded between 250 millimetres and 470 millimetres of rain.[11] Between 23 and 28 February, the BCC area received 400 millimetres to 1,100 millimetres (on average 795 millimetres), much of which fell between Friday 25 and Sunday 27 February. The monthly Brisbane rainfall total throughout February was second only to February 1893, when the city received 1,026 millimetres.[12] Even more significantly, the Brisbane City Gauge received 677 millimetres in three days, exceeding the previous three-day record of 600 millimetres in 1974. In 72 hours, Brisbane received around 80 per cent of the city's average annual rainfall and almost all the rainfall that London would get in an entire year.[13] The Alderley rain gauge reveals the magnitude of this event as it has one of the longest continuous records for rainfall in any Brisbane suburb (1899–2023). On 28 February, it received 345 millimetres and a massive 1,006 millimetres over six days. Incredibly, a home digital weather station in Mornington Street, Alderley recorded a total of 1,277.6 millimetres.[14]

Rainfall averaged over the entire Brisbane River catchment highlights some of the unusual differences between flood events. In the 1974 and 2022 floods the rainfall was similar over the first three days, but the 2022 event continued for around another 12 hours before suddenly stopping. The three-day catchment average rainfalls for Stanley River to Somerset Dam and Brisbane River to Wivenhoe Dam were significantly higher in 2022 than in 1974 and 2011 (see Table 9.1). Staggeringly, they were approximately 40 per cent higher than in 2011. Equally astonishingly, the three-day average rainfall downstream of Moggill was more than three times the volume recorded in 2011.[15]

Location	1974	2011	2022
Stanley River to Somerset Dam	429	447	627
Brisbane River to Wivenhoe Dam	296	292	409
Lockyer Creek	312	288	406
Bremer River	460	216	331
Brisbane between Wivenhoe Dam and Moggill	577	377	645
Brisbane River downstream of Moggill	623	155	637

Table 9.1: 9.00 am to 9.00 am three-day catchment average rainfalls (millimetres) in 1974, 2011 and 2022.[16]

Utilising Flood Storage

The Seqwater Flood Operations Centre was mobilised on 23 February 2022. Four senior flood engineers were deployed, although one was working remotely as a Covid-19 close contact, revealing the challenge of flood management during a pandemic. The first operational releases from Somerset Dam were made at 5.00 pm on 23 February. Water was released from Wivenhoe Dam at 10.00 pm on 25 February but ceased an hour later as downstream flows were joined by the waters of Lockyer Creek, Bremer River and local creeks. The Somerset Dam lake level peaked at 103.17 metres Australian Height Datum (AHD) on 27 February, the day of the dam's peak release. Wivenhoe releases restarted on 27 February at 4.00 am, and the Wivenhoe Dam lake level peaked at 74.61 metres AHD on 28 February, with peak releases occurring on 3 March. Flood releases ceased at Somerset Dam on 8 March and Wivenhoe the next day.[17] Engineer Stuart Khan says Wivenhoe received around three Sydney Harbours' worth of water in under three days and, critically, it received about 50 per cent more water in half the time compared with 2011.[18]

Unlike in 2011, Seqwater was able to speak directly to the media, a move that was welcomed by spokesperson Michael Foster as it allowed the organisation to keep the public abreast of the rapidly escalating and constantly changing situation. He says that 'this was one of the key differences from 2011, the ability to explain what was happening at Wivenhoe as it was happening'. Seqwater issued twice-daily situational reports (34 in all), held 24 videoconferences with relevant stakeholders, and shared datasets of predicted and actual dam releases.[19] Foster gave frequent press appearances on television and newspaper interviews explaining the dam release strategy.[20] As dam releases increased, Foster explained to an anxious public, 'That's the dam doing what it's supposed to do, reduce the natural flows.' He continued, 'I think Mother Nature has taught us many things and Mother Nature can change really quickly, so if we were to get more rain coming in next week [...] we need to ensure that the dam is ready to be able to deal with another event.' He also explained that 'sometimes the forecasts aren't right, sometimes forecasts can be really, really wrong'.[21] With the relentless rain, the forecasts were rapidly changing. The dissemination of regular dispassionate information stopped a knowledge vacuum forming or the flourishing of dam operation myths.

As in 2011, the Flood Operations Centre staff were constantly processing new information as automated processes imported radio-transmitted rainfall and river height data into the flood forecasting system every three minutes, and produced flood modelling every 15 minutes.[22] Information from 355 rainfall gauges and 245 water level gauges in South East Queensland catchments informed decisions and flood data were shared frequently between agencies, especially Seqwater and BoM.[23] Public notifications of dam releases had improved since 2011, as people who had signed up to the Dam Release Notification App received email and SMS updates, and recorded messages about the timing of dam releases were frequently updated and made available on a 1800 phone number.[24]

A Different Flood

It is difficult to compare floods when there have been changes in data collection, dam construction and varying initial water levels, but even with these disclaimers it is clear that 2022 was a substantial flood. The total inflow into Somerset Dam was greater in 2022 than in 2011, and would have only been exceeded in 1893 (had Somerset Dam existed). Inflows into Somerset Dam in February 2022 were 902,000 megalitres, compared with 820,000 megalitres in 2011, 710,000 megalitres in 1974 and the modelled figure of 1.34 million megalitres in 1893. However, the total inflow into Wivenhoe Dam in 2022 (2.3 million megalitres) was less than in 2011 (2.7 million megalitres).[25]

The releases from Wivenhoe were also smaller in 2022 than in 2011. While 1.97 million megalitres were released in 2022, a total of 2.75 million megalitres were released in 2011.[26] Downstream of Wivenhoe, the water levels at Ipswich and Moggill had already risen to 13.5 metres AHD and 11.5 metres AHD respectively before releases commenced. This meant that flood heights at Ipswich and Moggill had already peaked and were falling by the time the initial Wivenhoe releases of 3,200 cubic metres per second reached these stations. The delayed releases increased the duration of the flood but their timing reduced the flood heights reached downstream.

Along with Wivenhoe Dam's reduced inflow and releases in 2022 when compared with 2011, there were also significant procedural differences that affected the flood outcome in Brisbane. One was an operational change in the *Manual*, made in 2014, that allowed earlier dam releases at Wivenhoe. Water levels had to reach 67.25 metres AHD before releases were permitted in 2011, which in 2014 was reduced to 65.9 metres AHD. At the start of the 2011 flood event, Wivenhoe Dam was at the Full Supply Level (FSL) of 67 metres AHD, whereas in 2022 it measured 62.16 metres AHD, and the dam safety trigger level had been raised from 74 metres to 75 metres AHD. In practical terms, the flood managers had more storage capacity (approximately 1.5 million megalitres) in 2022 for floodwaters.[27]

Despite the advantage of the increased water storage capacity and the lower initial level, the volume of rain in 2022 presented major operational issues, as by 27 February the dam was reaching record peak heights. Wivenhoe Dam rose from 58.7 per cent of its FSL (61.36 metres AHD) on 24 February to 183.9 per cent (74.5 metres AHD, just 1.2 metres below the level of the first fuse plug spillway) on 27 February, a phenomenal increase in three days and not far below the 190.3 per cent reached in 2011.[28] As levels increased, the senior flood officers at Seqwater discussed a transition from the Flood Mitigation Strategy to the Dam Safety Strategy, which shifts the focus from flood mitigation to the prevention of the structural failure of the dam. Reflecting on this discussion, Michael Foster says, 'all it would have taken was two to three more hours of heavy rain and the Seqwater engineers would have likely to have needed to transition to dam safety releases, which would have resulted in increased flows downstream'.[29]

The 2011 event was primarily a riverine flood, with both the Bremer River and Brisbane River peaking higher than they did in 2022 (see Table 9.2). In comparison, the 2022 flood had three causes – riverine flooding, creek flooding and overland flow – all occurring at once. The behaviour of the creeks was a significant difference between the 2011 and 2022 floods, and in this regard the 2022 event was more like 1974. In 2022 creek behaviour varied greatly; some creek catchments experienced a 1 in 10 Annual Exceedance Probability (AEP) flood, while others were 1 in 2,000 AEPs.[30] Some, like Cabbage Tree Creek, flooded over 30 per cent more than in 2011. Further, the intense rain made flash flooding – the rapid inundation of low-lying areas – far more significant in 2022. After two years of La Niña rain, the soaked ground increased run-off and overland flow, which when combined with creek flooding meant many areas flooded in 2022 that were dry in 2011.[31] Oxley Creek in South Brisbane, a major flood contributor in 1974 with 638 millimetres of rain, received only 197 millimetres in 2011 but 642 millimetres in 2022. Kedron Brook, in north Brisbane, broke records in 2022 with 893 millimetres, compared with 315 millimetres in 2011 and 661 millimetres in 1974. The swollen creeks soon reclaimed their floodplains, flooding streets and homes in their paths.

Year	Ipswich	Moggill	Brisbane City
1893	24.5	24.5	8.35
1893	23.6	23.6	8.09
1974	20.7	19.95	5.45
2011	19.4	18.17	4.46
2022	16.72	14.09	3.85

Table 9.2: Comparative river flood heights between Ipswich, Moggill and Brisbane City (metres AHD). Heights for the 1893 floods are pre Somerset and Wivenhoe dams, and heights for the 1974 flood are pre Wivenhoe Dam.

The Rain Races Downstream

A 'Watch and Act' alert was issued by BoM in Ipswich at 11.00 am on 25 February, but was upgraded to a flash flooding warning for the inner city at 10.35 pm, with the first 'prepare to leave' warning released at 10.45 pm for areas around Bundamba, Woogaroo and Warrill creeks and the Bremer River. Warnings continued throughout the next day and heavy rain forced evacuations overnight in Goodna and Bundamba.[32] Ipswich Mayor Teresa Harding reported receiving flood warnings as late as 1.35 am on 27 February, and before 3.00 am the 'Council, police and SES were in Goodna with lights, sirens, door knocking and helping people to evacuate'.[33] An official Wivenhoe Dam release Emergency Warning was issued at 4.00 am on 27 February.

Kate Cantrell and her partner, Jessie, lived in an old Queenslander in Lawrence Street, North Ipswich, and while 'they didn't go completely under', Kate says, 'it was touch and go for a while'. Everyone else on the street (except the four neighbours on higher ground) completely flooded, including the daycare centre across the road (Figure 9.1). Kate recalls that 'some neighbours lost everything. A local Uber driver misjudged the rising water and flooded his car – he went under and had to be pulled out of his window by a good Samaritan.' The water rose 'higher than the 16-metre football posts' nearby. Kate and Jessie, who was four-months pregnant at the time, were without power for four days, and in January 2023 were still without a bathroom ceiling.[34]

Figure 9.1: The daycare centre in North Ipswich under water.
(Courtesy of Kate Cantrell)

Over in Helen Street, North Booval, Sue Kirk lived in a low-set rental house on Bundamba Creek. She had only been there for four months and was aware that the property had flooded in 2011 but, like many, she thought it might not happen again. She received a 'prepare to leave' text on 24 February but was never advised to evacuate, although she fled with her dog and chickens when the water reached her back fence. She relied on Facebook community pages to find an escape route as the roads were flooded. Neighbours left in kayaks, while Sue cut through a residential complex that had kindly opened their gates. She first learnt that her house was submerged via a photo posted on Facebook the next day, and nothing prepared her for the devastation when she returned days later after the roads reopened.

Sue's front door had swollen so much she had trouble entering the house, even the key resisted turning. She forced entry and the sight was 'gutting'. She explains that 'everything had moved. The brand-new fridge and the washing machine weren't even on the ground. The fridge was wedged between cabinetry and the wall and the washing machine was suspended between shelves and the tub, full of floodwater.' Her leather couch wore a 'fur of mould'. People helped with the clean-up but it was gruelling watching her possessions being tossed out. She lost everything, and her renter's insurance only covered the fridge and washing machine, but she says, 'no amount of money replaces losing photos and videos of your child'.[35] Financial packages, skewed towards helping home owners, do not help the large numbers of renters who live in low-lying affordable properties.

In Ipswich, almost 600 dwellings, 300 businesses and more than 250 vehicles were damaged, with a substantial loss of stock and livelihoods.[36] Roads and bridges were damaged, power was cut and the Mt Crosby Water Treatment Plant had to be taken offline temporarily.[37] Riverbanks and riparian areas were eroded or destroyed, as 'entire trees were ripped from the ground and carried downstream'. Landslips, unusual in Ipswich, 'occurred at various locations across the city'.[38] The riverwalk and the River Heart Parklands were devastated (Figure 9.2), and Colleges Crossing (a popular recreational spot) was virtually destroyed.

Figure 9.2: Ipswich Park underwater. (Photo by Margaret Cook)

The Ipswich Showgrounds were mobilised on 25 February as an evacuation centre. Managed by Red Cross for ICC, it supported over 4,000 local people over 12 days, providing food, shelter, counselling, medical treatment, and services to help find financial, housing and community support.[39] The riverine floodwaters followed their usual fluvial pathways, flooding several of the same suburbs as 2011, but numerous houses were spared with the reduced river flood height. This time, however, the intense rainfall caught many by surprise as the overland flow inundated homes well beyond the floodplain when stormwater drains overflowed, proving no match for the torrential rain.

Brisbane Caught Off-guard

While Ipswich flooded, on 26 February Brisbane's Lord Mayor, Adrian Schrinner, issued community service announcements about dangerous conditions as localised flooding occurred in low-lying areas of Brisbane, and issued videos via Facebook about preparing for bad weather and accessing the emergency alert system. Schrinner urged residents to 'stock up on sandbags', ensure they had 'essentials' and 'know when it is time to leave'. He warned that thousands of properties could be affected the next day on the high tide, with Premier Annastacia Palaszczuk indicating 1,413 properties would be flooded above floorboard height.[40]

Although forecasts predicted that the system would move south, the rain remained overhead and Brisbane residents 'were caught off-guard by fast-rising floods'.[41] BoM reported that the rainfall intensity was 'incredibly quick and incredibly fast' and Premier Palaszczuk expressed the thoughts of many: 'We never expected this rain, this rain bomb is just unrelenting. It's not a waterfall, it's like waves of water.'[42] The 'intense weather' she said, 'was like an unpredictable cyclone'. On 27 February the situation escalated further as BoM issued severe thunderstorm warnings for 'intense rainfall' from two systems.[43] Journalist Leisa Scott captured the frequently articulated refrain throughout the city as the rain kept falling: 'It'll stop soon, won't it?' Residents were checking BoM's website repeatedly, incredulous that the red radar images constantly sat there, as a 'technicolour monster hovering over the South East, malevolent and immovable'.[44]

As BoM issued warnings for thunderstorms, heavy rainfall and creek flooding on the evening of 26 February, the Lord Mayor tweeted a predicted flood height of 2.7 metres at the Brisbane City Gauge, lower than the major flood height. But with the constantly changing scenarios, the predicted river flood heights were revised five times in the next 11 hours.[45] The continuous revision of weather forecasts and data made information management and modelling flooding in an escalating disaster extremely challenging for meteorologists, dam operators and emergency managers. Council received 132 communications between 22 February and 7 March, and issued 75 severe weather warning alerts and 285 creek flood alerts. Alerts were out of date soon after (or before) their release, which proved trying for the general community, and left many unsure of what to do in the unfolding disaster as the swiftly rising floodwaters astonished Brisbane residents.

Graceville residents Mike Bayer and Gaenor Walker told journalist Michael Madigan, 'It came up so fast [...] We went to sleep and there was no water on the block and then we woke up at 2.00 am' (on 27 February) and 'it was up to our ankles'. They lost everything but their cat and passports.[46] Alison and Lyndon Hill were 'content to wait out the floods' in their Rosalie home, but their landlords, who had experienced the 2011 floods 'insisted they get out'. Alison told reporters that they trusted their landlords' experience, but left it too late to leave. Stranded in the home without power, they had to be paddled to safety by a friend.[47]

West End, one of Brisbane's most heavily developed suburbs since 2011, also experienced an unexpected rise in floodwaters on 27 February. After the 2011 floods, Amy O'Hara's family in Ryan Street, West End raised their house. As the waters rose early on the morning of 27 February, her father woke Amy and her sister to move everything upstairs. Water was already rising in nearby Hoogley Street and gushing out of the stormwater drains outside their home. As the water downstairs reached about 1 metre, Amy and her sister evacuated to a hotel. She kayaked back the next day to find her father and dog had stayed dry on the second floor.[48]

Michael Kelly has lived in a high-rise apartment in Buchanan Street, West End for 16 years. He experienced the 2011 flood and, in his words, 'foolishly thought another flood wouldn't come for about 20 years', taking comfort that he 'probably won't be here and have to go through it'. But he was also surprised that the water 'came unexpectedly and quite quickly'. On the afternoon of 26 February there was no sign of excess water on the footpaths outside his building, but by 8.00 pm it was ankle deep. At 1.30 am the next day, Michael was woken by a knock on his apartment door. It was the onsite manager warning everyone to move their cars from the car park as the basement pumps were struggling with the volume of water entering. Michael found moving his car challenging because, with the increased population in West End, high ground for parking is at a premium. Later that morning, the basement flooded and the power went out, and the lifts remained inoperable for six weeks. Similarly, rain rendered the lift in Kate Kirby's apartment block in Sherwood inoperable. It took months to repair and her elderly neighbours and those with health issues struggled. Flood repairs in apartments depend on the co-operation of the body corporate, and Kate says these issues have made many rethink high-rise living as the solution to Brisbane's housing crisis.[49]

A defining difference between the 2011 and 2022 events was that creek and overland flow flooded many places in Brisbane that were unaccustomed to floods. For residents on the southside, the quick-moving water followed familiar riverine flood paths, but many living on the northside were caught off-guard. A gorged Kedron Brook swamped Windsor and Grange, which were left dry in 2011, and Ithaca Creek flooded Ashgrove for the first time since 1974.

Brisbane felt the brunt of the rain on Sunday 27 February. Enoggera Reservoir (10 kilometres from the CBD) reached 230 per cent capacity, or about 5.5 metres more than the spillway could hold, and the waters poured into Fish and Ithaca creeks.[50] Enoggera Road was blocked at the bridge over Enoggera Creek, a bridge that locals could not remember flooding before.[51] Jamica Santos had lived near Enoggera Creek in Acacia Drive, Ashgrove for 25 years. In 2011 the floodwaters reached her driveway, but in 2022 the creek rose to just under two metres outside her home. She told *The Courier-Mail*, 'It was crazy, it just kept rising, it wouldn't stop. I was scared because of how quickly it was rising.' *The Courier-Mail* reported that around 4.30 am 'police had to break palings in their back fence to evacuate them'. Jamica recalls, 'I've never seen anything like it before, we were just watching all the fences drift by.'[52]

Only hours before they were rescued from their roof by a swift-water rescue team, Newmarket couple Debbie and Paul Edwards witnessed the 'river running through the house'. Water inundated roads and, from 27 February, Ashgrove was isolated as the local bridges were closed, shrouded in debris (Figure 9.3). A local community Facebook page reported multiple residents were left 'stranded and screaming', isolated and endangered by floodwaters.[53]

Figure 9.3: Local bridges, like the one at the entrance to Marist College Ashgrove, were rendered unusable. (Courtesy of Marist College Ashgrove Old Boys' Association)

Cathy O'Malley is a long-term resident of Stafford. Despite living beside Kedron Brook for 24 years, she had never been flooded. On 27 February, the creek floodwaters rushed into her backyard and rose rapidly, climbing from ground to knee height in 10 minutes. In another 10 minutes it reached the higher front yard. As the street flooded, stormwater drains rattled with the force of the water and wheelie bins raced by. Cathy's possessions, stored in plastic boxes under the house, floated out with the force of the water, and Kedron Brook was deeply scoured, with a landslip in Shand Street forcing home evacuations. Cathy believes that people didn't realise the extent of flooding in the northern suburbs, with the focus concentrated on the usual southside riverine flood.[54]

Cedric Chu lives in Butterfield Street, Herston, which backs onto Breakfast Creek, a tidal creek fed from The Gap and Ashgrove, which flooded extensively in 1974. His house didn't flood in 2011. Cedric believes BoM described the 2022 flood poorly, as they only distributed raw data. By contrast, the digital media, Brisbane Weather and Higgins Storm Chasing analysed the information and provided context to offer a 'layman's' understanding. Cedric called on his lived experience to understand the events unfolding in 2022. He knew that low pressure systems moving south are the ones to watch as they bring rain from the Pacific Ocean and two had developed. Conditions became nerve-wracking for him on 25 February as the floodwaters were rising with a falling tide, and the tropical lows were very slow moving and heading south. At midday the next day, social media warned Cedric of massive incoming rain with moisture being pulled from as far away as Nouméa. He predicted that 'things were going to be bad', so his family started sandbagging their home and erecting their own flood barrier. They evacuated at 4.30 pm as the rain continued to dump down and neighbours kayaked from their homes. Despite being on the higher part of the street, the water reached 2.1 metres in Cedric's house around 2.00 am. It had largely drained away by 6.00 am but the family were left for nine days without power and everything downstairs – the walls, the floors, furniture and possessions – was destroyed.[55]

Thirteen people lost their lives in the 2022 floods. This included a 34-year-old Moorooka man who drowned while trying to swim from a submerged car on Witton Road, and a 59-year-old man who tried to cross Cabbage Tree Creek Road at Fitzgibbon and died of a heart attack. A man's body was found in receding floodwaters in Stones Corner, and another 53-year-old man was found dead under a wharf at the Port of Brisbane, thought to have fallen out of a tender when crossing the river. A man in his seventies is presumed dead after he fell overboard from his yacht moored near Breakfast Creek.[56] Meryl Dray, an SES volunteer, died at Coolana, near Ipswich, on 25 February, when floodwaters swept the rescue vehicle she and her team were in from the road.

In 2022, 177 of Brisbane's 190 suburbs and 23,400 properties were flood-affected, compared with 94 suburbs and 14,100 properties in 2011.[57] While some had only minor inundation, Deloitte Access Economics estimates that 18,000 homes and businesses were damaged – 1,980 severely and 2,700 moderately.[58]

The Bruce, Warrego and Ipswich highways closed for several days, and approximately 2,770 Brisbane streets were impacted by the event.[59] A stream of debris, including private pontoons and trees, careered into ferry terminals, but the swinging gangways installed after the 2011 floods prevented worse damage for the CityCat (ferry) terminals and reduced the damage bill from around $120 million to $20 million (Figure 9.4). Only six terminals were substantially damaged and much of the network was operational again within months,[60] though one CityCat sank after it was struck by a houseboat that had been torn from its moorings.[61] The new riverwalk from New Farm to Newstead, built after 2011 and fixed to the riverbed by 37 concrete piles, only suffered cosmetic damage in 2022.[62] The Drift Restaurant, still lying damaged in the river since the 2011 floods, dislodged and crashed into the riverside bike path and was finally removed.[63]

Figure 9.4: St Lucia ferry terminal submerged in 2022.
(Courtesy of Miranda Joye)

Marine Safety Queensland recovered more than 6,700 tonnes of debris from the river, including 40 pontoons and 60 vessels deemed salvageable.[64] Pontoon debris was found as far away as K'gari (Fraser Island) and Noosa. Often made of polystyrene, pontoon pieces caused hazards for watercraft, were ingested by marine life and washed up on beaches.[65] An estimated 50 million tonnes of sediment moved through the catchment during the event, much of it forming a plume in Moreton Bay. Adding to this waste was the year's worth of landfill from damaged homes and businesses, with around 30,000 cubic metres of rubbish delivered to council refuse and recycling centres.[66]

As in 2011, there were moments of high drama during the 2022 event. A 70-year-old skipper had a lucky escape when his houseboat crashed into a ferry terminal and sank immediately on 27 February. Filmmaker Matthew Porter and his colleagues were making a car advertisement at the time and witnessed the accident, so they raised the alarm. Police tracked the skipper as he was dragged for 500 metres in fast-moving water until he reached the Howard Smith Wharves ferry terminal and was pulled to safety by members of the public.[67] The next day, a pontoon carrying a 550-tonne, 30-metre crane broke free of its moorings. Concerns that it would slam into parks or buildings, including the popular restaurant precinct Howard Smith Wharves, prompted evacuations in the local area and closure of the Story Bridge. The police tweeted around 2.00 pm: 'Anyone at Howard Smith Wharves, including surrounding businesses and the riverside walkway, are to EVACUATE IMMEDIATELY. Locals are advised to avoid the area, and unless absolutely necessary, STAY HOME.'[68]

Keeping the Public Informed

Throughout the 2022 event, regular press briefings with the Premier, Lord Mayor and disaster managers were broadcast on television and radio, and more extensive use was made of social media by the authorities than in 2011. BCC posted 288 social media communications to 3,175,251 followers on Facebook and 558,676 on Twitter.[69] However, despite Seqwater, BoM, local government and other agencies' intent to broadcast frequent warnings, the 2022 event revealed the fine balance between knowledge-sharing and bombardment with facts, as well as the additional challenge of sharing ever-changing real-time data in a comprehensible format. Premier Annastacia Palaszczuk told the waiting press on 26 February there was 'no concern for alarm'[70], and, after the flood event, residents complained that early communications like these created a false sense of security, which delayed them taking preventative measures.[71] Dissemination of information was also slow. Ipswich Mayor Teresa Harding criticised the insufficient time given for warning of dam releases, as a post-flood analysis in Ipswich found it took two to four hours after receiving data from BoM and Seqwater to issue flood information to the community.[72] Although BoM advised at 6.00 pm on Saturday 26 February that a major flood was likely the next day, many did not receive this warning for hours, some as late as Sunday evening when it was already too late.[73] Christine, in the rain-drenched suburb of

Alderley, received no warnings at all as her neighbourhood went under.[74]

The most scathing residents described it as a 'total communication failure'.[75] In Newcastle Street, Yeronga, Tim Dean evacuated his wife, two children and cat on Saturday evening, and said:

> The neighbours on the other side had to get us out of the water, the water was already up to my son's chest and the force of the water flowing was difficult to move in, like nothing I'd seen [...] We didn't see anybody coming to help, no police, no SES, nothing at all. They hadn't even bothered blocking the street.[76]

Premier Palaszczuk defended BoM by explaining that they always provided the most up-to-date warnings but the weather defied the forecasts, saying, 'It has been fast and it has been furious and it has had a big impact, this is the facts.' The forecast from Thursday was for conditions to ease but the 'system stayed over' the south-east. Palaszczuk stated, 'everyone expected the conditions to ease but they didn't [...] That is unpredictable. No one, not even the Bureau, saw that coming.'[77] She further explained, 'We didn't know that was going to happen, this is Mother Nature. I can't control Mother Nature, the people of this state can't control Mother Nature, and sometimes they throw stuff at us and we've got to deal with it.'[78]

To some extent this argument harked back to earlier defences as it blamed nature as wilful or evil and framed the flood hazard as external to human action. It also echoed Premier Anna Bligh's press statement in 2011 about 'wrestling back control from nature'.[79] However, Palaszczuk did have a point. This system was indeed unusual, but so too was Somerset's 1893 'wall of water' and the 'inland tsunami' experienced in Toowoomba in 2011. According to BoM, 'the weather in Queensland is complex, arguably more so than in most places in the world'. It is 'highly dynamic and can change rapidly over small distances in short timeframes' and at local scales.[80] The Bremer River can flood low-lying parts of Ipswich in six hours and flash flooding in summer thunderstorms is common in many parts of South East Queensland, a feature of living in the subtropics. Despite significant advances in meteorology, the only certainties are that nature remains unpredictable and well beyond human control.

A large problem with the reporting in 2022 was that BoM gives warnings for riverine flooding, not for creeks or overland flow. The BCC-controlled Weatherzone uses real-time telemetry and disseminates creek data but it does not forecast. In addition, Weatherzone is an opt-in service to which only 14 per cent of Brisbane residents had subscribed in 2022.[81] For the site to be more effective, it needs a much higher take-up rate. ICC has the web-based Disaster Dashboard that provides one site for disaster updates, traffic alerts, weather information and power outages. It too is a useful site but needs more promotion for greater community awareness of the resource.

The constantly changing information and the plethora of information sources contributed to the community confusion. Post-flood analysis found that people were unsure where to find information, and, when they did, the sources were not time stamped and were often out of date. Volumetric constraints on the Emergency Alert system meant alerts had to be sent out in batches and at one stage overload crashed the system.[82] Technology failure always presents challenges in floods: telegraph lines were washed away in 1893, telephone systems were flooded in 1974, websites crashed in 2011 and in 2022 text messaging could not keep up. A battery-operated radio has remained the steadfast communication source.

Comprehending warnings and the implications in a particular locale is difficult. As statistical climatologist Kate Saunders acknowledged, BoM 'issued weather warnings to the best of their ability but what was missing was translation for the general public to act upon'. What was available to residents was 'a PDF of the flood extent map to make decisions. This map only showed one possible flood scenario [...] This flood map also did not show the depth of the water, just whether there was water.'[83] An interactive, web-based map would be more useful as residents could then visualise the situation in their local area, assess the changing dynamics and determine the likelihood of their home flooding. Along with these limitations in resources and messaging, the methods used to disseminate information privileged the more affluent with home access to a computer. They also assumed digital and map literacy, and fluency in English. In Brisbane, 25 per cent of residents speak a language other than English at home (around 14 per cent in Ipswich).[84] Any communication strategies must consider culturally and linguistically diverse communities, an area of need that is being addressed by organisations including the Office of the Inspector General of Emergency Management and Red Cross. The language also needs to be direct, devoid of terminology whenever possible and interpreted to explain real impacts in identifiable locations. For example, a warning that the local creek will be 1.5 metres above normal high tide is more easily interpreted than a height at the City Gauge. Similarly, clear statements broadcast on television or social media that give practical advice to residents in a particular location, such as 'move your car to higher ground' or 'charge your device and prepare for power failure', are more helpful.[85]

In 2022, many people questioned the veracity of the facts when the information source was unclear and acted on their own lived experiences rather than instructions from authorities. They also phoned local government, friends and neighbours, or sought advice via social media. Many found Facebook community groups were the best source of information as they were seen as 'more location-specific and timely', and people didn't have to interrogate multiple websites to find relevant information.[86] These community pages are already moderated by trusted volunteers and are an underused resource in flood preparedness, warnings and the clean-up toolkit.

But webpages and social media depend on power supply,

which is often unavailable during floods. Nicki McCabe moved to Rinora Street, Corinda, near Oxley Creek, after 2011 and knew the house hadn't flooded in 2011 or 1974, so she felt relatively confident. What she didn't realise was that the floodwater would get so high it would isolate the area. She found herself 'relatively dry but marooned in her estate' and without electricity in 2022. The community Facebook page regularly posted where to get food and help, but as her phone went flat she was disconnected from this local intelligence. She instead relied on a battery-operated radio and the ABC, and scrounging every opportunity to recharge her phone. Nicki and her neighbours were completely cut off – 'they couldn't see, hear or connect with the organised support', including emergency accommodation or free meals at community centres. It was, she said, 'as if they were in a different city'. Finding essential supplies and three meals a day, all within walking distance, became 'almost a full-time job'. A grocer in Sherwood offered the community her fridge to save food from perishing in unpowered homes. One of Nicki's equally isolated neighbours initiated a Facebook group for the immediate neighbourhood and established a donation station at the end of the street where people could deliver ice (a vital and rare commodity), sausages and bread (for a sausage sizzle), a generator (charging station) and Nicki contributed gas bottles. Nicki had no power, no food or means of cooking, but she felt a sense of guilt eating as she hadn't flooded. She said, 'others were doing it tough' – their homes were flooded to the rooftop and they were sleeping in cars as they had 'nowhere to go'. She laments, 'there were some very fragile folk around who were feeling very alone'.[87]

Mud Army 2.0

As the floodwaters receded, the clean-up began. The BCC created Mud Army 2.0 on 1 March and 16,747 volunteers registered through Volunteering Queensland to help with the 1,569 requests for help. But on 2 March the region faced volatile weather conditions of 'extremely unstable' storms, with the potential for hail and heavy rainfall on 3 March. The potential wild weather prompted a request from the Premier for all but essential workers to stay home for 48 hours, so Lord Mayor Adrian Schrinner asked the Mud Army to stand down. With creeks saturated and unable to absorb any more rain, Deputy Police Commissioner Shane Chelepy warned those who had flooded 'there is a possibility your home will be inundated again' and to avoid returning home.[88] Fortunately, by 4 March the rain had largely ceased. The Mud Army was again mobilised on 5 March and a group of 1,795 people were sent to 1,039 homes over 180 streets in 21 flood-affected suburbs to remove damaged possessions (Figure 9.5). But, unlike the original Mud Army in 2011, the Mud Army 2.0 was only deployed for one day. On 6 March, Schrinner emailed: 'Due to today's incredible effort, Brisbane City Council has confirmed that the Mud Army 2.0 can put down their tools and volunteers are no longer needed to clean up Brisbane on Sunday.' Instead, the Defence Force and Council would continue the clean-up.[89]

Figure 9.5: West End clean-up. (Courtesy of Jan Bowman)

An informal mud militia took matters into their own hands. Alison Lees, a single mum of three children and a pensioner, who lived in Cliveden Avenue, Corinda, was a grateful recipient of the kindness of friends and strangers. Although flooded in 2011, the house in Corinda was all she could afford after her divorce and she sought comfort that another major flood would be years away.

Facebook, the Graceville Presbyterian Church and her children's school rallied, sending helpful volunteers. She said it took 'worry and jobs off my hands'. People arrived, allocated tasks and sorted things, and she declared the help 'amazing'.[90] Others fed the Corinda community. Shelly Stewart and Donna Bogaart converted 10 bread loaves, 3 kilograms of meat, 3 tubs of butter and 86 slices of cheese into sandwiches. Shelly had been a Mud Army recruit in 2011, but decided she would put her 'old bones' and catering company 'On a Roll' to good use feeding the community.[91]

West End resident Michael Kelly paid tribute to the many people who responded very quickly to the needs of flooded locals. The local federal member organised a sausage sizzle for a couple of days, with local cafes and organisations also providing food. Michael said, 'it is exhausting sorting through flooded belongings and the momentum of people around you pushes you on'. People stayed in the local area as they didn't have anywhere to go. However, by the fourth week he could see the psychological toll, especially in parents with young children as they tried to sort their homes, and go to work and school, while dealing with physical and emotional exhaustion. Michael recalls, 'what stood out to me was the connection of community'. Everyone 'really united together and pitched in to help. It was really encouraging.'[92]

After the floods, residents found the best way to help those affected was by delivering food to those who had no power or kitchens for cooking. In 2022 there were numerous restaurants and cafes that delivered free food and coffee to locals, and coffee shops in West End also provided workspaces with internet and power for people to recharge their phones. Other residents received vouchers to buy petrol for generators or cleaning products, but the supply of items such as towels and ice proved just as helpful. Practical help was also paramount, with plumbers, electricians and tradespeople working on weekends to help residents rebuild.

Looking Back to 2011

Immediately after the 2011 floods, Premier Anna Bligh declared 'some very tough decisions' about rebuilding lay ahead, suggesting that some suburbs may not be rebuilt in the same way. In her words, quoted by *The Courier-Mail* on 20 January: 'We owe it to future generations to bite the bullet and make the right [decisions]. The last thing we want to do is rebuild in the same place and see that home flooded again in two or three years' time.'[93]

But many Queenslanders did not heed Bligh's warning. They simply rebuilt, facilitated by weak planning laws and building codes that allowed them to do so. Many could not afford to relocate or, determined to stay, repaired their flood-damaged homes. Few altered the design or building materials of their properties to increase flood resilience, as insurance and council regulations permitted such inaction. Further, the introduction of compulsory flood insurance encouraged many to stay in the knowledge that future damage would be paid for collectively. Insurance became the bandaid solution to floodplain management, despite some policies being prohibitively expensive. Thus Queensland avoided systemic changes in behaviour or policies.

For many, especially for those unaffected in 2011, the floods receded into memory. The real estate industry recovered, with the fears of a 30 per cent decrease in values predicted in 2011, and described by Australian property monitor Andrew Wilson as 'hysterical', not coming to pass.[94] There was a short-term dip in the property market of between 5 and 10 per cent; however, as the decline was similar in other Australian capital cities, flooding may not have been a significant contributor. Owners repaired properties for sale and advertisements boasted again of full property restoration, without revealing prior flood damage as a causal factor. Within a decade the river had reverted to a benign landscape feature, the floodplains again a developer's paradise, and the region experienced a boom with property prices reaching dizzying heights in 2022.

There were many factors that had encouraged flood complacency.

The response to the 2011 event and the QFCI did little to improve human understanding of floods. A class action was lodged by 6,800 people against the Queensland Government, Seqwater and SunWater for negligence in the operation of Wivenhoe and Somerset dams in the 2011 floods. On 29 November 2019, Supreme Court Justice Robert Beech-Jones found in favour of the plaintiff and claimants, stating that the engineers had not complied with the flood manual and breeched their duty of care.[95] The court did not find that flooding would not have occurred but rather that the actions of the engineers had exacerbated the floods downstream of the dam. In 2021 Seqwater successfully appealed and in May 2021 the NSW Supreme Court approved a settlement payment of $440 million by the Queensland Government and SunWater to 6,500 claimants for damage sustained. The drawn-out process caused pain for many and gave some people very little compensation. The QFCI, public debate and class action reaffirmed in popular thinking that Wivenhoe Dam remained the guarantee of protection – if only it was operated differently.[96]

The 2014 changes to the dam operating manual also gave people false hope that Wivenhoe Dam would withhold future floods, fed by Premier Campbell Newman's assurances to *Courier-Mail* readers that these measures 'will save homes and businesses from the heartbreak of another flood'.[97] As letters to the *Courier-Mail* editor revealed, some of the public did not share Newman's faith in the dams' future flood prevention, maintaining 'Tweaking Wivenhoe rules won't stop floods'. One writer, Sherwood resident Tony Horton, feared the rhetoric would encourage people to build in high-risk areas.[98] Newman's narrative that the floods had been mismanaged offered comfort to those who lived on the floodplain, and he had plenty of vocal supporters in the development industry. Real estate agent Patrick Dixon reported in 2015 that the 'general consensus from buyers is that [the 2011 flood] was a bureaucratic bungle that shouldn't have happened'.[99] The ABC News reported on 10 January 2016 that Fig Tree Pocket agent Cathy Lammie had found 'many flood victims in her area believed it was a man-made flood. That is why so many of them have stayed and rebuilt.'[100]

Taking Proactive Measures

Despite false hopes by residents and developers that floods had been assigned to history, authorities were taking more proactive measures to mitigate the hazard. One of the most successful strategies was moving much of the town of Grantham after it was destroyed by the 2011 floods. A $30 million land swap scheme relocated 110 homes to higher ground, and these homes escaped flooding in 2022, unlike homes on the lower original town site.[101]

Following the 2011 floods the state government also created the Queensland Reconstruction Authority (QRA) as the lead agency responsible for disaster recovery and resilience policy in the state. Part of its remit was to address the QFCI recommendation that a flood study should be available for every urban area in Queensland. In 2011–12 the QRA completed the first state-wide catchment-based floodplain mapping identifying the State's floodplains.[102] A partnership between the Queensland Government, Seqwater, and the local governments of Brisbane, Ipswich, Somerset and Lockyer Valley completed a study that analysed the entire river system downstream of Wivenhoe Dam, as well as revised hydrologic and hydraulic models. The Brisbane River Strategic Floodplain Management Plan followed in April 2019. These documents significantly augmented available data that informs flood management.

Only two days before the 2022 flood, on 24 February, ICC adopted the Ipswich Integrated Catchment Plan that identified 84,000 residents living on the floodplain and 36,380 buildings exposed to flooding (17 per cent in the highest flood risk categories). A 1 in 100 AEP event would inundate more than 15,000 buildings above ground level and leave the city with $1.8 billion in damages ($490 million to residences). The plan was the culmination of two years' work and the most comprehensive flood study ever undertaken by ICC, providing 47 recommendations to improve the city's flood resilience.

Hazard reduction strategies have advanced significantly in the last five years, most notably with the creation of BCC's Flood Resilient Homes Program, which was introduced in 2018 and delivered in partnership with Brisbane Sustainability Agency and James Davidson Architects. The program retrofits houses to make them more flood resilient by modifying designs, changing construction materials and raising the residential areas of buildings. It has been described by the QRA as a 'good practice example of leadership in flood risk management in Queensland'.[103] Participation in the program is voluntary, with 286 properties assessed and 144 homes completed by 2022 (including one house raising) at a cost to BCC of $9,878,860. The Flood Resilient Homes Program can claim success. After the 2022 event, BCC contacted 100 homeowners from the program, and found that 75 people were impacted by floods, of which 62 said the resilience works mitigated damage. BCC is seeking three-tier government funds to expand the scheme.[104]

Since the 2022 floods there have been further government initiatives in the direction of 'flood resilience', with the introduction of schemes that move away from engineering solutions towards better building and town planning. In May 2022 the Queensland government introduced a $741 million Resilient Homes Fund with Commonwealth and State Disaster Recovery funds to be administered by QRA.[105] The intent was encapsulated in the slogan 'build back better'. Homeowners could apply for funds to raise or retrofit their homes, or join a voluntary buy back scheme. There appears to be a public appetite for proactive measures with more than 5,700 homeowners having registered for the Resilient Homes Fund in January 2023.[106]

Retrofitting homes to maximise flood recovery and reduce the hazard is a welcome move, but sometimes it is wiser not to build back. There are many houses in extremely vulnerable areas, deemed by authorities as having high risk, that should be moved. A $350 million Voluntary Home Buy-Back program is part of the $741 million Resilient Homes Fund, also administered by the QRA. The intention is to buy 500 homes, distributed among eight Queensland councils.[107] Under the scheme, home owners will sell their properties to the local councils, the homes will be removed from the floodplain, and the land will be zoned for 'non habitable use'.

In January 2023, the first three homes were demolished in Goodna. Paul Harding was one of the first to accept a buy-back contract as his Goodna house flooded halfway up his second storey in 2022. He says when he heard the contract was signed he was 'doing cartwheels down the street' as he thought he'd be 'stuck with the house' with no chance of selling. He knows floods will come again and now his family faces a happier future.[108] One year after the 2022 flood, ICC has already bought back 40 homes from the 160 negotiations underway. It is an encouraging start for what needs to happen in many parts of South East Queensland (and Australia), but, as the qualifying criteria are tough and the program comes to an end in June 2023, the reality is that many will miss out.

Living with Floods

Christine lives in Alderley, in a single-story post–World War II home that backs onto a creek that feeds into Kedron Brook. Although the creek was regulated into a stormwater channel after the 1974 floods, sections of the land are often 'soft', even in dry times, and in heavy rain the water naturally flows into its familiar path, marked by a tree line. Christine and her husband were largely unaffected by the 2011 floods but in 2022 'there was water everywhere'. Christine says, 'I have never seen a water level like it. Things went under that have never even come close before.' Her 'backyard became a swimming pool' as the creek began 'flowing backwards as Kedron Brook could not take in any more water'. She says, 'It was a different flood [and] you can't forget that, you have to remember that all the time.' They had considered building underneath their home, as had many in the neighbourhood, but won't be now. As Christine explains, '[people] have forgotten the power of Mother Nature and paid the price. You have to respect the site you are living on and unless you are prepared to live with consequences, you must work within the parameters of where you are living.' She knows that floods will come again, and every flood will be different.[109]

Under the banner headline 'The brown snake has turned on us again', journalist Leisa Scott described the 'horror' of the 2022 flood as a 'flashback' to 2011. She expressed the thoughts of many South East Queensland residents: how could it come again so soon after a 'one-in-100 flood' only 11 years earlier? But, as the water receded and the river resettled 'into its languid meanderings', she stated that residents, 'will try, again, to reset the rhythm of our lives'.[110] Perhaps the new rhythm could be more attuned to nature's hydrological cycles, rather than return to business as usual.

With two major floods in relatively quick succession – 2011 and 2022 – both distinct events with different outcomes, we have been given a sharp reminder of the region's subtropical climate, propensity to flood and the complex network of our rivers and creeks. Weather remains difficult to predict and can quickly change. The risk of extreme flooding will increase with climate change as the hazard grows through urban density, and we must make proactive changes to reduce the risk rather than being caught by surprise when the next flood inevitably occurs. We cannot rely on dams to prevent all flooding. Even if Wivenhoe Dam could hold back all the upstream floodwaters, heavy rainfall downstream will fill the creeks and stormwater systems and inundate parts of the city. No manual or structure can accommodate every possible outcome. As every hydrologist will tell you, 'no two floods are the same'.

Conclusion: Floods Will Come Again

While there is a growing acceptance that floods are natural events, and it is human factors that have caused the hazard, many people still believe that Mother Nature is to blame or that floods can be prevented. The faith in engineering and technology to flood-proof Brisbane has persisted, despite centuries of flooding. The nineteenth-century rhetoric of 'taming', 'controlling' and 'harnessing' the river with technocratic means to prevent floods has prevailed into the twentieth and twenty-first centuries, along with the untrammelled enthusiasm to develop the floodplain.

With few exceptions after flooding, newspapers rarely offer articles or informed debate on non-structural mitigation strategies that include public education, floodplain management, land-use planning or building codes. The fallacy that the complexities of hydrology can be reduced to a single strategy, codified and guided by the successful application of a dam-operating manual, endures. Dams can reduce flood peaks and withhold smaller floods, but they have a finite capacity and they are not a panacea. And, as Brisbane residents witnessed in 2022, water falling downstream of the dam resulting in creek flooding and overland flow can be just as devastating as 'controlled' riverine flooding. Have these recent events shifted the faith in dams towards a greater understanding of the complexities of flood behaviour and the need for other proactive measures? Only time, or the next flood, will tell.

*

This book has explored the evolving relationship between the Brisbane River system and its floodplain dwellers from colonial settlement in the 1820s to the floods of 2022. Despite centuries of Turrbal and Jagera knowledge, and almost 200 years of settler experience and hydrological research into devastating floods, successive generations have adopted the same approach: attempt to control the river.

European explorers and early settlers were impressed by the bounty offered by the river and its fertile banks. The floodplains were cleared, subdivided and developed, actions imbued with notions of improvement, progress and human superiority over nature. The settlers displayed little understanding that the floodplain is an integral part of the river's ecological structure and nature's flood mitigation tool. When the 1893 floods threatened dreams of urban settlement and linear progress, the government called on engineers to modify the river, first with dredging, truncation and building training walls, and later with the construction of Somerset Dam. This created a dependency on dams to mitigate floods. After the 1974 floods, the completion of the larger Wivenhoe Dam continued this one-dimensional flood control policy, despite an increasing reliance on non-structural solutions interstate and internationally.

With the inferred flood protection provided by dams, building on the floodplain grew concomitantly with the hazard. Successive state governments were heavily dependent on property as an economic stimulant, creating an interdependence of government, political parties, industry, developers and unions who all backed, or at least did not question, floodplain development. A growth imperative, vested interests and a community antipathy to regulations made land management politically unpalatable. Intergovernmental obfuscation over responsibility for riverine flood mitigation allowed development on the floodplain to flourish. With increasing faith in dams, management of the floodplain seemed redundant, especially as drought eroded flood memory and made the substantial numbers of new arrivals to South East Queensland increasingly unaware of the inherent risk of flood in a subtropical climate. Governments and those in property-related industries did little to dispel the myth that Brisbane had been flood-proofed by Wivenhoe Dam.

The 2011 floods undermined the flood immunity myth but only briefly challenged the wisdom of floodplain development. Even a crude comparison of the effects of the 1974 and 2011 floods highlights that the human-induced hazard grew substantially. The policy of relying on dams, at the expense of other flood mitigation strategies, had been found wanting. But rather than call for change to the state government's dependency on dams for flood mitigation in favour of adopting more resilient practices, the debate degenerated into a blame game. Suggestions of state or local government culpability were diverted by a media focus on the failure of the dam or the engineers operating it. These ideas persisted in a class action that did little to inform South East Queenslanders about the real risk of the region's flood hazard and prevented discussion of the need for legislation to curtail future floodplain development. While the hydrological reality is that dams cannot prevent floods, only mitigate them, the dominant and persistent belief is that properly operated dams will prevent flooding.

As the 2022 floods demonstrated, if the rain is heavy enough over a short duration, nothing can prevent floods. Wivenhoe Dam withheld voluminous amounts of rain, but, as in the 2011 event, dam releases were essential. South East Queenslanders also had a harsh lesson that riverine flooding is not the region's only flood hazard. As large quantities of rain fell downstream of the dam and into the extensive network of creeks, localised flooding was largely unpreventable. Stormwater systems struggled with the deluge of hundreds of millimetres of rain in a short space of time and overland flooding was inevitable. Flood mitigation cannot solely rely on dams – it also requires measures to control land use on riverine floodplains as well as near creeks and low-lying areas susceptible to flash flooding.

*

Brisbane's flood history has been shaped by notions of environmental control, as well as the perceived need to manage both droughts and floods and the inherent tension this causes. A dependency on dams has encouraged minimal regulation of the floodplain, increased the flood hazard and reduced resilience. Diminishing flood memories allow complacency, buttressed by the delusion that humans have controlled nature by taming the river. But the quick succession of substantial floods in 2011 and 2022 should erode myths that floods are infrequent and always occur in the same way. In the words of wildfire specialist Max Moritz and historian Scott Gabriel Knowles, 'to save people and property, we need to abandon the myth of control'.[1] We need to learn to live with the river.

As a society we have reached a tipping point. Future floods are inevitable. While the timing, temporal and spatial characteristics of the next flood are unknown, its arrival is certain. With climate change there is an increased chance of more intense rain and flooding because every additional degree in temperature means the atmosphere can hold around 7 per cent more moisture.[2] With a warming climate, most scientists predict that future floods will be greater than those in 1841 and 1893. We have built Somerset and Wivenhoe dams to mitigate floods, but there are no other suitable dam sites. This strategy has reached its logical conclusion. As we continue to build on the floodplain, we increase the flood hazard and the cost of reconstruction. Have we reached the stage that moving people is more economically viable than staying on the floodplain? The move towards resilient home construction and buy-back schemes gives hope for an alternative future where the region addresses its flood realities.

As the urban footprint of South East Queensland grows, more impermeable surfaces are created, creeks are filled in and fluvial pathways are blocked or altered, making it increasingly difficult for water to escape. Along with business and residential relocation schemes, we can improve urban areas to reduce flooding with nature-based measures. Known as 'blue-green solutions', such measures include planting vegetation to soak up water and reduce erosion, and building rainwater parks, tanks and permeable footpaths to help absorb rain. South East Queensland needs to embrace every flood mitigation strategy available, but the best strategy is to stop making matters worse. Brisbane already has the most densely developed floodplain in Australia and we need to restrict building in areas more vulnerable to flooding. Governments should implement stronger legislation, regulations, town plans and building codes to discourage, or prohibit, further floodplain development.

South East Queensland's response to floods has almost entirely been reactionary, a problem that is shared nationally. The Australian Productivity Commission in 2014 found that 97 per cent of federal 'disaster money' is spent on the clean-up up after disasters rather than prevention.[3] This focus on rescuing and rebuilding allows the cycle of destruction to escalate. As we saw in 2011 and 2022, the community rallied after flood disasters to form a Mud Army and help those who had been affected. When faced with warnings of impending major flooding, could we not form a Flood Army to help move people, animals and possessions to higher ground in advance of the floodwaters? Are there ways to harness existing community networks or social media to disseminate accurate information quickly in advance of, and during, the next flood to help people make informed decisions? As the flood memories fade and thoughts move to the next hydrological cycle of droughts and bushfires, can we educate the public about the real risks? How else can we change the way we build and where we live to reduce the number of homes impacted by flooding? This is the time to prepare and implement hazard reduction strategies. A shift towards proactive measures could save lives and millions of dollars. With our changing climate and urban growth there is an increasing urgency to embrace innovative mitigation strategies.

Ultimately governments (state and local) must determine the level of flood risk the community is prepared to accept. If governments and the wider community are not prepared to reduce the hazard through greater regulation of the floodplain or public education, then we must accept the residual flood risk. As a society we have been responsible for increasing the flood hazard and must live with the consequences. When floods occur, we cannot look for individuals to blame for collective systemic failure. We also cannot assume that future disasters will play out in the same way as they have in the past. As Joseph Powell reminds us in his history of water resources, 'floods and droughts will always return, as is their wont, but truly adaptive societies do not choose to suffer the same calamities time and again'.[4] Sophisticated societies adapt to reduce the hazard and increase human resilience. If braver, more substantial planning changes and appropriate land resumptions had been made after the 1974 floods, the impact of the 2011 and 2022 floods would have been much reduced.

Time will tell if South East Queensland remains locked in a cycle of destruction and rebuilding where governments continue to refuse to constrain development on the floodplain. But government initiatives such as the QRA and Resilient Homes Fund indicate a political will and community support to adapt our floodplain management strategies. As we've seen from the stories of those who lost homes and livelihoods during flood events, public education is also needed to help us develop a deeper environmental awareness that floods are an essential and inevitable part of a river's hydrological cycle, one that the dams can only mitigate and not prevent, and can never be truly predicted or controlled. Permanent settlement on the floodplain has created an urban flood hazard that only humans can address. If we could find the courage to make the systemic changes needed to allow us all to live with floods then, as a society, we might foster a harmonious relationship with the Brisbane River, Maiwar, as the Turrbal and Jagera people have for centuries. Perhaps in time we will accept that it is a river with a city problem and not the other way around.

Acknowledgements

No book is written in isolation, either through the scholarship that has come before it or those people and experiences that assist along the journey. This book began as a PhD at The University of Queensland under the skilful supervision of Dr Melissa Harper and Professor Peter Spearritt, and with the financial support of the Australian Government Research Training Program Scholarship. The 2022 floods prompted the addition of a new chapter.

The water fraternity – hydrologists and civil engineers – have been extremely generous with their time and knowledge. They helped me comprehend the complexities of river hydrology and hydrography, megalitres, cumecs, flow rates and more, providing me with insights into flood behaviour and management that I would never have discovered on my own. The assistance and data provided by Seqwater is much appreciated, and many thanks to the Floods Community of Practice, the Queensland Disaster Management Research Advisory Panel, and disaster managers and scholars for their generous sharing of knowledge. I especially wish to acknowledge Geoffrey Cossins, Geoffrey Heatherwick, Peter Baddiley, Terry Malone and Mike Foster for constant help and patience.

Interviews with riverside dwellers who endured the 1974, 2011 and 2022 floods, including those that Robyn Buchanan and I conducted in 2011 (now on the ICC website), provided information on the human impact of floods and responses. Thanks especially to John Adams, Kate Cantrell, Cedric Chu, Robyn Flashman, Jean and Graham Gahan, Michael Kelly, Kate Kirby, Sue Kirk, Nicki McCabe, Rachel Nolan, Cathy O'Malley, Beryl and Ken Wilson, and Christine (last name withheld) for their interviews, and to Chas Keys for helping me determine interstate comparisons. Discussions with Turrbal elder Joe Kirk taught me about Indigenous understandings of rivers as did a Museum of Brisbane exhibition. My kayaking field trip to the confluence of the Stanley and Brisbane rivers and visits to the site of Caboonbah Homestead, and Somerset and Wivenhoe dams – all pivotal flood places – reaffirmed R. H. Tawney's school of thought that 'historians need strong boots' to understand history.

Librarians and archivists are vital allies in any historical endeavour and I am indebted to the assistance of the Queensland State Archives staff and Cheryl McNamara of the National Archives in Brisbane and her Canberra colleagues. Many fruitful hours were spent at BCC Archives with archivist Annabel Lloyd and Robert Noffke. State Library of Queensland, National Library, Fryer Library, ICC heritage branch, Dandiiri Schools and Community Library, and Ipswich City Council Library staff (especially Sally Hetherington) deserve great thanks. I am grateful to those who have provided photos: Jan Bowman, Kate Cantrell, John Doody, Sally Hetherington, Miranda Joye, Jackie Ryan, Catherine Solomon, BCC Archives, Marist College Ashgrove Old Boys' Association, Newspix, Picture Ipswich and State Library of Queensland.

Attendance at conferences exposed me to the scholarship and intellectual generosity of environmental historians. I particularly wish to acknowledge those who attended the Foreign Bodies, Intimate Ecologies Conference at Macquarie University, February 2016, and the 'Green Streams' at the Australian Historical Association conferences that helped my work find its intellectual home. The greatest boost in this regard was attending the National Environmental History PhD Workshop, run by Libby Robin, Tom Griffiths, Heather Goodall and Jane Carruthers at the Australian

National University in 2016. Many of the students I met that week have become an invaluable support group. Thanks also to all the stimulating audience questions at conferences and book talks as these helped shaped my thinking for the 2022 chapter. I appreciate the generosity of people who shared stories and photos in response to Facebook call-outs and to my readers for their encouragement to update the book.

Thank you to Nick Earls and Alexandra Payne for your early enthusiastic support for publication and to Madonna Duffy and her team at University of Queensland Press for embracing this project. To my editor, Felicity Dunning, thank you! From the outset you understood this book and gently nurtured and shaped the prose for appreciation for a wider audience, with infectious enthusiasm (twice!).

Immense gratitude goes to my close friends and family who have weathered this experience with me, without complaints of neglect. Thanks especially to Jodi Frawley, Donna and Kevin Bracker, Corey Cassidy, Sandy Horneman-Wren and the Bartetzko family. To my parents, Ian and Helen Pullar, I am thrilled that you instilled in me a lifelong love of history and reading, and to you and my sister, Jean Yates, thank you for your invaluable editing skills and proofreading. To my brother and sister-in-law, Stuart and Susan Pullar, thanks for sharing your flood stories and social networks. Special thanks to my sons, Andrew and Cameron, for their unending support and faith in me to write this book. To my husband, Nick, who prepared diagrams and maps, critiqued innumerable drafts and endured hours of discussion with infinite patience, my love and thanks are not enough for making this challenge possible.

Notes on Sources

While there are histories of interstate and overseas rivers and floods, many of which are cited in the endnotes, there are few that deal with Brisbane River floods. Consequently, I depended heavily on primary sources. Newspapers provided a rich lode, aided considerably by the National Library of Australia's digitised newspapers (Trove) and cuttings collections held by the State Library of Queensland and ICC. Not all articles in the cuttings collection have dates or page numbers, and these have been identified where possible. Newspapers are referenced when directly quoted, but I generally draw on articles in the months around the specific floods. Oral histories, diaries, photographs, television footage and letters provided essential insights. Official documents used include government departmental annual reports, parliamentary debates, legislation, town plans, maps, council records, and dam operation manuals supplemented by engineering reports.

Each major flood had key documents – the Queensland Hydraulic Engineer's reports for 1893; reports by BoM and the Department of Social Security and papers from a flood symposium held by the Institution of Engineers for 1974; the Queensland Flood Commission of Inquiry documents for 2011; Seqwater and BoM reports for 2011 and 2022; and reports for BCC and ICC, as well as those by the Queensland Reconstruction Authority and the Office of the Inspector General of Emergency Management in 2022. Papers produced by engineer hydrologist Geoffrey Cossins (many held in the BCC Archives) proved an invaluable resource. The National Archives of Australia, Queensland State Archives and BCC Archives hold many catalogued files on the Brisbane River (especially for the 1893 and 1974 floods) and considerable information about the 2011 and 2022 floods can be found online. Seqwater provided flood height data, all rainfall data was taken from the BoM website and census figures came from the Australian Bureau of Statistics, unless otherwise stated. The map of the Brisbane River Catchment was drawn by Nick Cook using base data from Queensland Spatial Catalogue and Queensland Globe.

Current flood maps can be found for Brisbane at floodinformation. brisbane.qld.gov.au/fio/ and Ipswich at www.ipswichplanning.com. au/flood-map-information.

Notes

Introduction: A Meandering River

1   U. Lübken, 'Rivers and Risk in the City: The Urban Floodplain as a Contested Space', in S. Castonguay & M. Evenden (eds), *Urban Rivers: Remaking Rivers, Cities, and Space in Europe and North America*, University of Pittsburgh Press, Pittsburgh, 2012, p. 131.

2   M. Cioc, *The Rhine: An Eco-Biography, 1815–2000*, University of Washington Press, Seattle, 2002, p. 33.

3   D. Malouf, *A First Place*, Random House Australia, Sydney, 2014, p. 7.

4   Quoted in H. Goodall, 'The River Runs Backwards', in T. Bonyhady & T. Griffiths (eds), *Words for Country: Landscape and Language in Australia*, University of New South Wales Press, Sydney, 2002, p. 41.

5   H. Goodall, 'The River Runs Backwards', p. 36.

6   K. Wittfogel, *Oriental Despotism: A Comparative Study of Total Power*, Yale University Press, New Haven, 1957.

7   This term, used by Sara Pritchard to describe the Rhône in France, is equally applicable to most modern rivers. S. Pritchard, *Confluence: The Nature of Technology and the Remaking of the Rhône*, Harvard University Press, Cambridge, 2011, pp. 6, 11.

8   R. White, *The Organic Machine: The Remaking of the Columbia River*, Hill and Wang, New York, 1995, pp. 1, 108.

9   The following are rare exceptions: J. Steele, *The Brisbane River*, Rigby, Brisbane, 1976; H. Gregory, *The Brisbane River Story: Meanders through Time*, Australian Marine Conservation Society, Brisbane, 1996; R. Buchanan, *The Bremer River*, Ipswich City Council, Ipswich, 2009.

10   S. Pyne, *Burning Bush: A Fire History of Australia*, Henry Holt & Company, New York, 1991, p. xii.

11   P. Troy, 'Introduction: The Water Services Problem', in P. Troy (ed.), *Troubled Waters: Confronting the Water Crisis in Australia's Cities*, ANU E Press, Canberra, 2008, p. 1.

12   Only in Southern Africa is the annual variability greater. B. L. Finlayson & T. A. McMahon, 'Australia v the World: A Comparative Analysis of Streamflow Characteristics', in R. F. Warner (ed.), *Fluvial Geomorphology of Australia*, Academic

Press, Sydney, 1988, p. 27; J. Kemp et al, 'River Response to the European Settlement in the Subtropical Brisbane River', *Anthropocene*, no. 11, December 2015, p. 3.

Chapter 1: Encountering the Floodplain

1   S. Ruska, 'Moodagurra and the forming of the Brisbane River', *Brisbane Blacks Monthly*, 2 October 2012. Shannon Ruska is a storyteller and a Nunukul Yuggera man. This account was provided by the Brisbane Museum and the Dandiiri Library and Community Centre. Uncle Joe Kirk, Turrbal and Wakka Wakka elder, rejects the serpent story, instead telling the story of the freshwater eel, or Duegum, the spiritual totem of Jagera people, creating the Brisbane River. Joe Kirk, interview with author, 22 May 2017.
2   Neville Bonner, transcript of interview by Robyn Buchanan, Ipswich City Council, 1995, pp. 2–3.
3   C. Petrie, *Tom Petrie's Reminiscences of Early Queensland*, Watson Ferguson and Co., Brisbane, 1904, pp. 89–91, 148; W. Clark, 'A Jubilee Retrospect – The City of South Brisbane', *The Queenslander*, 7 August 1909, p. 21; Joe Kirk, interview with author.
4   R. Kerkhove, *Aboriginal Campsites of Greater Brisbane: An Historical Guide*, Boolorong Press, Brisbane, 2015, p. 1.
5   E. Coxen, 'Notes on Floods in the Brisbane River'. Read before the Royal Society of Queensland, 21 August 1893, BCC Archives, BCA File 1577.
6   A. Meston, 'Floods and Droughts', *The Queenslander*, 29 March 1890, pp. 599–600. The meaning 'big flowing water' for Magenjie is given by C. Moynihan, 'To the editor', *The Queenslander*, 17 August 1901, p. 328.
7   'Flood Prevention', *The Queensland Times, Ipswich Herald and General Advertiser*, 2 November 1929, p. 8.
8   I. Jones, 'The Floods of the Brisbane River'. Read before the Historical Society of Queensland, 28 July 1931, p. 288.
9   J. Steele, *The Explorers of the Moreton Bay District 1770–1830*, University of Queensland Press, Brisbane, 1992, p. 151; C. Petrie, *Tom Petrie's Reminiscences of Early Queensland*, p. 75; T. Bonyhady & T. Griffiths (eds), *Words for Country: Landscape and Language in Australia*, pp. 69–70.
10 Quoted in J. Steele, *The Brisbane River*, p. 13.
11 Quoted in J. Steele, *The Explorers of the Moreton Bay District 1770–1830*, pp. 101–116.
12 P. Read, *Returning to Nothing: The Meaning of Lost Places*, Cambridge University Press, Cambridge, 1996, p. 3.
13 V. Strang, *Uncommon Ground: Cultural Landscapes and Environmental Values*, Berg, Oxford, 1997, p. 217.
14 Queensland remained part of the Colony of New South Wales until separation in 1859.
15 J. Steele, *The Explorers of the Moreton Bay District 1770–1830*, pp. 160, 164.
16 J. C. Scott, *Seeing Like a State: How Certain Schemes to Improve the Human Condition Have Failed*, Yale University Press, New Haven, 1998, pp. 11–12.
17 *Sydney Gazette and New South Wales Advertiser*, p. 2.
18 Quoted in J. Steele, *The Explorers of the Moreton Bay District 1770–1830*, p. 136.
19 Quoted in J. M. Powell, *Plains of Promise, Rivers of Destiny: Water Management and the Development of Queensland 1824–1990*, Boolarong Publications, Brisbane,

1991, p. 7; J. Steele, *The Explorers of the Moreton Bay District 1770–1830*, pp. 160, 164, 192, 199.

20   H. Gregory, *The Brisbane River Story*, p. 22.

21   *The Brisbane Courier*, 2 March 1893, p. 4.

22   'The Brisbane River 100 Years Ago', *The Brisbane Courier*, 22 March 1930, p. 10.

23   J. C. Scott, *Seeing Like a State*, pp. 55–58; G. Bolton, *Spoils and Spoilers*, George Allen and Unwin, Sydney, 1981, pp. 17, 59; W. R. Johnston, *Brisbane, The First Thirty Years*, Boolarong Publications, Brisbane, 1988, p. 34.

24   Quoted in W. R. Johnston, *Brisbane, The First Thirty Years*, p. 34.

25   Quoted in G. Greenwood & J. Laverty, *Brisbane 1859–1959: A History of Local Government*, Oswald Ziegler, Brisbane, 1959, p. 35.

26   R. Buchanan, *The Bremer River*, pp. 21–23, 112.

27   'Moreton Bay', *The Australian*, 24 February 1842, p. 1.

28   L. Macquarie, 'Government and General Orders, Government House, Sydney, Wednesday, 5th March 1817', *Sydney Gazette and New South Wales Advertiser*, 22 March 1817, p. 1.

29   T. Sherratt, 'Human Elements', in T. Sherratt, T. Griffiths & L. Robin (eds), *A Change in the Weather: Climate and Culture in Australia*, National Museum of Australia, Canberra, 2005, p. 6.

30   T. Sherratt, 'Human Elements', p. 4.

31   T. Griffiths, *Forests of Ash: An Environmental History*, Cambridge University Press, Cambridge, 2001 pp. 32–35; P. Coates, 'Can Nature Improve Technology?', in M. Reuss & S. H. Cutcliffe (eds), *The Illusory Boundary: Environment and Technology in History*, University of Virginia Press, Charlottesville, 2010, p. 44.

32   'Random Sketches by a Traveller through the District of East Moreton', *The Moreton Bay Courier*, 12 March 1859, p. 3.

33   *An Act for Regulating the Occupation of Unoccupied Crown Lands in the Unsettled District of 1890*, Act 24, no. 11, Victoria.

34   J. D. Lang, *Queensland, Australia: A Highly Eligible Field for Emigration, and the Future Cotton-field of Great Britain*, Edward Stanford, London, 1861, pp. 60–62, 77.

35   'Labour', *The Moreton Bay Courier*, 4 July 1846, p. 2.

36   Auction notice, *The Moreton Bay Courier*, 9 June 1849, p. 3.

37   W. Davenport, *Harbours and Marine: Port and Harbour Development in Queensland 1824–1985*, Harbours and Marine, Brisbane, 1986, p. 49.

38   W. Davenport, *Harbours and Marine*, p. 208.

39   For information on dredging, see W. Davenport, *Harbours and Marine*, pp. 207–208; H. Gregory, *The Brisbane River Story*, p. 118; I. Cameron, *125 Years of State Public Works in Queensland 1859–1984*, Boolarong Publications, Brisbane, 1989, p. 29.

40   'Local Intelligence', *The Moreton Bay Courier*, 20 June 1846, p. 3; 'The Government Puddle Again', *The Moreton Bay Courier*, 26 February 1859, p. 2.

41   Letter to editor, 'The Water Supply', *The Moreton Bay Courier*, 24 March 1858, p. 2; 'The Supply of Water', *The Moreton Bay Courier*, 23 March 1850, p. 2.

42   Quoted in R. L. Whitmore, *Queensland's Early Waterworks*, Department of Natural Resources Queensland, Brisbane, 1997, pp. 3–9.

43   Joe Kirk, interview with author.

44   R. L. Whitmore, *Queensland's Early Waterworks*, pp. 79, 89–93; Joe Kirk, interview with author; 'The Ipswich Water Works', *The Telegraph*, 23 March 1878, p. 3; R. Buchanan, *The Bremer River*, pp. 67–69; 'Domestic Intelligence Ipswich', *The Moreton Bay Courier*, 31 July 1847, p. 2.

45 H. Gregory, *The Brisbane River Story*, p. 78.
46 'The Moreton Bay District', *The Star* (Ballarat), 18 September 1856, p. 1.
47 Arthur Martin & Co.'s Advertisements, *The Telegraph*, 24 January 1885, p. 10.
48 'A Hexagon Land Syndicate', *The Telegraph*, 19 June 1884, p. 4.
49 R. L. Lawson, *Brisbane in the 1890s: A Study of an Australian Urban Society*, University of Queensland Press, Brisbane, 1973, p. 12.
50 'The Flood in Brisbane', *The Darling Downs Gazette*, 15 March 1890, p. 5.
51 A. Meston, 'Floods and Droughts', *The Queenslander*, 29 March 1890, pp. 599–600.

Chapter 2: Mighty Outbreak of Nature's Forces: The 1893 Floods

1 'Buninyong Hurricane. Mr. Wragge's "Red Letter Day"', *The Week*, 24 February 1893, p. 13. In 1893, the terms 'hurricane' and 'cyclone' were both used for the same meteorological phenomena.
2 'Floods in Southern Queensland', *The Brisbane Courier*, 3 February 1893, p. 5.
3 C. Wragge, *Nature*, 4 May 1893, p. 3.
4 Bureau of Industry, Roads, Mining and General Works Committee, *Brisbane Water Supply and Flood Prevention: Interim Report of the Special Committee*, 1933, p. 12, Queensland State Archives, ID 276173.
5 Henry Plantagenet Somerset to the Commissioner, cited in *Esk Record*, 18 June 1932, p. 1. Henry Somerset similarly informed the 1927 Gutteridge Royal Commission: A. G. Gutteridge, 'Commission of Enquiry, Brisbane Water Supply Report', *Queensland Parliamentary Papers*, vol. 2, 1928.
6 J. B. Henderson, 'Floods, Brisbane and Mary Rivers: Second Interim Report', Annual Report of Hydraulic Engineer for Water Supply, *Queensland Votes and Proceedings*, vol. 3, 1895, p. 1469.
7 'Floods in Southern Queensland', *The Brisbane Courier*, 3 February 1893, p. 5.
8 'Bellevue', *The Queensland Times*, 11 February 1893, p. 8.
9 G. Harris, 'Reminiscences of My Early Days in Ipswich', Fryer Manuscript, 1923.
10 'The Flood in Ipswich', *Toowoomba Chronicle and Darling Downs General Advertiser*, 7 February 1893, p. 2.
11 'Wednesday's Intelligence', *The Queensland Times*, 11 February 1893, p. 10.
12 'The Colliery Disaster', *The Queensland Times*, 11 February 1893, p. 10; P. McQuade, J. McQuade, M. Cuthbertson, A. Smart & C. Walker, *Magisterial Enquiry into the Cause of Death of Thomas Wright, George Wright*, 27 May 1893, Queensland State Archives, ID 248808, no. 312. For a detailed account, see J. Phillips, *The Wrights of Tivoli*, Ipswich, 2002, pp. 83–89.
13 'Floods at Ipswich', *The Queensland Times*, 4 February 1893, p. 5; 'Disastrous Floods in the Bremer and Brisbane', *The Queensland Times*, 7 February 1893, p. 3.
14 'Floods in Southern Queensland', *The Brisbane Courier*, 3 February 1893, p. 4; 'Summary of News', *The Brisbane Courier*, 3 February 1893, p. 4.
15 'The Late Floods', *The Brisbane Courier*, 9 February 1893, p. 2.
16 'Floods in Southern Queensland', *The Brisbane Courier*, 3 February 1893, p. 5.
17 'Disastrous Floods', *The Brisbane Courier*, 6 February 1893, p. 3.
18 'The Brisbane Courier', *The Brisbane Courier*, 6 February 1893, p. 2.
19 'Victoria Bridge Gone', and 'The Floods', *The Brisbane Courier*, 6 February 1893, pp. 2–4.
20 'The Great Floods', *The Town and Country Journal*, 18 February 1893, p. 27.

21 'Disastrous Floods', *The Brisbane Courier*, 6 February 1893, p. 2; *The Brisbane Courier*, 8 February 1893, p. 2.

22 'Toowong', *The Week*, 10 February 1893, p. 5.

23 'Engelsburg', *The Queensland Times*, 9 February 1893, p. 5.

24 'Meteorology of Australasia', *The Brisbane Courier*, 17 February 1893, p. 5.

25 'The Southern Floods', *The Daily Northern Argus* (Rockhampton), 17 February 1893, p. 5.

26 H. Somerset, *Esk Record*, 18 June 1932, p. 1; Transcripts of Commission of Inquiry Brisbane Water Supply Report, Fifth Day, 19 August 1927, BCC Archives, BCA File 0770; M. Cook & A. Lloyd, 'Unpacking a Legend', *Circa*, no. 6, 2018, pp. 21–27.

27 Bureau of Industry, Roads, Mining and General Works Committee, *Brisbane Water Supply and Flood Prevention*, p. 12.

28 'Latest Flood News', *The Brisbane Courier*, 20 February 1893, p. 5.

29 T. Pugh, *Pugh's Almanac and Queensland Directory*, Brisbane, 1894, p. 76.

30 'The Weather and Storms', *The North Queensland Register* (Townsville), 22 February 1893, p. 32.

31 'Floods at Ipswich', *The Telegraph*, 24 February 1893, p. 3; 'The Flood in Ipswich', *The Queenslander*, 4 March 1893, p. 421; 'The Recent Floods', *The Brisbane Courier*, 24 February 1893, p. 5.

32 'Goodna and Ipswich', *The Brisbane Courier*, 3 March 1893, p. 6.

33 'Milton and Toowong', *The Queenslander*, 25 February 1893, p. 372.

34 'Another Terrible Flood in Brisbane', *The Sydney Morning Herald*, 20 February 1893, p. 5.

35 'On One-tree Hill', *The Telegraph*, 8 February 1893, p. 5.

36 'Kangaroo Point', *The Telegraph*, 7 February 1893, p. 2; 'Indooroopilly', *The Telegraph*, 27 February 1893, p. 6.

37 Eleanor Bourne Papers, State Library of Queensland Manuscript, OM8–129.

38 'Yeronga and Rocklea', *The Queenslander*, 11 February 1893, p. 278.

39 'Swan Hill and Windsor', *The Telegraph*, 6 February 1893, p. 3.

40 'Silt in the River', *The Telegraph*, 28 February 1893, p. 4.

41 'On One-tree Hill', *The Telegraph*, 8 February 1893, p. 5.

42 J. B. Henderson, 'Floods in Brisbane River, and Schemes for Abatement of their Disastrous Effects', Annual Report of the Hydraulic Engineer for Water Supply, *Queensland Votes and Proceedings*, vol. 4, 1896, p. 2.

43 James Florence Inquest, Queensland State Archives, ID 348808, no. 59.

44 'Great Floods in Queensland', *The Town and Country Journal*, 18 February 1893, p. 28; John Power Inquest, Queensland State Archives, ID 248808, no. 124; 'Magisterial Inquiries', *The Brisbane Courier*, 24 February 1893, p. 3.

45 George Keogh Inquest, Queensland State Archives, ID 348808, no. 71.

46 'Suicide at Indooroopilly', *The Queensland Times*, 7 March 1893, p. 3; 'Gatton', *The Week*, 17 March 1893, p. 23.

47 'The Weather and Storms', *The North Queensland Register*, 22 February 1893, p. 32.

48 'A Journal of the Floods: Some Personal Experiences', *The Worker*, 11 February 1893, p. 2.

49 'The Flood in Ipswich', *Capricornia* (Rockhampton), 25 February 1893, p. 12. Emily O'Gorman noted in the 1844 Gundagai floods in New South Wales that knowledge of previous floods became a liability: E. O'Gorman, *Flood Country: An Environmental History of the Murray-Darling Basin*, CSIRO Publishing, Collingwood, Victoria, 2012, p. 24.

50 'The Flood in Wivenhoe Pocket', *The Queensland Times*, 21 February 1893, p. 6; Telegraph Newspaper Company, *Souvenir of Foods*, February 1893; 'Fernvale', *The Queenslander*, 18 February 1893, p. 323.

51 'The Floods', *The Darling Downs Gazette*, 11 February 1893, p. 4.

52 'From River Terrace', *The Telegraph*, 8 February 1893, p. 2.

53 'The Brisbane Courier', *The Brisbane Courier*, 6 February 1893, p. 2.

54 'The Brisbane Courier', *The Brisbane Courier*, 8 February 1893, p. 2.

55 'The Late Floods', *The Brisbane Courier*, 10 February 1893, p. 6.

56 *Central Flood Relief Fund of Queensland 1893*, Central Executives Report to the Subscribers, Queensland State Archives, ID 1139524.

57 'A Day of Humiliation', *The Brisbane Courier*, 22 February 1893, p. 7.

58 'National Sins', *The Week*, 24 February 1893, p. 16; 'Day of Humiliation', *The Telegraph*, 22 February 1893, p. 4; 'Day of Humiliation and Prayer', *The Queenslander*, 17 June 1893, p. 1111.

59 'Day of Humiliation', *The Telegraph*, 22 February 1893, p. 4.

60 'The Brisbane Courier', *The Brisbane Courier*, 20 February 1893, p. 4.

61 As noted by T. Steinberg, *Acts of God: The Unnatural History of Natural Disaster in America*, Oxford University Press, Oxford, 2000, p. xxi; A. Kelman, *A River and Its City: The Nature of Landscape in New Orleans*, University of California Press, Berkeley, 2003, p. 187.

62 'The Brisbane Courier', *The Brisbane Courier*, 20 February 1893, p. 4.

63 'The Brisbane Courier', *The Brisbane Courier*, 8 February 1893, p. 2.

64 'The Flood at Fig-tree Pocket', *The Queenslander*, 11 March 1893, p. 477.

65 T. Griffiths, 'The Language of Catastrophe: Forgetting, Blaming and Bursting into Colour,' *Griffith Review 35* (Autumn 2012), p. 52. This trend has been noted by M. Everard, *The Hydro-Politics of Dams: Engineering or Ecosystems*, Zed Books, London, 2013, p. 155; E. O'Gorman, *Flood Country*, p. 24; D. Blackbourn, *The Conquest of Nature: Water, Landscape and the Making of Modern Germany*, W. W. Norton and Company, New York, 2006, pp. 191–193; S. Pritchard & T. Zeller, 'The Nature of Industrialisation', in M. Reuss & S. H. Cutcliffe (eds), *The Illusory Boundary: Environment and Technology in History*, University of Virginia Press, Charlottesville, 2010, p. 85.

66 'North Ipswich', *The Queensland Times*, 21 February 1893, p. 5; 'East Ipswich', *The Queensland Times*, 21 February 1893, p. 5; 'The Flood', *The Telegraph*, 7 February 1893, p. 2; *The Darling Downs Gazette*, 20 February 1893, p. 3.

67 'Ipswich', *The Queenslander*, 25 February 1893, p. 373.

68 'Latest Flood News', *The Brisbane Courier*, 13 February 1893, p. 2.

69 'To the Memory of Constable Sangster', *The Queensland Times*, 28 February 1893, p. 2.

70 'The Floods', *The Maryborough Chronicle*, 7 February 1893, p. 2; 'The Recent Floods', *The Brisbane Courier*, 10 February 1893, p. 5; 'Booroodabin and Valley', *The Telegraph*, 17 February 1893, p. 6.

Chapter 3: Taming the River

1 A. R. L. Wright, 'Relieving Canal', *The Telegraph*, 14 February 1893, p. 3.

2 K. A. Wittfogel, *Oriental Despotism*.

3 'Day of Humiliation', *The Telegraph*, 22 February 1893, p. 4.

4 'Pints and Pars', *The Week*, 24 February 1893, p. 17.

5   *The Brisbane Courier*, 25 February 1893, p. 4; 'Flood Prevention and Navigation Works', *The Brisbane Courier*, 6 November 1896, p. 4; 'Flood Prevention Schemes', *The Brisbane Courier*, 19 January 1898, p. 4.

6   'Flood Prevention Schemes', *The Brisbane Courier*, 19 January 1898, p. 4.

7   'Royal Society of Queensland Monthly Meeting', *The Brisbane Courier*, 22 March 1898, p. 7.

8   'The Brisbane Courier', *The Brisbane Courier*, 10 February 1893, p. 4.

9   Exchange no Robbery, letter to editor, 'Modern River Dwellers', *The Brisbane Courier*, 21 February 1893, p. 3.

10 'Take your choice', *The Telegraph*, 9 February 1893, p. 2.

11 'Letters to the Editor', *The Brisbane Courier*, 14 January 1898, p. 6.

12 Letter from J. W. Powell, Director-General, United States Geological Survey, to J. P. Thomson, cited in 'Discussion', *Proceedings and Transcripts of the Queensland Branch of the Royal Geographical Society*, vol. XV, 1899–1900, p. 53.

13 G. F. White, *Human Adjustment to Floods*, PhD thesis, University of Chicago, Chicago, 1942, p. 1.

14 M. Everard, *The Hydro-Politics of Dams*, p. 155.

15 G. F. White, *Human Adjustment to Floods*, p. 1.

16 M. Cioc, *The Rhine*, p. 39; D. Blackbourn, *The Conquest of Nature*, pp. 191–193.

17 J. B. Henderson, 'Floods, Brisbane and Mary Rivers: Second Interim Report', pp. 1469–1470. For more information on Henderson, see R. L. Whitmore, *Eminent Queensland Engineers*, Institution of Engineers Australia, Queensland Division, Brisbane, 1984; R. Whitmore, *Hydraulic Henderson: Water Resources Pioneer*, Engineers Australia, Queensland Division, Brisbane, 2009; M. Cook, 'John Baillie Henderson: A Hydrologist in Colonial Brisbane', *International Review of Environmental History*, vol. 4, no. 1, 2018, pp. 69–92.

18 'Annual Report of Hydraulic Engineer on Water Supply', *Queensland Parliamentary Papers*, vol. 3, 1910, p. 8.

19 'Annual Report of the Water Supply Department', *Queensland Votes and Proceedings*, vol. 3, 1894, pp. 1455–1456.

20 J. Powell, *Plains of Promise, Rivers of Destiny*, p. 40; H. Eklund, 'Irrigation Activities 1919–1920', *Water Supply Department Queensland Bulletin*, no. 1, 1920, p. 4, Queensland State Archives, ID 291292; 'Annual Report of the Hydraulic Engineer', *Queensland Parliamentary Papers*, vol. 3, 1903, p. 797.

21 J. Powell, *Plains of Promise, Rivers of Destiny*, p. 89.

22 'Annual Report of the Hydraulic Engineer', *Queensland Parliamentary Papers*, vol. 3, 1903, p. 797.

23 J. Powell, 'Snakes and Canons: Water Management and the Geographical Imagination in Australia', in S. Dovers (ed.), *Environmental History and Policy: Still Settling Australia*, Oxford University Press, Melbourne, 2000, p. 59.

24 J. Powell, *Plains of Promise, Rivers of Destiny*, p. 90; J. B. Henderson, 'Floods, and the Mitigation of their Evil Effects', Annual Report of the Hydraulic Engineer for Water Supply, *Queensland Votes and Proceedings*, vol. 3, 1895, p. 990; J. B. Henderson, 'Floods, Brisbane and Mary Rivers', p. 1469; R. Whitmore, *Hydraulic Henderson*, p. 28.

25 'Government and Floods', *The Brisbane Courier*, 10 January 1894, p. 4.

26 'Floods in the Brisbane', *The Brisbane Courier*, 5 February 1895, p. 3.

27 J. B. Henderson, 'Floods in Brisbane River, and Schemes for Abatement of their Disastrous Effects', pp. 295–308.

28 G. Cossins, 'Early Hydrology of the Brisbane Area', *Engineering Update*, vol. 5, no. 1, April 1997, p. 22; Geoffrey Cossins, interview with author, 12 August 2015.
29 J. B. Henderson, 'Floods in Brisbane River, and Schemes for Abatement of their Disastrous Effects', p. 307. See also O. Powell, 'Brisbane Floods: 1893 to the Summer of Sorrow', *Queensland Historical Atlas*, 15 April 2015.
30 'Flood Prevention', *The Brisbane Courier*, 20 June 1896, p. 9.
31 Lusta, letter to editor, 'Prevention of Floods and Silting up of the River', *The Brisbane Courier*, 12 March 1898, p. 7.
32 T. O'Connor & G. L. Lotz letters to editor, 'Flood Prevention', *The Brisbane Courier*, 26 June 1896, p. 7; 14 June 1895, p. 2.
33 F. J. Fuller, letter to editor, 'Flood Prevention', *The Brisbane Courier*, 19 January 1898, p. 7.
34 J. B. Henderson, 'Floods in Brisbane River, and Schemes for Abatement of their Disastrous Effects', p. 297.
35 C. E. Bernays, letter to editor, 'Flood Prevention', *The Brisbane Courier*, 19 January 1898, p. 7.
36 'The Port of Brisbane', *The Brisbane Courier*, 10 March 1898, p. 5.
37 'Flood Mitigation, Local Authorities' Conference', *The Brisbane Courier*, 15 February 1898, p. 2.
38 J. Powell, *Plains of Promise, Rivers of Destiny*, pp. 60, 66; 'H. R. A. and H. Association's Monthly Reading', *The Maitland Weekly Mercury* (NSW), 8 October 1898, p. 12; J. M. Powell, 'Enterprise and Dependency: Water Management in Australia', in T. Griffiths & L. Robin (eds), *Ecology and Empire: Environmental History of Settler Societies*, Melbourne University Press, Melbourne, 1997, p. 105; R. Whitmore, *Hydraulic Henderson*, p. 8; E. O'Gorman, *Flood Country*, p. 70; H. Goodall, 'Fresh and Salt: Introduction', *Transforming Cultures eJournal*, vol. 1, no. 2, June 2006, p. iv.
39 J. Pennycuick, *Report on Scheme for the Abatement of Floods in the Brisbane River*, Government Printer, Brisbane, 1899, pp. 2–5; 'Flood Prevention Scheme, Colonel Pennycuick's Work', *The Queenslander*, 2 December 1899, p. 1081; J. B. Henderson, 'Floods in Brisbane River, and Schemes for Abatement of their Disastrous Effects', p. 300. Middle Creek Dam was located upstream of Wivenhoe Dam where Lake Wivenhoe now is.
40 'Colonel Pennycuick's Reply', *The Brisbane Courier*, 31 March 1900, p. 8.
41 G. Cossins, 'Early Hydrology of the Brisbane Area', p. 23.
42 J. Dobson, 'Physical/ Engineering Aspects of the Estuary', in P. Davie, E. Stock & D. L. Choy (eds), *The Brisbane River*, The Australian Littoral Society, Brisbane, 1990, pp. 203–204.
43 'The Port of Brisbane', *The Brisbane Courier*, 11 March 1898, p. 5.
44 W. Davenport, *Harbours and Marine: Port and Harbour Development in Queensland from 1824–1985*, Queensland Department of Harbours and Marine, Brisbane, 1986, p. 205; 'The Port of Brisbane', *The Brisbane Courier*, 11 March 1898, p. 5.
45 'The Port of Brisbane. Suggested River Improvements', *The Brisbane Courier*, 15 April 1898, p. 6.
46 'The Port of Brisbane', *The Brisbane Courier*, 11 March 1898, p. 5.
47 I. Tyrrell, *True Gardens of the Gods: Californian-Australian Environmental Reform, 1860–1930*, University of California Press, Berkeley, 1999, p. 121.
48 'The Port of Brisbane Mr Lindon Bates's Report', *The Brisbane Courier*, 23 December 1898, p. 4; 'The Lindon Bates Dredges', *The Brisbane Courier*, 21 May 1900, p. 4.

The capability of Bates's dredges was later subjected to a public inquiry. 'London Bates Dredges. Inquiry to be Held', *The Brisbane Courier*, 31 January 1902, p. 4.

49 'Widening the River. Gardens Point Sacrificed', *The Brisbane Courier*, 1 July 1911, p. 5.

50 'Improvements to River Banks', *The Brisbane Courier*, 17 January 1907, p. 4; H. Gregory, *The Brisbane River Story*, p. 50.

51 'Brisbane River', *The Brisbane Courier*, 4 January 1929, p. 14; H. Gregory, *The Brisbane River Story*, p. 50; *The Queensland Chamber of Manufacturers Year Book*, 1954, vol. 8, p. 41; 'Brisbane River', *The Telegraph*, 21 January 1927, p. 5.

52 'The Port of Brisbane', *The Brisbane Courier*, 13 January 1896, p. 5.

53 'Annual Report of the Department of Harbours and Marine', *Queensland Parliamentary Papers*, vol. 1, 1936, p. 3.

54 'Brisbane River', *The Telegraph*, 21 January 1927, p. 5.

55 'Engineers Afloat. Waterfront Inspection. Brisbane River Development', *The Telegraph*, 2 April 1924, p. 9.

56 'Centenary of Brisbane River', *The Brisbane Courier*, 3 November 1922, p. 6; 'Brisbane River. A Notable Asset. Miles of Wharves', *The Brisbane Courier*, 4 January 1929, p. 14.

57 'River Improvements', *The Telegraph*, 24 February 1897, p. 4.

58 'Wharf to Replace Hamilton Riverside Park?', *The Telegraph*, 18 July 1935, p. 12; 'Gardens Point. Cutting it Away. Ten Acres to Disappear', *The Telegraph*, 22 August 1913, p. 2.

59 'The Brisbane River', *The Telegraph*, 1 December 1923, p. 8.

60 G. F. White, *Human Adjustment to Floods*, p. 51.

61 'Stradbroke Island Water Supply', *The Brisbane Courier*, 6 June 1905, p. 2.

62 J. Powell, *Plains of Promise, Rivers of Destiny*, p. 94.

63 G. Cossins, 'The Overlooked Heritage of Somerset Dam: A Story of Droughts Floods Disagreeable Water and Lost Chances', in Sheridan & Norman (eds), *Engineering Heritage Matters: Conference Papers of the 12th National Conference on Engineering Heritage, Toowoomba, 29th September to 1 October 2003*, Engineers Australia, Barton, ACT, 2003, p. 51; J. Cole, *Shaping a City: Greater Brisbane 1925–1985*, William Brooks, Brisbane, 1984, p. 65; J. Powell, *Plains of Promise, Rivers of Destiny*, p. 94.

64 G. Gutteridge, 'Commission of Enquiry, Brisbane Water Supply Report', *Queensland Parliamentary Papers*, vol. 2, 1928, p. 780.

65 E. O'Gorman, 'Unnatural River, Unnatural Floods, Regulation and Responsibility on the Murray River in the 1950s', *Australian Humanities Review*, vol. 48, 2010, p. 95.

66 G. Gutteridge, 'Commission of Enquiry', pp. 848, 851.

67 'Colonel Pennycuick's Reply', *The Brisbane Courier*, 31 March 1900, p. 15.

68 W. E. Bush, *Water Supply Extensions and Flood Mitigation*, Brisbane City Council, Brisbane, 1930, pp. 14–15, 29.

69 B. Carroll, 'William Forgan Smith: Dictator or Democrat?', in D. Murphy, R. Joyce, M. Cribb & R. Wear (eds), *The Premiers of Queensland*, University of Queensland Press, Brisbane, 2003, p. 215.

70 Queensland Bureau of Industry, *Special Committee on Brisbane Water Supply and Flood Prevention, Report on Recommendations*, Queensland Bureau of Industry, Brisbane, 1934; Bureau of Industry, Roads, Mining and General Works Committee, *Brisbane Water Supply and Flood Prevention: Interim Report of the Special Committee*, 1933, pp. 2, 14, Queensland State Archives, ID 276173.

71 Queensland Bureau of Industry, *Somerset Dam*, Bureau of Industry, Brisbane, 1958, p. 10.

72 Queensland Bureau of Industry, *Special Committee on Brisbane Water Supply and Flood Prevention, Report on Recommendations*, p. 6.

73 H. W. Herbert, 'If Rain is Heavy Enough Somerset Dam Won't Save Brisbane', *The Courier-Mail*, 4 March 1953, p. 2.

74 Queensland Bureau of Industry, *Special Committee on Brisbane Water Supply and Flood Prevention, Report on Recommendations*, p. 6.

75 'When Brisbane had Big Water Crisis', *The Telegraph*, 6 November 1946, p. 5; 'Somerset Dam Averted Serious Floods Damage', *The Queensland Times*, 2 March 1950, p. 2.

76 'Site Visited', *The Queensland Times*, 17 December 1934, p. 10.

77 D. Nye, *American Technological Sublime*, MIT Press, Cambridge (MA), 1994. See also D. Blackbourn, *Conquest of Nature*, pp. 191–195; Z. Sofoulis, 'Big Water, Everyday Water: A Sociotechnical Perspective', *Continuum: Journal of Media and Cultural Studies*, vol. 19, no. 4, 2005, pp. 445–463.

78 Queensland State Public Relations Bureau, *Somerset Dam*, State Public Relations Bureau, Brisbane, 195–?, pp. 10, 195.

79 E. M. Shepherd, Coordinator General's Department, *Flood Conditions in the St Lucia University Campus*, 24 February 1972, Queensland State Archives, ID 569498.

80 C. Barton, 'Opening Address', in *Proceedings of Symposium January 1974 Floods Moreton Region*, Institution of Engineers, Australia, Queensland Division, Brisbane, 1974, p. 5.

Chapter 4: Encroaching on the Floodplain

1 *The Bendigo Independent*, 11 February 1893, p. 3.

2 BCC Minutes of Proceedings, 2 November 1914, and correspondence in BCA 612; Orleigh Park comprises subdivisions 132 to 184 and subdivisions 211 to 236 of western suburban allotments 44 and 45; R. E. Burton, Manning Street, South Brisbane, to Town Clerk, City South Brisbane, 25 April 1916, BCA 612; J. MacMillan to Town Clerk, South Brisbane Council, 9 March 1916, BCA 612; 'South Brisbane', *The Telegraph*, 26 January 1915, p. 10.

3 'Stone Axe Heads Stanley River Find', *The Telegraph*, 4 November 1930, p. 2.

4 J. Cole, *Shaping a City*, pp. 39, 407–409.

5 W. A. Jolly, *Greater Brisbane 1929*, Watson, Ferguson and Co. Ltd, Brisbane, 1929, p. 20.

6 J. Cole, *Shaping a City*, pp. 407–409.

7 J. Cole, *Shaping a City*, p. 41.

8 'Commercialism Before Beauty', *The Daily Standard*, 12 October 1926, p. 9.

9 BCC Ordinances, Chapter 75, Drainage Problem Areas, pp. 1–2; The Town Plan of the City of Brisbane, 1965, Chapter 8, Part 8, Clause 2, p. 62; *Queensland Government Gazette* CXX, no. 73, 21 December 1965, pp. 1777–1846.

10 Scorer & Scorer in association with Gutteridge, Haskins & Davy, & D. J. McCulloch, *Report on the Master Scheme for the Town Planning of the City of Ipswich, 1949*, pp. 38, 131.

11 *Acquisition of Land Act 1967*, Section 19(3); C. Robertson, 'Compensation Lost, Compensation Found: Injurious Affection and the Integrated Planning Act Labyrinth', *Proctor*, April 2002, p. 20.

12   D. I. Smith & J. W. Handmer, 'Urban Flooding in Australia: Policy development and implementation', *Disasters*, vol. 8, issue 2, 1984, pp. 111–113.

13   Quoted in R. Wear, *Johannes Bjelke-Petersen, The Lord's Premier*, University of Queensland Press, Brisbane, 2002, p. 186; P. Spearritt, 'The Water Crisis in Southeast Queensland: How Desalination Turned the Region into Carbon Emission Heaven', in P. Troy (ed.), *Troubled Waters: Confronting the Water Crisis in Australia's Cities*, Australian National University, Canberra, 2008, p. 22.

14   R. Wear, 'Johannes Bjelke-Petersen: Straddling a Barbed Wire Fence', *Queensland Historical Atlas*, 23 September 2010; *Queensland Parliamentary Debates*, 21 August 1947, p. 128.

15   W. Steele & J. Dodson, 'Made in Queensland: Planning Reform and Rhetoric', *Australian Planner*, vol. 51, no. 2, 2014, pp. 141–150.

16   C. Jones to J. Bjelke-Petersen, 7 September 1972, Letter 8026 B409Y, Queensland State Archives, ID 5400011; *Queensland Parliamentary Debates*, 5 March 1974, p. 2671.

17   'Building and Land', *The Brisbane Courier*, 13 July 1926, p. 19.

18   J. Cole, *Shaping a City*, p. 123; 'Greater Brisbane Population Statistics', *The Daily Mail*, 20 December 1925, p. 15; 'Population of 380,220 in Brisbane', *The Courier-Mail*, 21 April 1945, p. 3; P. Spearritt, 'The 200 km City: Brisbane, the Gold Coast, and Sunshine Coast', *Australian Economic History Review*, vol. 49, no. 1, 2009, p. 96; Bureau of Census and Statistics, 'Population Growth with the Brisbane Statistical Division, 1856–1971', Brisbane, 1973, p. 6.

19   'See Brisbane Growing', *The Courier-Mail*, 10 June 1950, p. 3; Government Statistician, Brisbane, 'Building Operations in Queensland – Fourth Quarter and Year, 1954', *Queensland Government Statistician Bulletin*, no. 15, 1955.

20   'Brisbane Flooded', *The Worker*, 11 February 1931, p. 6.

21   Bureau of Industry, Roads, Mining and General Works Committee, *Brisbane Water Supply and Flood Prevention*, p. 13.

22   'City Flood Problem Likely to Get Worse', *The Sunday Mail*, 9 April 1972, p. 15.

23   'Land is Available in Many Areas', *Truth*, 11 June 1950, p. 24.

24   'A Suburb is Progressing', *The Queensland Times*, 19 January 1950, p. 2.

25   'Moreton Region Man Made Environment', Coordinator General, Brisbane, 1973, p. 94; 'Chain of Homes from Brisbane to Ipswich', *The Courier-Mail*, 5 January 1953, p. 3.

26   'At Ipswich Higher than 1908 Level', *The Week*, 13 February 1931, p. 30; R. H. Napier to E. Shepherd, 10 December 1970, Queensland State Archives, ID 569498; R. Buchanan, *Ipswich in the 20th Century*, Ipswich City Council, Ipswich, 2004, p. 113.

27   P. Spearritt, 'The 200 Kilometre City', p. 99; J. Cole, *Shaping a City*, pp. 239–240.

28   Bureau of Census and Statistics, 'Population Growth within the Brisbane Statistical Division, 1856–1971', Brisbane, 1973, p. 9.

29   S. Macey, 'Perception of Flood Hazard and Adjustment in Brisbane', Master of Arts thesis, University of Queensland, Brisbane, 1978, pp. 61, 66.

30   'River Lot Buyers Could be Shy Now', *The Telegraph*, 2 February 1974, p. 6; Advertisement, *The Courier-Mail*, 7 December 1974, p. 29. The average male income in Queensland in 1972–73 was $96.90 per week: Australian Bureau of Statistics, 'Average Weekly Earnings', December Quarter 1973, no. 6.18, p. 2.

31   'Driest Spell since 1902', *The Courier-Mail*, 30 September 1936, p. 14.

32   'City Gripped by Record Drought', *The Courier-Mail*, 2 September 1946, p. 1; 'Inigo Rain Forecast Stirs City', *The Courier-Mail*, 27 August 1953, p. 3.

33 A. Partridge, Commissioner for Irrigation, Annual Report, *Queensland Parliamentary Papers*, vol. 2, 1928, pp. 747, 752.

34 'Flood Risks', *The Queenslander*, 27 January 1927, p. 15.

35 'Building Sites', *The Daily Standard*, 28 November 1933, p. 8.

36 G. F. White, *Human Adjustment to Floods*, p. 52.

37 'Somerset Dam is City's Wet Weather Safety-valve', *The Courier-Mail*, 8 March 1950, p. 2.

38 'The Flood Story that Brisbane Knew Nothing About', *The Sunday Mail*, 5 March 1950, p. 3; 'Somerset Dam Averted Serious Flood Damage', *The Queensland Times*, 2 March 1950, p. 2.

39 'Somerset Dam Saves Serious Flooding in Brisbane City Area', *The Cairns Post*, 3 February 1951, p. 1; 'Dam Keeps Flood from City', *The Courier-Mail*, 3 February 1951, p. 3.

40 'Somerset Dam Could Stop £3 Million Flood Damage', *The Courier-Mail*, 24 November 1954, p. 8.

41 'Wall at Dam "Saved City"', *The Courier-Mail*, 29 March 1955, p. 3.

42 V. Gair, 29 March 1955, letter 409A, Queensland State Archives, ID 540011.

43 Queensland State Public Relations Bureau, *Somerset Dam*, p. 7.

44 H. W. Herbert, 'If the Rain is Heavy Enough', *The Courier-Mail*, 4 March 1953, p. 2.

45 'Somerset Dam Could Stop £3 Million Flood Damage', *The Courier-Mail*, 24 November 1954, p. 8; 'Somerset Dam Holding Back Big Volume of Floodwater', *The Queensland Times*, 14 July 1954, p. 3.

46 'Brisbane Emergencies', *The Central Queensland Herald* (Rockhampton), 31 March 1955, p. 16; V. Gair, letter B409A, *Flood Prevention and Mitigation Part 1*, 29 March 1955, Queensland State Archives, ID 540011.

47 E. O'Gorman, 'Unnatural River, Unnatural Floods, Regulation and Responsibility on the Murray River in the 1950s', p. 137.

48 H. W. Herbert, 'If the Rain is Heavy Enough', *The Courier-Mail*, 4 March 1953, p. 2.

49 'Wall at Dam "Saved City"', *The Courier-Mail*, 29 March 1955, p. 3.

50 The Commissioner for Consumer Affairs to Coordinator General on 28 July 1971, Secretary to Commissioner for Consumer Affairs, Flood Data – Brisbane River, 5 August 1971; Advertisement, *The Courier-Mail*, 28 May 1971, p. 17; T. V. McAulay, Town Clerk to Chief Engineer, Department of Coordinator General, 11 January 1971, Queensland State Archives, ID 569498.

51 'Oxley and Sherwood', *The Queenslander*, 18 February 1893, p. 322.

52 Hooker Centenary, *New Horizons*, Hooker Centenary Pty Ltd, Brisbane, 1960, p. 197; '£8m. Development Plan for Brisbane', *The Canberra Times*, 11 November 1961, p. 5; 'In Queensland this Week', *The Canberra Times*, 2 November 1961, p. 2.

53 Geoffery Cossins, interview with author, 12 August 2015.

54 Secretary Hooker-Rex to the Department of Coordinator General, 3 April 1962, BCA 1577; Chief Engineers, Department of Coordinator General to Town Clerk, BCC, 30 October 1970, BCA 1577.

55 T. V. McAulay, Town Clerk to Chief Engineer, Department of Coordinator General, 14 January 1971, Queensland State Archives, ID 569498.

56 Jean Gahan and Graham Gahan, interview with author, 19 August 2016.

57 Australian Bureau of Statistics, 'Population and Dwellings in Local Government Areas', *Bulletin*, no. 6, 1971, pp. 1, 4.

58   Ipswich Flood heights from R. G. Gamble, 'Ipswich Floods 1974', *Queensland Division Technical Papers*, vol. 16, no. 25, November 1975, pp. 1–10.
59   Robyn Flashman, interview with author, 17 August 2016.
60   D. Rose, 'It Was Even Worse in 1893', *The Courier-Mail*, 29 January 1974, p. 4.
61   Queensland Department of the Coordinator General of Public Works, *Future Brisbane Water Supply and Flood Mitigation Report on Proposed Dam on the Brisbane River at Middle Creek or Alternatively Wivenhoe and Flood Mitigation for Brisbane and Ipswich*, vol. 1, June 1971, p. 87; J. Chapman, M. Davis & N. Elliot, 'Australia Day Washout', Department of Social Work, University of Queensland, Brisbane, March 1974, p. 11, Appendix 2.
62   Queensland Department of the Coordinator General of Public Works, *Future Brisbane Water Supply and Flood Mitigation Report*, pp. 37–38.

Chapter 5: The River Prevails: The 1974 Flood

1   *Queensland Parliamentary Debates*, 5 March 1974, p. 2652.
2   Department of Social Security, *Queensland Flood Report Australia Day 1974*, Commonwealth of Australia, Canberra, 1981, p. 4; A. J. Shields, 'Synoptic Meteorology of Flood Period', in G. Cossins & G. Heatherwick (eds), *January 1974 Floods, Moreton Region: Proceedings of Symposium*, The Institution of Engineers, Australia, Queensland Division, Brisbane, 1974, p. 8.
3   'Doors as Rafts', *The Courier-Mail*, 26 January 1974, p. 3.
4   'Risk Decision is All Mine: Clem', *The Telegraph*, 29 January 1974, p. 3; 'Jones Defends Dam Decision', *The Telegraph*, 30 January 1974, p. 31; 'Dam Opened', *The Telegraph*, 31 January 1974, p. 3; 'Mayor Orders Big Dam Shut', *The Courier-Mail*, 30 January 1974, p. 13; G. Cossins, 'The Operation of Somerset Dam During the Flood of January 1974', Memo, BCC Archives, BCA 1577; Geoffrey Cossins, interview with author, 12 August 2015.
5   Geoffrey Cossins, interview with author.
6   D. Tucker, 'Alderman Clem Jones as Lord Mayor of Brisbane: A Study of Plebiscitary Leadership', *Australian Journal of Public Administration*, vol. 53, no. 2, 1994, pp. 201–212.
7   'Levels Rise at Kilcoy', *The Courier-Mail*, 31 January 1974, p. 2.
8   Geoffrey Cossins, interview with author; *Queensland Parliamentary Debates*, 5 March 1974, p. 2690; For a detailed account of events, see M. Cook, 'Did Clem Jones Save Brisbane from Flood?', *Queensland Historical Atlas*, 30 April 2015.
9   *Queensland Parliamentary Debates*, 5 March 1974, p. 2681.
10   Figures from G. Cossins, 'Flood Mitigation in the Brisbane River', in G. Cossins & G. Heatherwick (eds), *January 1974 Floods, Moreton Region*, pp. 152, 157.
11   G. Heatherwick, 'Flood Forecasting and Warnings Moreton Region', in G. Cossins & G. Heatherwick (eds), *January 1974 Floods, Moreton Region*, p. 66.
12   Bureau of Industry, Roads, Mining and General Works Committee, *Brisbane Water Supply and Flood Prevention*, pp. 2, 14.
13   Director of Meteorology, *Brisbane Floods, January 1974*, Department of Science Bureau of Meteorology, Canberra, 1974 p. 29; G. Heatherwick, 'Flood Forecasting and Warnings Moreton Region', p. 65.
14   Geoffrey Heatherwick, interview with author, 21 September 2015.
15   Geoffrey Cossins interview by B. McDonald, unpublished transcript held by G. Cossins.

16   T. Bell (ed.), *State Emergency Service, Queensland: 30th Anniversary Book*, Counter Disaster and Rescue Department of Emergency Services, Brisbane, 2005, p. 5.

17   Beryl Wilson, interview with author, 15 August 2016.

18   'Six Years After: The Flood of '74', *Sunday Mail Colour*, 27 January 1980, p. 6.

19   T. Bell, *State Emergency Service, Queensland*, p. 5.

20   H. Lunn, 'After the Deluge, the Post Mortem', *The Australian*, 20 February 1974, p. 11.

21   *Queensland Parliamentary Debates*, 5 March 1974, pp. 2633–2634, 2638.

22   G. Cossins, 'The Overlooked Heritage of Somerset Dam', p. 45.

23   B. McDonald, 'Six Years After: The Flood of '74', *The Sunday Mail*, 27 January 1980, p. 4.

24   E. Robinson, *Once in a Lifetime: A Personal Narrative of The Great Flood of 1974*, 5 March 1974.

25   'Highest since 1955', *The Courier-Mail*, 26 January 1974, p. 3; 'Great Floods Kill Three, Damage in Millions. And More Coming', *The Sunday Mail*, 27 January 1974, p. 1.

26   'Few Suburbs Escaped Damage from the Floods', *The Queensland Times*, 28 January 1974, p. 2.

27   'The Whole World Under Water', *The Queensland Times*, 30 January 1974, p. 6.

28   'Few Suburbs Escaped Damage from the Floods', *The Queensland Times*, 28 January 1974, p. 2.

29   'Floods Take About 43 Homes in Ipswich Area', *The Queensland Times*, 30 January 1974, p. 1.

30   Editorial, 'The Way Back to Normal', *The Courier-Mail*, 2 February 1974, p. 1.

31   *Queensland Parliamentary Debates*, 5 March 1974, p. 2646.

32   *Queensland Parliamentary Debates*, 5 March 1974, p. 2639.

33   P. Swannell & L. T. Isaacs, 'An Assessment of the Consequences of the 1974 Flood in the Jindalee Area', February 1974, pp. 13, 18, Appendix; J. Bragg, 'Brisbane has to Live with Floods', *The Sunday Mail*, 3 February 1974, p. 6.

34   Information taken from January 1974 newspapers, Queensland State Archives Inquest files, Series 36 Coronial Files and *Queensland Parliamentary Debates*, 5 March 1974, p. 2649.

35   'Rescue Disaster as Floods Hit New Top', *The Courier-Mail*, 29 January 1974, p. 1; 'Soldier Dies, One Lost in Flood', *The Sydney Morning Herald*, 29 January 1974, p. 1; Statement by B. Lickiss, MLA, 13 February 1974, Queensland State Archives, ID 540061; *Queensland Parliamentary Debates*, 5 March 1974, p. 2627; Premier to Mrs Hourigan and Mrs Kerr, 1 February 1974, Queensland State Archives, ID 540040.

36   'Bremer Damage Severe', *The Telegraph*, 1 February 1974, p. 5.

37   C. Amey to the Premier of Queensland, 20 March 1974; *Floods and Cyclones – December 1973/January 1974 Cyclone 'Una' and 'Wanda'*, Queensland State Archives, ID 540161, Part 6.

38   'Brisbane Licks its Muddy Wounds', *The Courier-Mail*, 30 January 1974, p. 3.

39   *Queensland Parliamentary Debates*, 5 March 1974, p. 2646; Director of Meteorology, *Brisbane Floods*, p. 36; Memorandum, 23 July 1974; *Floods and Cyclones – December 1973/January 1974 Cyclone 'Una' and 'Wanda'*, Queensland State Archives, ID 540161, Part 6.

40   *Report on floods*, Queensland State Archives, ID 540040; *Notes for discussion with Prime Minister: Secondary Industries*, Queensland State Archives, ID 540040; 'Some Small Firms on the Brink of Collapse', *The Courier-Mail*, 5 February 1974, p. 3;

Snowy Mountains Engineering Corporation, *Brisbane River Flood Investigations: Final Report*, 1975, p. 57.

41 J. A. Butler, Managing Director, Tickle Wholesale Distributors Ltd to the Premier, 8 March 1974, Queensland State Archives, ID 540062, Part 3; Snowy Mountains Engineering Corporation, *Brisbane River Flood Investigations*, p. 31.

42 '$2 million "gone like the morning mist"', *The Courier-Mail*, 29 January 1974, p. 3.

43 Snowy Mountains Engineering Corporation, *Brisbane River Flood Investigations*, pp. 69–70.

44 *Queensland Parliamentary Debates*, 5 March 1974, p. 2631.

45 *Report on floods*, Queensland State Archives, ID 540040.

46 G. Cossins, 'The Operation of Somerset Dam During the Flood of January 1974'.

47 Australian Bureau of Statistics, *Queensland Year Book 1975*, Australian Bureau of Statistics Queensland Office, Brisbane, 1975.

48 Editorial, 'Mr. Whitlam is Absent', *The Courier-Mail*, 30 January 1974, p. 4.

49 H. Lunn, *Joh: The Life and Political Adventures of Sir Johannes Bjelke-Petersen*, 2nd edition, University of Queensland Press, Brisbane, 1984, pp. 158–160; Lodge cartoon, *The Australian*, 14 February 1974, p. 8; *Queensland Parliamentary Debates*, 5 March 1974, p. 2691.

50 E. Robinson, *Once in a Lifetime*, 5 March 1974.

51 G. Gahan to H. Gahan, 26 January to 12 February 1974, personal collection.

52 'City Mop-up Choked by Car Tangles', *The Sunday Mail*, 3 February 1974, p. 1.

53 P. O'Gorman to K. Spann, Under Secretary, Premier's Department, 30 July 1974, Queensland State Archives, ID 540166; P. O'Gorman & K. V. Wildermuth to Under Secretary, Premier's Department, 22 July 1974, Queensland State Archives, ID 540166.

54 'One Day it will be Worse', *The Courier-Mail*, 2 February 1974, p. 1.

Chapter 6: Dam Dependency

1 Editorial, 'Inquiry Needed on Flooding', *The Courier-Mail*, 1 February 1974, p. 4.

2 'Make Developers Pay – Egerton', *The Telegraph*, 30 January 1974, p. 7; A. Underwood, 'Buck-passing on Flood Area Development', *The Courier-Mail*, 4 February 1974, p. 4.

3 'The "Fast Buck" Cost is High', *The Courier-Mail*, 28 January 1974, p. 6.

4 K. Thomas, letter to editor, 'Developers', *The Courier-Mail*, 31 January 1974, p. 4.

5 H. Lunn, 'Little Bit of a Panic', *The Australian*, 4 February 1974, p. 9.

6 'Claim of No Blame', *The Courier-Mail*, 1 February 1974, p. 7.

7 A. Underwood, 'Buck-passing on Flood Area Development', *The Courier-Mail*, 4 February 1974, p. 4; See also L. Keogh, 'City of the Damned: How the Media Embraced the Brisbane Floods', *Queensland Historical Atlas*, 16 April 2015.

8 *Queensland Parliamentary Debates*, 5 March 1974, p. 2682; J. Cole, *Shaping a City*, p. 407; A. Underwood, 'Buck-passing on Flood Area Development', *The Courier-Mail*, 4 February 1974, p. 4.

9 Editorial, 'Must be No More Delay', *The Courier-Mail*, 28 January 1974, p. 4.

10 *Queensland Parliamentary Debates*, 5 March 1974, pp. 2675, 2682.

11 '$13 m. Plan to Stop Flooding', *The Courier-Mail*, 30 January 1974, p. 7.

12 'Risk Decision is All Mine: Clem', *The Telegraph*, 29 January 1974, p. 3. In court cases against Reid in 1971 and Clement in 1972, BCC had lost both cases to prevent building in low-lying areas. A. G. Brown, 'Land use control in the Moreton region

with special reference to flood mitigation in urban centres', in *Queensland – Study of land use control in the flood prone areas of Moreton Region*, p. 11, National Archives of Australia, A3491 1974/411.

13   H. Lunn, 'Little Bit of a Panic', *The Australian*, 4 February 1974, p. 9.

14   'Make Flood Areas Parks', *The Sunday Mail*, 27 January 1974, p. 5; 'Make Developers Pay – Egerton', *The Telegraph*, 30 January 1974, p. 7.

15   Editorial, 'Must be No More Delay', *The Courier-Mail*, 28 January 1974, p. 4; See also D. Evans & T. Ryan, 'Eight Dead as Brisbane Floods Continue to Rise', *The Australian*, 29 January 1974, p. 1.

16   P. Slovic, *The Perception of Risk*, Earthscan Publications, London, 2000; A. Kelman, *A River and its City: The Nature of Landscape in New Orleans*, University of California Press, Berkeley, 2003; D. Crichton, 'International Historical, Political, Economic, Social, and Engineering Responses to Flood Risk,' in J. Lamond, C. Booth, F. Hammond & D. Proverbs (eds), *Flood Hazards: Impacts and Responses for the Built Environment*, CRC Press, Boca Raton, 2012, pp. 155–175.

17   A. Underwood, 'Buck-passing on Flood Area Development', *The Courier-Mail*, 4 February 1974, p. 4.

18   Ibid.

19   J. Bragg, 'Brisbane has to Live with Floods', *The Sunday Mail*, 3 February 1974, p. 6.

20   I. Miller, 'Inquiry Call on Floods', *The Telegraph*, 31 January 1974, p. 2.

21   Editorial, 'Inquiry Needed on Flooding', *The Courier-Mail*, 1 February 1974, p. 4.

22   J. N. Allom to Premier, 6 July 1974, *Floods and cyclones – December 1973/January 1974 Cyclone 'Una' and 'Wanda'*, Queensland State Archives, ID 540161, Part 6, letter 410T.

23   E. Bacon, Honourable Secretary, Union of Australian Women to the Premier, 6 March 1974, *Floods and Cyclones – December, 1973/January 1974 Cyclone 'Una' and 'Wanda'*, Queensland State Archives, ID 540062, Part 3, letter 410T.

24   'Support Sought on Flood Inquiry', *The Courier-Mail*, 29 July 1974, p. 8.

25   Quoted in R. L. Heathcote & B. G. Thom (eds), *Natural Hazards in Australia*, Australian Academy of Science, Canberra, 1979, p. 445.

26   *Queensland Parliamentary Debates*, 5 March 1974, pp. 2627, 2632, 2640–2641, 2696.

27   T. Grigg, *A Comprehensive Evaluation of the Proposed Wivenhoe Dam on the Brisbane River: An Examination of the Economic, Financial, Social and Environmental Effects*, Coordinator General's Department, Brisbane, June 1977.

28   These current figures have increased marginally from the time of design. Queensland Department of Energy and Water Supply, *Wivenhoe and Somerset Dams Optimisation Study Report*, Department of Energy and Water Supply, Brisbane, 2014, pp. 22–23.

29   Station number 540684. T. Grigg, *A Comprehensive Evaluation of the Proposed Wivenhoe Dam on the Brisbane River*, p. 82.

30   Interdepartmental committee on flood mitigation, Brisbane areas, 74/1294, in *Queensland – Study of land use control in the flood prone areas of Moreton Region*, 6 September 1974, pp. 2–3, National Archives of Australia, A3491 1974/411.

31   D. Rose, 'This Could Happen Again', *The Courier-Mail*, 4 September 1974, p. 4.

32   *Queensland Parliamentary Debates*, 5 March 1974, pp. 2671–2672; *Queensland Parliamentary Debates*, 10 April 1974, p. 3819.

33   T. Grigg, *A Comprehensive Evaluation of the Proposed Wivenhoe Dam on the Brisbane River*, p. 91.

34   'State Pushes for Dam Help', *The Courier-Mail*, 20 February 1974, p. 9.

35   J. Bragg, 'Brisbane has to Live with Floods', *The Sunday Mail*, 3 February 1974, p. 6.

36 T. Crofts, 'It's Our Flood Hope', *The Telegraph*, 31 January 1974, p. 8.

37 'Flood Threat Past: Sir Joh', *The Courier-Mail*, 19 October 1985, p. 18; See also L. Keogh, 'City of the Dammed'.

38 'Flood Threat Past: Sir Joh', *The Sunday Mail*, 19 October 1985, p. 18.

39 Z. Sofoulis, 'Big Water, Everyday Water', p. 452.

40 J. Bjelke-Petersen, *Don't You Worry About That!: The Bjelke-Petersen Memoirs*, Collins/Angus Robertson Publishers Australia, Sydney, 1990, p. 256.

41 Wivenhoe Dam Memo, Wivenhoe Dam – Publicity, 1985, Queensland State Archives, ID 568998.

42 J. Bjelke-Petersen Press Release, circa 1985, Queensland State Archives, ID 568998.

43 'Flood Threat Past: Sir Joh', *The Courier-Mail*, 19 October 1985, p. 18.

44 R. A. Pielke, Jr, 'Nine Fallacies of Floods', *Climate Change*, vol. 42, issue 2, 1999, p. 416.

45 SCARM, *Floodplain Management in Australia: Best Practice Principles and Guidelines*, CSIRO Publishing, Collingwood, Melbourne, 2000, p. 75; NSW Planning and Environment Commission, *Statement of Policy*, Circular 15, 16 August 1978.

46 B. Hayden to G. Whitlam, 3 May 1973, National Archives of Australia, A1209 1974/7416 Flood control and mitigation – Queensland.

47 Kevin Newman, the Minister for National Development, informed Parliament in 1979. Cited in *Future responsibility for Flood Forecasting and Warning Report*, 1980, p. 15, National Archives of Australia, 45/53 Part 2, Series no. J 1324.

48 Department of Minister and Cabinet notes for file, National Archives of Australia, A1209 1974/7416 Flood control and mitigation – Queensland.

49 J. Caulfield, 'Development Interests and Growth in the Local Economy', in J. Caulfield & J. Wanna (eds), *Power and Politics in the City: Brisbane in Transition*, Macmillan, Melbourne, 1995, pp. 97–118.

50 J. Davis, *Planning Legislation and Practice in Queensland: Swings or Roundabouts?*, Southern Downs Regional Council, 11 July 2011, pp. 1–9.

51 D. I. Smith, *Urban Flooding in Queensland – A Review*, Department of Natural Resources, Queensland, 1998, pp. iv–xiii; *State Flood Risk Management Policy Discussion Paper*, Queensland Government Natural Resources and Mines, 2002, pp. vii, 2.

52 *State Flood Risk Management Policy Discussion Paper*, pp. 6–8.

53 Brisbane City Council, *Queensland Floods Commission of Inquiry (QFCI) Submission Two*, 8 April 2011, p. 14; State Planning Policy 1/03, p. 7.

54 D. I. Smith, *Urban Flooding in Queensland*, p. 29. This has been revised to a 1-in-75-year event, still more frequent than 1 in 100 used for the DFL.

55 The DFE used a flood flow of 6,800 cubic metres per second to determine a DFL of 3.7 metres at the Port Office. This DFE varied upstream to allow for the river's slope, with heights varied to 7.99 metres at the mouth of Oxley Creek, 8.05 metres at Graceville and 9.51 metres at the Sherwood Arboretum.

56 Brisbane City Council, *QFCI Submission Two*, p. 9.

57 Joint Flood Taskforce, *Joint Flood Taskforce Report for the Brisbane City Council*, March 2011, p. 35.

58 '$13 m. plan to stop flooding', *The Courier-Mail*, 30 January 1974, p. 7; J. Bragg, 'Brisbane has to Live with Floods', *The Sunday Mail*, 3 February 1974, p. 6.

59 'The Real Tragedy is yet to Come, says Ald Clem', *The Australian*, 29 January 1974.

60 *Brisbane City Council Annual Report 1973–1974*, Brisbane City Council, Brisbane, p. 12.

61   K. Feeney, 'Flood Buyback will Transform 6 Ha of Properties into Parks', *Brisbane Times*, 21 September 2012.

62   Moreton Shire, which amalgamated with Ipswich in 1995, introduced the 1974 flood level as the DFL.

63   The Pioneer River that flows through Mackay is number one, with a 3- to 8-hour warning time. Peter Baddiley, interview with author, 3 March 2017; W. R. Wilkie, Regional Director to Director of Meteorology, 5 August 1980, National Archives of Australia, 45/53, Part 2, Series no. J 1324.

64   The flood flow was 9,560 cubic metres per second. Sinclair Knight Merz, *Brisbane River Study Final Report*, June 1998, vols 1 & 2.

65   Queensland Crime and Misconduct Commission, *Brisbane River Flood Levels: A CMC Report on the Brisbane City Council's Handling of the Flood Study Reports*, Crime and Misconduct Commission, Brisbane, March 2004, p. 12.

66   A Q100 flood would have a flood flow of 9,560 cubic metres per second. H. Thomas, 'Dire Study Rejected and Later Hushed Up', *The Australian*, 13 January 2011, p. 2; *Brisbane River Flood Levels*, March 2004.

67   Brisbane City Council, *QFCI Initial Submission*, 11 March 2011, p. 2.

68   *Joint Flood Taskforce Report*, p. 17; Brisbane City Council, *QFCI Submission Two*, p. 14. This level was known as Q50. This is the height for new roads.

69   Brisbane City Council, *QFCI Submission Two*, p. 15.

70   Brisbane City Council, *Urban Renewal Brisbane: 20 Year Celebrations*, Brisbane City Council, Brisbane, 2011.

71   D. A. Wilhite, 'Breaking the Hydro-Illogical Cycle: Changing the Paradigm for Drought Management', *Earth*, 57, no. 7, 2012, pp. 70–71.

72   J. Seeney, 'Matters of Public Interest', *Hansard*, 9 March 2010, p. 650; 'Water Users Holding Key to Desalination Plants', *The Courier-Mail*, 15 July 2010.

Chapter 7: The Untameable Torrent: The 2011 Flood

1   D. Grant, 'Touched Yet Untouched by Week from Hell', *Gold Coast Bulletin*, 15–16 January 2011, p. 10.

2   C. Holmes & QFCI, *QFCI Final Report*, QFCI, Brisbane, 2012, p. 32.

3   Australian Government Bureau of Meteorology (BoM), *Report to QFCI*, March 2011, pp. 13–17, 54.

4   BoM, *Report to QFCI*, pp. 13–17, 54; M. Barnes, State Coroner, *Office of the State Coroner Findings of Inquest into the Deaths Caused by the South-East Queensland Floods of January 2011*, 5 June 2012. In South East Queensland, 22 people lost their lives, with another three missing and feared dead. All but one death occurred in the Toowoomba and upper Lockyer Valley region.

5   BoM, *Report to QFCI*, pp. 13–17, 43.

6   BoM, *Report to QFCI*, p. 47; *Joint Flood Taskforce Report*, p. 4; Peter Baddiley (BoM hydrologist), interview with author, 3 March 2017. Independent calculations indicated significantly more rain occurred over Wivenhoe Dam than gauges recorded. *Brisbane Flood January 2011*, Independent Review of Brisbane City Council's Response to the 9–22 January 2011 Flood, p. 12.

7   *Joint Flood Taskforce Report*, p. 4; Seqwater, *January 2011 Flood Event: Report on the Operation of Somerset Dam and Wivenhoe Dam*, Seqwater, Brisbane, 2011, p. 23; Terry Malone (Seqwater), interview with author, 25 January 2017.

8   Anna Bligh joint press conference, 12 January 2011, included in Anna Bligh

Statement to QFCI, 6 February 2012.

9   A. Caldwell, R. Viellaris & S. Vogler, 'Devastation on a Scale Never Seen Before', *The Courier-Mail*, 13 January 2011, p. 2; Z. Jackson, 'City Braces for Water to Peak', *The Queensland Times*, 12 January 2011, p. 14; M. Condon, 'Memories Come Spilling Back', *The Courier Mail*, 12 January 2011, p. 75; M. Condon, 'Facing Armageddon', YouTube, 20 January 2011.

10 P. Foley, 'Be Warned: Huge Flood is Overdue', *The Queensland Times*, 19 October 2010, p. 1.

11 BoM, *Report to QFCI*, p. 3; Peter Baddiley, interview with author; Rachel Nolan, interview with author, 18 October 2017.

12 Stephen Robertson, MP, to Gary Humphreys, Seqwater Grid Manager, 22 October 2010, and Gary Humphreys to Stephen Robertson, 24 December 2010, both included in Stephen Robertson statement to QFCI, April 2011.

13 A. Bligh, *Through the Wall*, Harper Collins, Sydney, 2015, p. 213.

14 Seqwater, *Manual of Operational Procedures for Flood Mitigation at Wivenhoe Dam and Somerset Dam*, Revision 7, November 2009.

15 J. Tibaldi, *First Statement to QFCI*, 25 March 2011, p. 8.

16 Robert Ayre was a former Water Resources Commission engineer from 1983, then consultant and SunWater employee from 2000. He served as a flood engineer in 1996–97 and 2000–02 when he became Senior Floods Operations Engineer. He was co-author of the *Real Time Flood Operations Model*. Terrence Malone worked at BoM from 1986 until 2006, then SunWater in 2007 and 2008, and Seqwater from 2009. John Tibaldi worked as an engineer in the Water Resources Commission and SunWater from 1983, and became the Principal Engineer, Dam Safety at Seqwater in 2008. John Ruffini, a professional hydrologist since 1985, joined Queensland Water Resources in 1989 and served as Flood Operations Engineer from 1996.

17 Seqwater, *January 2011 Flood Event*, p. 31.

18 Seqwater, *January 2011 Flood Event*, p. iv; R. Nathan, 'Brisbane 2011: Lessons from Large Floods', *IPENZ Proceedings of Technical Groups*, vol. 37, no. 1, 2005, p. 11.

19 D. I. Smith & J. Handmer (eds), *Flood Warning in Australia*, Centre for Resource and Environmental Studies, Australian National University, Canberra, 1986, pp. 51–52; Terry Malone, interview with author. Since 2011, there are now about 350 rain gauges.

20 Queensland Department of Energy and Water Supply, *Wivenhoe and Somerset Dams Optimisation Study Report*, p. 6.

21 Seqwater, *January 2011 Flood Event*, p. iv.

22 *Flood Jan. 2011*, Oral history collection, Picture Ipswich.

23 T. Dalton, 'The Flood 2011', *The Courier-Mail Special Issue*, 22–23 January 2011, p. 35.

24 *Flood Jan. 2011*, Picture Ipswich.

25 Ibid.

26 J. Johnston, 'They Swam for Their Lives with Just the Clothes on Their Backs', *Gold Coast Bulletin*, 14 January 2011, p. 9.

27 N. Marsh, *Island in the Flood: The Story of the Bellbowrie, Moggill and Anstead Floods*, N. Marsh, Bellbowrie, 2011, pp. 62–65.

28 N. Marsh, *Island in the Flood*, p. 28.

29 L. Scott, 'The Flood 2011', *The Courier-Mail Special Issue*, 22–23 January 2011, p. 27.

30 L. Millar, 'An Unfamiliar Homecoming', in ABC, *Flood*, Harper Collins, Sydney, 2011, p. 49.

31 M. Condon, 'Tragedy that Stopped City's Beating Heart', *The Courier-Mail*, 13 January 2011, p. 75.

32 M. Condon, 'A Bridge Over Troubled Waters', *The Courier-Mail*, 14 January 2011, p. 24.

33 T. Dalton, 'The Flood 2011', *The Courier-Mail Special Issue*, 22–23 January 2011.

34 ABC, *Flood*, p. 112.

35 P. Syvret, 'Sirens Puncture the Silence of a Slow-moving Disaster', *The Courier-Mail*, 13 January 2011, p. 78.

36 T. Dalton, 'The Village of the Damned', *The Courier-Mail*, 17 January 2011, p. 11; Agnew P&F Association, *Flood Horror and Tragedy*, ProVision, Lilydale, Victoria, 2011, p. 210.

37 QFCI & Queensland Premier and Minister for Reconstruction, *QFCI Interim Report*, QFCI, Brisbane, 2011, p. 27.

38 T. Dalton, 'Spirit Reigns Supreme', *The Courier-Mail*, 14 January 2011, p. 8.

39 Agnew P&F Association, *Flood Horror and Tragedy*, pp. 264, 274, 288, 300.

40 *Fact Sheet: Brisbane City Council 12-month Flood Recovery Report*, January 2012; Carl Wulff (ICC CEO) submission to QFCI, 2 September 2011, p. 6; Queensland Department of Energy and Water Supply, *Wivenhoe and Somerset Dams Optimisation Study Report*, p. 38.

41 M. Barnes, State Coroner, *Office of the State Coroner Findings of Inquest into the Deaths Caused by the South-East Queensland Floods of January 2011*, 5 June 2012.

42 *Brisbane Flood January 2011*, Independent Review of Brisbane City Council's Response to the 9–22 January 2011 Flood, p. 35; 'New Social Networks Offer Info', *The Queensland Times*, 13 January 2011, p. 9; J. Zubrzycki, 'World Watches Images of Catastrophe in Awe', *The Australian*, 13 January 2011, p. 6.

43 '2011 Floods: Through Your Eyes', *The Queensland Times*, 31 January 2012, p. 2.

44 S. Vogler & R. Viellaris, 'Thousands Set to Flee as Deluge Day Nears', *The Courier-Mail*, 12 January 2011, p. 6; A. Caldwell, R. Viellaris & S. Vogler, 'Devastation on a Scale Never Seen Before', *The Courier-Mail*, 13 January 2011, p. 2.

45 M. Condon, 'Memories Come Spilling Back', *The Courier-Mail*, 12 January 2011, p. 75.

46 A. Caldwell, R. Viellaris & S. Vogler, 'Devastation on a Scale Never Seen Before', *The Courier-Mail*, 13 January 2011, p. 2.

47 L. Brady, 'City in the Spotlight as Flood Water Rises', *The Queensland Times*, 13 January 2011, p. 8; J. Huxley, 'After Mother Nature's Cruel Hand, Communities Reunite with Wary Eye on the Sky', *The Sydney Morning Herald*, 15–16 January 2011, p. 1; T. Dalton, 'Our Three Brutal Months', in 'A Summer Like No Other', *The Courier-Mail Special Issue*, 5 March 2011, p. 3; R. Craddock & B. Williams, 'Grim Journey into Mother Nature's Fury', *The Courier-Mail*, 15–16 January 2011, p. 11.

48 S. Parnell, 'The River that Turned the City into a Mudflat', *The Australian*, 13 January 2011, p. 1; R. MacDonald, 'Bureaucrats, Miners, Even God in Firing Line as Blame Game Begins', *The Courier-Mail*, 19 January 2011, p. 27.

49 M. Colman, 'Waiting as the River Ruled', in '2010–2011 A Summer Like No Other', *The Courier-Mail Special Issue*, 5 March 2011, p. 18.

50 S. Parnell, 'City Feels the Sting of the River it Loved Too Much', *The Australian*, 14 January 2011, p. 2; J. Walker & S. Parnell, 'Floodwaters Show No Mercy', *The Australian*, 13 January 2011, p. 1; L. Scott, 'Coronation Drive One Long Road of Slush', *The Courier-Mail*, 15–16 January 2011, p. 85.

51   S. Rodgers, 'Mud and Misery', & K. Campbell, 'Citizens Reign', in *The 2010–2011 Floods Crisis*, APN Special Commemorative Publication, February 2011, pp. 3, 19.

52   A. Bligh, *Through the Wall*, p. 240.

53   A. Bligh, *Through the Wall*, p. 236.

54   'Coping with Crisis', *The Sunday Mail*, 2 January 2011, p. 42.

55   Anna Bligh Media Statements, 13 January 2011.

56   L. Megarrity, 'Anna of the Floods', *Australian Book Review*, issue 372, June/July 2015, p. 57.

57   B. Beban, letter to editor, *The Australian*, 13 January 2011, p. 15; J. Birmingham, 'Has Anna Earned Herself a Second Chance?', *Brisbane Times*, 13 January 2011, p. 15.

58   Editorial, 'High Praise for Region's Exemplary Leadership', *The Courier-Mail*, 15–16 January 2011, p. 42; N. M. de Bussy & A. Paterson, 'Crisis Leadership Styles – Bligh Versus Gillard: A Content Analysis of Twitter Posts on the Queensland Floods', *Journal of Public Affairs*, vol. 12, no. 4, 2012, pp. 326–332, 329.

59   T. Dalton, 'Kindness Comes to Muddy Street', *The Courier-Mail*, 15–16 January 2011, p. 6.

60   ABC, *Flood*, p. 88; Brisbane City Council, *QFCI Initial Submission*, p. 25.

61   L. Wilson, 'State goes it alone in shunning insurance', *The Australian*, 3 February 2011, p. 1.

62   M. Griffiths, 'Brisbane Floods to Cost City $440 Million', *PM*, ABC News, 8 February 2011.

63   S. Parnell, 'The River that Turned the City into a Mudflat', *The Australian*, 13 January 2011, p. 1.

64   C. Holmes & QFCI, *Final Report*, p. 146.

65   N. Marsh, *Island in the Flood*, p. 11.

66   QFCI, *Final Report*, p. 163.

67   QFCI, *Final Report*, p. 192; D. Houghton, 'Paying for a River View', *The Courier-Mail*, 22–23 January 2011, p. 63; H. Thomas & M. Rout, 'History Forgotten in Rush to Riverfront Luxury', *The Australian*, 18 January 2011, pp. 1, 4.

68   D. Topp, *Tennyson Breach*, Boolarong Press, Brisbane, 2012, p. 115; QFCI, *Final Report*, p. 192; Queensland Ombudsman, *Investigation of Brisbane City Council's Tennyson Reach Parkland Transactions*, February 2013.

69   *The Queensland Times, 1974 Floods Commemorative Feature*, 1 February 1994, p. 17.

70   For example: S. Kroll-Smith, *Recovering Inequality: Hurricane Katrina, the San Francisco Earthquake of 1906 and the Aftermath of Disaster*, University of Texas, Austin, 2018; B. Winter, P. M. Blaikie, T. Cannon & I. Davis, *At Risk: Natural Hazards, People's Vulnerability and Disasters*, Routledge, London, 2003; G. Bankoff, G. Frerks & D. Hilhorst, *Mapping Vulnerability: Disasters, Development and People*, Earthscan, London, 2008.

71   *Joint Flood Taskforce Report*, p. 31.

Chapter 8: Flood Management with Hindsight

1   H. Thomas, 'Damned if They Do, Damned if They Don't', *The Australian*, 15–16 January 2011, p. 13.

2   State Disaster Management Group Minutes, 17 January 2011, p. 8; In Anna Bligh Submission to QFCI, 6 February 2012.

3   'Question Time', *The Courier-Mail*, 18 January 2011, p. 1.
4   Editorial, 'Queenslanders Stood Strong During Disaster', *The Weekend Australian*, 15–16 January 2011, p. 15.
5   QFCI, *Transcript of Proceedings, Day 1*, 10 February 2011, p. 3.
6   M. O'Brien, *Brisbane Flooding January 2011: An Avoidable Disaster*, submission to QFCI, 20 March 2011, p. 4.
7   M. Solomons, 'Dam Saves City but Punishes Farmer', *The Courier-Mail*, 18 January 2011, p. 13; R. Callinan, 'Engineers Cut Flow Gushing from Dam', *The Australian*, 13 January 2011, p. 2.
8   H. Thomas, 'Bligh's Tough People Owed a Tough Inquiry', *The Australian*, 14 January 2011, p. 2; M. Raymond, 'January 2011 Brisbane River Floods and Examination by Media of the Dam Operations', Australian National Committee on Large Dams, 2011, p. 7; H. Thomas, 'The Great Avoidable Catastrophe: An Inquiry's Challenge', *The Weekend Australian*, 22–23 January 2011, p. 10; H. Thomas, 'Releases Too Little, Too Late', *The Australian*, 21 February 2011, p. 6.
9   H. Thomas, 'The Great Avoidable Catastrophe', *The Weekend Australian*, 22–23 January 2011, p. 10.
10 H. Thomas, 'Engineer Bores a Hole in Dam Untruths', *The Weekend Australian*, 19–20 March 2011, p. 3.
11 Insurance Council of Australia, *Flooding in the Brisbane River Catchment, January 2011*, ICA Hydrology Panel, Sydney, 20 February 2011.
12 H. Thomas, 'Engineer Bores a Hole in Dam Untruths', *The Weekend Australian*, 19–20 March 2011, p. 3.
13 J. B. Henderson, 'Floods in Brisbane River, and Schemes for Abatement of their Disastrous Effects', p. 303.
14 C. Holmes & QFCI, *Final Report*, p. 30; R. Barrett, 'Early Releases Would Have Been Futile', *The Australian: Nation*, 13 April 2011, p. 7.
15 John Tibaldi, Third statement to QFCI, 11 April 2011, p. 2.
16 QFCI, *Interim Report*, p. 82.
17 H. Thomas, 'Water Storage Levels "Made Damage Worse"', *The Australian*, 18 January 2011, p. 2.
18 R. Nathan, 'Brisbane: Lessons from Large Floods', *Water*, December 2012, p. 44.
19 H. Thomas & D. Uren, 'Dam in Sights of Flood Inquiry', *The Australian*, 18 January 2011, p. 1.
20 QFCI, *Interim Report*, p. 37
21 Cummins had an association with Australian Dams and Water Consulting, the firm commissioned to review the Wivenhoe Dam manual on the recommendation of the QFCI Interim Report.
22 Robert Ayre, Seventh statement to QFCI, 1 February 2012.
23 QFCI, *Transcripts of Proceedings*, 3 February 2012, p. 5204.
24 S. Maslen and J. Hayes, 'Experts under the Microscope: The Wivenhoe Dam Case,' *Environmental Systems and Decisions Journal*, vol. 34, 2014, p. 188.
25 Engineers Australia, *Comments on QFCI Final Report*, July 2012, p. 11.
26 QFCI, *Interim report*, p. 62.
27 H. Thomas, 'What the Floods Inquiry Didn't Hear: Wivenhoe "Breached the Manual"', *The Australian*, 23 January 2012, p. 1; H. Thomas, 'Missed Again: Unearthed Emails Point to Wivenhoe Breach', *The Australian*, 24 January 2011, p. 1.
28 N. Paull, 'Flood inquiry won't hurt government: Fraser', *Brisbane Times*, 5 February 2012.

29 C. Holmes & QFCI, *Final Report*, p. 192.

30 C. Holmes & QFCI, *Final Report*, p. 31.

31 Advice of John Jerrard QC concerning examination of material provided to the Crime and Misconduct Commission, pp. 48–49.

32 M. Madigan, 'Report Backs Dam Release Action', *The Courier-Mail*, 25 September 2012, p. 7.

33 S. Vogler & M. Solomons, 'Seeney Defends Lag in Recovery', *The Courier-Mail*, 9 January 2013, p. 10.

34 M. Solomons & T. Thompson, 'State Drags Chain on Inquiry's Main Points', *The Courier-Mail*, 8 January 2013, p. 6.

35 Editorial, 'Triumph of the Spirit', *The Courier-Mail*, 22–23 January 2011, p. 65.

36 T. Thompson & J. Robertson, 'Bad Planning Decisions Blamed', *The Courier-Mail*, 14 April 2011, p. 6.

37 Johnston Dixon, 'Special Floods Class Action Supplement', *River Report*, 2013, pp. 6–7.

38 A. Fraser, 'Dream Homes at a Perilous Price', *The Australian*, 18 January 2011, p. 11.

39 J. Grant, letter to editor, 'Seek Flood Result', *The Courier-Mail*, 12 May 2011, p. 31.

40 S. Cousins, 'Wivenhoe Releases Could've Prevented Floods? Nonsense, Say Experts', *Crikey*, 16 February 2011.

41 A. Fraser, 'Ebbs and Flows of Riverfront Sales', *The Australian*, 18 October 2012, p. 33; E. Lutton, 'Floods and Property: Brisbane Five Years On', *Domain*, 10 November 2015.

42 P. Syvret, 'A year after the Queensland floods, memories return', *The Courier-Mail*, 7 January 2012, p. 49.

43 C. Holmes & QFCI, *Final Report*, p. 38.

44 Editorial, *The Sydney Morning Herald*, 14 January 2011, p. 12.

45 S. Lunn, 'The Untamable Torrent', *The Weekend Australian, Inquirer*, 15–16 January 2011, p. 1.

Chapter 9: No Two Floods Are the Same: The 2022 Flood

1. C. Hanna, 'Brisbane homes flooded as "rain bomb" continues to threaten lives in south-east Queensland', *The Guardian*, 27 February 2022.

2. B. Smee & T. Shepherd, 'Major flood warning issued for Brisbane after "rain bomb" unleashes havoc on south-east Queensland and northern NSW', *The Guardian*, 28 February 2022; A. Klein, 'Record flooding in Australia driven by La Niña and climate change', *New Scientist*, 28 February 2022.

3. C. Hanna, 'Brisbane homes flooded'; G. Redfearn, 'Anatomy of a "rain bomb": Scientists strive to understand phenomenon that caused Australia's east coast floods', *The Guardian*, 5 March 2022.

4. G. Redfearn, 'Anatomy of a "rain bomb"'.

5. Queensland Government, Inspector General of Emergency Management (IGEM), *South East Queensland Rainfall and Flooding February to March 2022 Review Report 1: 2022–2023*, p. 12.

6. Australian Government Bureau of Meteorology (BoM), *Special Climate Statement 76 – Extreme rainfall and flooding in south-eastern Queensland and western New South Wales*, 25 May 2022, p. 3.

7. R. Rosel, '389 mm in 3 hrs: Highest rainfall totals in southeast Queensland', *The Courier-Mail*, 25 February 2022.

8. BoM, Ipswich Alert Station 40831.

9. Queensland Reconstruction Authority (QRA), *Companion Document 2021–22 Southern Queensland Floods State Recovery and Resilience Plan 2022–23*, p. 8; Phoenix Resilience, *February–March 2022: Ipswich Flood Review: Operational Review Report*, p. 10; BoM.

10. QRA, *Companion Document 2021–22*, p. 8.

11. Queensland Government, IGEM, *South East Queensland Rainfall and Flooding*, p. 60.

12. Ibid., p. 28.

13. Climate Council, *A Supercharged climate: Rain bombs, flash flooding and destruction*, 2022.

14. Christine (last name withheld), interview with author, 25 January 2022.

15. HARC, *February 2022 Flood Event: Report on the Operation of Somerset Dam and Wivenhoe Dam*, April 2022, p. ix.

16. Ibid., p. 10.

17. Ibid., p. 4.

18. G. Redfearn, N. Evershed & J. Nicholas, 'What caused the "rain bomb"? How the unprecedented Queensland and NSW Floods Unfolded', *The Guardian*, 1 March 2022; BoM, *Special Climate Statement 76*, p. 14.

19. HARC, *February 2022 Flood Event*, p. viii.

20. For example, 'Michael Foster from SEQ Water explains the Wivenhoe Dam release strategy', *ABC News*, 28 February 2022.

21. H. Johnson, 'One dam huge problem', *The Courier-Mail*, 1 March 2022, p. 4.

22. Queensland Government, IGEM, *South East Queensland Rainfall and Flooding*, p. 59.

23. HARC, *February 2022 Flood Event*, p. 5.

24. Ibid., p. 116.

25. Ibid., pp. 11–12.

26. Ibid., p. 10.

27. Ibid., p. x.

28. S. Richards, 'A breakdown of how south-east Queensland's flood crisis played out', *abc.net.au*, 19 March 2022.

29. Michael Foster, interview with author, 22 February 2022.

30. Hon. P. de Jersey, *Brisbane City Council 2022 Flood Review*, 9 May 2022, p. 12.

31. Ibid., p. 12.

32. Phoenix Resilience, *February–March 2022: Ipswich Flood Review*, p. 12; B. Bennion, 'Questions on late warnings', *The Ipswich Tribune*, 2 March 2022, p. 5.

33. Ibid., p. 5.

34. Kate Cantrell, information supplied to author, 18 January 2023.

35. Sue Kirk, interview with author, 29 January 2023.

36. QRA, *Companion Document 2021–22*, p. 8; Phoenix Resilience, *February–March 2022: Ipswich Flood Review*, p. 14.

37. M. Silk, 'Floating crane loose in Deadly Qld floods', *The Canberra Times*, 28 February 2022.

38. Phoenix Resilience, *February–March 2022: Ipswich Flood Review*, p. 14.

39. Ibid., p. 30.

40. 'Brisbane suburbs in flood's firing line as heavy rain and high tide combine', *The Courier-Mail*, 27 February 2022; S. Lai, 'Queensland Storm "like an unpredictable cyclone"', *9 News Australia*, 27 February 2022. Premier asks millions to stay home', *Channel Nine News*, 27 February 2022.

41. B. Smee, '"We didn't really expect it": Brisbane residents caught off-guard by

fast-rising floods', *The Guardian* online, 27 February 2022.

42. S. Lai, 'Queensland storm'.
43. Ibid.
44. L. Scott, 'Swollen, muddy torrent is a flashback to the horror of '11', *The Courier-Mail*, 1 March 2022, p. 6.
45. P. de Jersey, *Brisbane City Council 2022 Flood Review*, p. 77.
46. M. Madigan, 'Big river flows into thousands of our lives', *The Courier-Mail*, 1 March 2022, p. 8.
47. Ibid.
48. M. Madigan, 'Big river flows into thousands of our lives', p. 8.
49. Kate Kirby, interview with author, 19 January 2023.
50. B. Smee, '"We didn't really expect it"'.
51. B. Smee & T. Shepherd, 'Major flood warning issued for Brisbane'.
52. M. Madigan, 'Big river flows into thousands of our lives', p. 8.
53. N. Innes, S. Scott, D. Buckley, F. Ripper & T. Chamberlain, 'Brisbane floods: Multiple rescues as water levels rise', *The Courier-Mail*, 27 February 2022.
54. Cathy O'Malley, interview with author, 29 January 2023.
55. Cedric Chu, interview with author, 8 October 2022.
56. S. Richards, 'A breakdown of how south-east Queensland's flood crisis played out', *abc.net.au*, 19 March 2022; D. Buckley, 'Qld flood death toll highest in more than a decade', *The Courier-Mail*, 10 March 2022.
57. P. de Jersey, *Brisbane City Council 2022 Flood Review*, p. 13.
58. Deloitte Access Economics, *The social, financial and economic costs of the 2022 South East Queensland Rainfall and Flooding Event*, QRA, June 2022, p. 13.
59. S. Richards, 'A breakdown of how south-east Queensland's flood crisis played out'.
60. QRA, *2021–22 Southern Queensland Floods State Recovery and Resilience Plan*, p. 84.
61. J. McKay, T. Chamberlain & J. Kerr, 'Deluge claims another victim, Records fall as rivers swell', *The Courier-Mail*, 2 March 2022, p. 3.
62. QRA, *2021–22 Southern Queensland Floods State Recovery and Resilience Plan*, p. 27.
63. Ibid., p. 26.
64. Queensland Government, IGEM, *South East Queensland Rainfall and Flooding*, p. 92.
65. QRA, *2021–22 Southern Queensland Floods State Recovery and Resilience Plan*, p. 9.
66. Deloitte Access Economics, *The social, financial and economic costs of the 2022 South East Queensland Rainfall and Flooding Event*, p. 21.
67. B. Smee & T. Shepherd, 'Major flood warning issued for Brisbane'.
68. S. Dobeson, 'Parts of Brisbane CBD evacuated with crane loose in river', *MyGC.com.au*.
69. P. de Jersey, *Brisbane City Council 2022 Flood Review*, p. 78.
70. *A Current Affair* Staff, 'Brisbane residents angered by lack of flood warnings', *9 Now*, 28 February 2022.
71. Queensland Government, IGEM, *South East Queensland Rainfall and Flooding*, pp. 35–36.
72. Phoenix Resilience, *February–March 2022: Ipswich Flood Review*, p. 28; B. Bennion, 'Questions on late warnings', p. 5.
73. P. de Jersey, *Brisbane City Council 2022 Flood Review*, p. 80.
74. Christine (last name withheld), interview with author, 25 January 2022.

75. Queensland Government, IGEM, *South East Queensland Rainfall and Flooding*, p. 65.
76. J. Sinnerton, S. Kovacevic & E. Williams, 'Fury at lack of deluge warning', *The Courier-Mail*, 3 March 2022.
77. J. Marszalek & J. McKay, 'Premier: "Bureau didn't see it coming"', *Gold Coast Bulletin*, 1 March 2022, p. 5.
78. M. Silk, 'Floating crane loose in Deadly Qld floods'.
79. A. Bligh, *Through the Wall: Reflections on Leadership, Love and Survival*, Sydney, HarperCollins, 2015, p. 240.
80. Queensland Government, IGEM, *South East Queensland Rainfall and Flooding*, p. 60.
81. Ibid., p. 77.
82. Ibid., pp. 28 & 60–65.
83. J. Sinnerton, S. Kovacevic & E. Williams, 'Fury at lack of deluge warning'; Queensland Government, IGEM, *South East Queensland Rainfall and Flooding*, p. 67.
84. Phoenix Resilience, *February–March 2022: Ipswich Flood Review*, p. 21.
85. P. de Jersey, *Brisbane City Council 2022 Flood Review*, pp. 79–80.
86. Queensland Government, IGEM, *South East Queensland Rainfall and Flooding*, p. 36.
87. Nicki McCabe, interview with author, 19 January 2023.
88. B. Smee, 'South-east Queensland residents brace for more storms just days after severe flooding', *The Guardian*, 3 March 2022.
89. K. Kyriacou, S. Payne & G. Clelland, 'Residents joined by saintly strangers as clean-up continues', *The Sunday Mail*, 7 March 2022, p. 16.
90. E. Williams & F. Ripper, 'Mud militia out in force after Mud Army told to stand down', *The Courier-Mail*, 4 March 2022, p. 8.
91. Ibid.
92. Michael Kelly, interview with author, 12 January 2023.
93. A. Caldwell, 'Danger zones may not be developed', *The Courier-Mail*, 20 January 2011, p. 2.
94. E. Lutton, 'Floods and Property: Brisbane five years on', *Domain*, 10 November 2015.
95. J. Beech-Jones, Rodriguez & Sons Pty Ltd v Queensland Bulk Water Supply Authority trading as Seqwater (No 22) (2019) NSWSC 1657, New South Wales: Judgment Summary, Supreme Court, 2019.
96. Inspect my Home, *What to consider before buying property in a Brisbane flood zone*, 2 March 2021, <www.inspectmyhome.com.au/blog/buying-property-in-a-brisbane-flood-zone/>.
97. S. Vogler, 'New release rules aim to save homes', *The Courier-Mail*, 1 April 2014, p. 4.
98. T. Horton, J. Hodgkinson & D. Brandt, Urraween, letters to editor, *The Courier-Mail*, 2 April 2014, p. 22.
99. P. Dixon quoted in E. Lutton, 'Floods and Property'.
100. L. Hamilton-Smith, 'Emotional impact of south-east Queensland's 2011 floods remains, five years on', *ABC News*, 10 January 2016.
101. J. Simmonds, *Rising from the Floods: Moving the Town of Grantham*, Bad Apple Press, Sydney, 2020.
102. QRA, *Annual Report 2011–12*, Queensland Government, p. 9.
103. Cited in P. de Jersey, *Brisbane City Council 2022 Flood Review*, p. 56.

104. Ibid., pp. 55–7.
105. QRA, *$741 million Resilient Residential Recovery package approved*, Queensland Government, 2022.
106. Queensland Government, *First at-risk Ipswich homes demolished under voluntary home buy-back program*, Media statement, 24 January 2023.
107. The Queensland Cabinet and Ministerial Directory, *Flood-impacted homeowners accept buy back offers*, Media statement, Queensland Government, 16 October 2022.
108. QRA, *Paul Harding, Goodna – Voluntary Home Buy-Back Program*, Media statement, Queensland Government, 2023.
109. Christine (last name withheld), interview with author, 25 January 2022.
110. L. Scott, 'Swollen, muddy torrent is a flashback to the horror of '11', p. 6.

Conclusion

1.   M. A. Moritz & S. G. Knowles, 'Coexisting with Wildfire', *American Scientist*, vol. 104, no. 4, July–August, 2016.
2.   Climate Council, *Everything you need to know about floods and climate change*, 2 March 2022, <www.climatecouncil.org.au/resources/climate-change-floods/>.
3.   Australian Government Productivity Commission, *Natural Disaster Funding Inquiry Report*, 2014.
4.   J. Powell, *Plains of Promise, Rivers of Destiny*, p. 320.

Index

Italicised page numbers within this index refer to references in figures.